D1564139

CHARLES WADDELL
CHESNUTT

CHARLES
WADDELL

"*Each of us inevitable,*

Each of us limitless—each of us with his or her right upon the earth,

Each of us allow'd the eternal purports of the earth,

Each of us here as divinely as any is here."

WALT WHITMAN

CHESNUTT

Pioneer of the Color Line

BY HELEN M. CHESNUTT

CHAPEL HILL — *The University of North Carolina Press*

CHARLES WADDELL CHESNUTT IN 1899

ACKNOWLEDGMENTS

SEVERAL years after my father's death in November, 1932, I began to look over his papers, manuscripts, and correspondence. Among these I found many old newspapers and magazines, some manuscript journals which he had written as a young teacher in North Carolina, many letters, and a number of scrapbooks filled with newspaper clippings and magazine articles about his writings at the turn of the century. Much of this material had been packed away in boxes in the attic, and, almost forgotten, had been gathering dust through the years. As I read and studied them I thought, "This record of my father's life ought to be preserved to serve as an inspiration to other young people who find life difficult and challenging." My mother agreed; so with her warmest encouragement and that of my two sisters and my brother I undertook the task.

My nephew and I spent one entire summer vacation dusting and sorting and filing the material. Many of the papers were yellowed, faded, and very brittle. It seemed wise, therefore, to have them copied so that when the actual work began they would be easy to read. Letters, too, were worn and often almost illegible, and they had to be copied. All this took several years and many typists worked at it. To all of them I am deeply indebted—especially to Mrs. Ardelia Bradley Dixon, now Senior Clerk at Cleveland Central High School, and to Mrs. Bessie Smith Bobo, who spent their spare time for years working on the documents and later on the manuscript itself.

For permission to quote letters, I am grateful to Mr. Ferris Greenslet, for the Houghton Mifflin Company letters; to Mr.

Arthur W. Page, for the letters of Walter Hines Page; to Mrs.
Portia Washington Pittman, for the letter of Booker T. Washington; to Mr. Jay Clifford, for the letter of Carrie W. Clifford, and
to Mary Dickerson Donahey and Martha Smith for letters written
to me.

The staff members of the Cleveland Public Library were un-
failing in their courtesy and patience in answering my many
queries. For reading the manuscript and giving me encouragement and good counsel, I am especially indebted to Miss Alta M.
Bien, Head of the English Department at Central High School;
to Dr. Lyon N. Richardson, Professor of English and Director of
the University Libraries of Western Reserve University; to Mr.
Arna Bontemps, Librarian of Fisk University; and to Mr. Carl
Van Vechten. I am grateful, too, to Dr. Charles S. Johnson,
President of Fisk University, for helping to make publication
possible.

Last but by no means least, I owe warmest thanks to my two
sisters, Ethel and Dorothy, for their encouragement and co-operation—to Dorothy especially, who year after year walked hand in
hand with me, giving me the benefit of her memory, her judgment,
her criticism, and her devoted help in lightening my daily burdens.

HELEN M. CHESNUTT

February 14, 1952

CONTENTS

CHARLES WADDELL CHESNUTT

1

North Carolina: Departure and Return

CHLOE SAMPSON and her daughter Ann Maria were leaving Fayetteville; they had had their fill of insecurity and fear. Of fear especially, for Ann Maria was a beautiful and spirited girl with a brilliant mind, and she felt very deeply that the lot of the free colored people of North Carolina had become insupportable, was, in fact, one of genuine danger. Their suffrage had been taken away. Laws forbidding marriage between white and free colored people had been passed. They had now no more civil rights than the slaves and were practically in the same condition.

Ann Maria was a born teacher, and had been secretly teaching slave children to read and write. She did this at great risk to herself, for in the decade before the Civil War such teaching was becoming very dangerous. After many passionate discussions, in which Ann Maria made it quite clear to her mother Chloe that she would not passively accept the fate ordained for her by the iron custom of the South, they decided to leave the Old North State for the Northwest—land of promise and hope. In the year 1856 they joined a little band of free colored people who were preparing to go North by wagon train.

Like other pilgrims of other times they were seeking to escape from the rigid restrictions under which they were living and to find a clearer and freer atmosphere, in which they could feel physical and spiritual security. There was already in Cleveland, Ohio, a colony of people who had gone there some years earlier; so the wagons were turned toward that beautiful little city on the shores of Lake Erie. In the group of pilgrims was a young man, Andrew Jackson Chesnutt. He was on his way to Indiana to join his uncle, who had settled there some years before and was a well-known and respected citizen.

The journey was long and tedious. Discouragement and fear and bitter hardship cast their blight over the spirits of the group. At times they ran into positive danger, and often it seemed the wiser course to abandon their hopes and return to North Carolina. But Ann Maria browbeat them, railed at them, cajoled them and laughed at them, poured out her charm, her indomitable courage, and sparkling wit to lift their spirits and lead them forward. Andrew fell in love with her, and Ann Maria began to dream too. But the time of parting came. Andrew left the wagon train and went westward to Indiana. The wagons continued on toward Cleveland.

There Chloe Sampson bought a little house on Hudson Street, near Garden Street, in a modest but attractive neighborhood. People of German descent had settled there, and Garden Street was named from their flourishing flower gardens. The atmosphere of safety, the kindness and sympathy of neighbors, white and colored, made Ann Maria happy. She would live here all her life, would marry, perhaps, rear her children here, and give them a happy childhood and, above all, peace and security.

Meantime, in Indiana, Andrew's uncle was helping him with his education. His prospects were very bright, but his thoughts kept turning northward. He could think of nothing but Ann Maria, and so one day he left Indiana and went to Cleveland. There in July, 1857, Ann Maria Sampson and Andrew Jackson Chesnutt went down to the Probate Court and obtained a marriage license. On the following day, July 26, 1857, they were married.

They made their home with Ann Maria's mother in the house on Hudson Street. Andrew found a job as driver-conductor on the first horsecars that ran on Woodland Avenue. The line, called the Kinsman Street Omnibus Line, had been opened in 1857 and ran out Woodland Avenue (then called Kinsman Street) from the depot to Woodland Cemetery.

On June 20, 1858, Charles Waddell Chesnutt was born. Ann Maria was content—her boy should have every advantage that any child could have, a happy childhood, a good education, opportunity for mental and spiritual growth. He should stand upright and fill a man's place in the world. He should become a scholar and a gentleman, and all the dreams and hopes that in her own case had been unfulfilled should come to full fruition in this child of hers. Although several other children were born to her, none meant to her what Charles meant. In his early years, she endeavored to fill his heart with fine ideals and lofty principles, to imbue his mind with the spirit of courage and high endeavor. She tried to make him feel that loyalty and duty were sacred obligations.

Shortly after Charles was born, the little family moved to Oberlin. Ann Maria thought that it would be a good thing to be near Oberlin College—an institution founded upon the principles of human equality and equal opportunity for all—so that Charles could be educated there. Andrew found employment as assistant to a wheelwright, John Scott, the husband of Andrew's aunt.

At that time Oberlin was a station of the Underground Railroad and a center of anti-slavery sentiment. Andrew of course became very much interested in the work of the Underground Railroad and had the exciting experience of participating in the famous Oberlin-Wellington rescue case in 1858. On September 13 of that year two slave-catchers, accompanied by a United States marshal, arrested a fugitive slave who had been living near Oberlin for several years. When the news reached Oberlin, the citizens were outraged. A large crowd of men, including a college professor and several of the students, on horseback and in buggies, tore after the slave-catchers, caught up with them in Wellington, and rescued the slave. The affair caused great excitement and a number of the rescuers were arrested at once for violation of the Fugitive Slave Law, Andrew among them. However, the warrant against him was nulled, because one of the "t's" in his name was put in the middle instead of with the other at the end, thus constituting what the judge, who was unfriendly to the Fugitive Slave Law, construed as a misnomer. So Andrew was saved from a sojourn in jail.

The second son, Lewis, was born in Oberlin on January 16, 1860, and Ann Maria found that the care of two babies close together made life so difficult that she needed her mother's help. Andrew now realized that Cleveland offered better opportunities for earning a living than Oberlin, and they returned to Cleveland, to the house on Hudson Street. Andrew got his old job back, and things moved on serenely for a while. Another son, Andrew, and

then a daughter were born. The little girl died soon after birth
and was buried in the Erie Street Cemetery. When the Civil War
broke out, Andrew enlisted as a teamster and served throughout
the war in the Union Army. Meanwhile Ann Maria and her three
little boys were well cared for by her mother; and Charles, when
he was old enough, attended the Cleveland Public Schools.

At the close of the Civil War, finding himself near Fayetteville,
Andrew went to see his father. The old man seemed to him so
feeble that he decided to remain. He sent for Ann Maria and the
children.

Ann Maria was heartbroken. Were all her hopes and dreams
to be worth nothing? Must she return to the South? Could it be
that Charles and the two younger boys must leave this land of
hope and light and return to the land of darkness and despair?
She raged against her fate; she said she'd never go back—but she
went, leaving her mother, who preferred to remain in Cleveland.

The journey south in 1866 was quite different from the earlier
wagon train journey north. They went by rail and steamboat—
first to Washington and then to North Carolina. The journey was
really pleasant; the three charming little boys made many friends.
Charles and Lewis thoroughly investigated everything on the boat
and the other passengers made much of them. Ann Maria began
to believe that things might be better in the South. She schooled
herself to become reconciled to her fate. When Andrew met them,
she had regained her old courage and ambition. Andrew's father
set him up in business in a grocery store in Gillespie Street between the Market House and Russell Street. Ann Maria went
about the business of keeping house and rearing her children.

Those were stirring times, those days of Reconstruction just
after the close of the war. Almost at once, schools for colored
people were established by the Freedmen's Bureau, which was
created on March 3, 1865, for the purpose of caring for the
emancipated slaves and the abandoned lands at the close of the
war. The colored people of the South for several years were under
the almost absolute control of this Bureau. The commissioner
at the head of it was General O. O. Howard, who had had a
distinguished career during the war and was deeply interested in
Negroes. The school established in Fayetteville was named after
him, the Howard School. Later on he was responsible for the
establishment of Howard University in Washington, D. C., for

the higher education of the Negro, and was at the head of it for several years.

It was to the Howard School that Charles and Lewis were sent. The principal of the school was Robert Harris, whose family some years before the war had gone to Cleveland to live. Robert and his brother Cicero had attended the Cleveland High School and were well educated for the time. When the war ended and schools for colored people were established in the South, the two brothers had returned to North Carolina—Robert to Fayetteville, and Cicero to Charlotte—where they both began teaching in the colored schools.

Fayetteville was fortunate in having Robert Harris as principal of the Howard School. He was a man of irreproachable character and high ideals. His position in Fayetteville was, on a smaller scale, like that of Booker T. Washington later. He procured money from the Peabody Fund, the Freedmen's Bureau, and other sources for the education of colored youth. But he did more than this. By his tact and moderation, he won and held the good will of all classes of the community. He enjoyed the confidence of the leading men of the town as well as that of the parents and the pupils themselves. His example and precept promoted among the colored people a higher standard of morality and good conduct than existed in almost any other southern town of that period. Ann Maria's children were fortunate to come under the influence of this remarkable man and Ann Maria was thankful for it.

So the years passed. Andrew became a county commissioner and justice of the peace for Cumberland County. Charles was learning all that could be taught him in the Howard School. After school he helped his father in the store—kept the books, waited on customers, swept out the place—and listened to and reflected upon everything he heard. The store was the natural meeting place for all the people of the neighborhood. Here the more intelligent met and discussed freely the latest political developments. Here the more ignorant told each other stories of superstition and conjuration, and here the boy Charles took in everything with his wide-open ears. After the store was closed, he talked over all that he had heard with Ann Maria at home.

Charles was nine years old when he saw a man killed in cold blood. One day while helping in the store, he heard a great com-

motion in the street. People were streaming past, shouting, and
women were screaming. Charles joined the crowd making for the
Market House. There at the corner of the Market House, a
colored man had just been shot and killed by a white man for
the alleged "nameless crime." However, there was no mob vio-
lence. The murderer was tried and convicted of homicide, and
Charles became acquainted with the power of the law.

Ann Maria was failing in health. Three little girls, Clara, Mary,
and Lillian, were born to her after her return to Fayetteville.
Charles was her prop and stand-by. When freed from the duties
of the schoolroom and the store, he helped Ann Maria at home
—washing the clothes, nursing the babies, minding the other
children, cleaning the house, anything to relieve his idolized
mother from the burdens of a life too hard for her. In the midst
of all these duties, he found time to read. There were few books
in his home and no libraries in the town, but there was a very
good bookstore run by Mr. George Haigh, a member of one of
Fayetteville's first families. Mr. Haigh took an interest in Charles
because he was such an intelligent and well-bred little lad, and
gave him the freedom of the store. Every moment that Charles
could spare from his busy life was spent in browsing in the bookstore, and every cent that he could call his own he spent in buying
second-hand books.

After the birth of Lillian, Ann Maria did not recover, and when
Charles was thirteen years old his mother died, leaving him
desolate indeed. Grandmother Chloe, who had married Moses
Harris, a carpenter, in Cleveland, and had returned with him to
Fayetteville to be near her daughter and grandchildren, took
charge of the children after Ann Maria's death. Charles had
promised his mother that he would watch over his brothers and
sisters, a promise which had made Ann Maria's last days happy.
So Charles mothered the other children and helped his grandmother with the housework.

Grandmother Chloe, however, was none too pleased to have
the children settled upon her—the work was too confining and
she was getting old. She sent for her niece Mary Ochiltree, a girl
about eighteen years old, who lived out in the country where
there were no schools, and told her that if she would come into
Fayetteville and help her with the children, she could attend the
Howard School and further her education. Mary accepted gladly.

Cousin Mary, as the children called her, was very good to them, and Andrew found himself thinking of her as a possible successor to Ann Maria. She was young and attractive, gentle and efficient with the children. Before very long, Andrew's home was running smoothly again with the six children in the care of the new mother, Cousin Mary, as they continued to call their father's second wife.

2

A Very Young Teacher

WHEN CHARLES was fourteen, his father decided that it was time
for him to help with the family expenses. A friend of Andrew's, a
saloon-keeper in the town, offered Charles the job of keeping
his books and doing odd jobs about his establishment. When the
boy told Robert Harris that he was going to leave school to work
in a saloon, Harris was so distressed that he dismissed his class
and went to see Charles's father. The result was that Charles was
appointed pupil-teacher in the Howard School at a modest salary.
He now fell under the direct influence of Robert Harris, who encouraged in him the aspirations and hopes with which his mother
had inspired him.

At the age of fourteen Charles wrote his first story, a serial, and
published it in a small weekly newspaper run by a colored man.
Andrew, meanwhile, had failed in the storekeeping business because of having given too much credit to his customers and had
moved out to his farm on the Wilmington Road, about two miles
from Fayetteville. So after his day's work as pupil-teacher Charles
helped his father on the farm. On Saturdays he peddled needles,
pins, thread, buttons, and the like, from door to door in the
country districts, until he was fifteen years old. But his earnings
were not enough. The soil of Andrew's farm was poor; it required
the most arduous toil to raise any kind of crop upon it. The house
was a log cabin, roomy enough, but with no conveniences of any
kind. A new family was coming along, and more money was
needed to keep things going. So Charles again consulted his

teacher and friend, Robert Harris, who sent him to Charlotte, North Carolina, to assist his brother Cicero Harris, principal of a school there.

Cicero Harris was a spiritual man, who, like his brother Robert, had a great influence upon Charles's life. They shared the same room, taught together all day, and ate their meals together. Charles remained in Charlotte as assistant to Cicero Harris for three years, learning how to teach and how to discipline the great boys and girls who were often much older than he. During these years at Charlotte, Charles spent his summers teaching in remote country districts where the school term lasted for only two or three months a year. He needed to earn the extra money, for his father still depended on his help to support the growing family in Fayetteville.

The boy was often lonely and homesick, longing for his father and his brothers and sisters, yearning for someone congenial to talk with, to confide in. The country people, backward and ignorant and often jealous, offered little companionship. There was no diversion of any kind, and Charles spent all his leisure in reading and study and in writing the journal which he started at this time. This journal reveals the tremendous efforts he had to make to get his summer teaching positions and shows the loneliness and discouragement that he often experienced. In July, 1874, he was promised a teaching position at Malley Creek, but when with high hopes he reached the place, he found there was no money to pay a teacher. He then returned to Charlotte, hired a saddle horse, and rode down to Morrow's Turnout to find a school, but all the schools were running and no teachers were needed. He tried other districts in Mecklenburg County but found no school. At Moore's Sanctuary he was told that the people had used up the school funds in building a schoolhouse, and had no money left for a teacher. He heard of another school in Gaston County and walked twenty-three miles to apply for it; but again funds were lacking and the school was not to be opened. Exhausted both physically and spiritually, he decided to go home and rest for a week or two. He finally succeeded in getting a little school at Mount Zion, near Fayetteville. There were forty-four pupils in this school, several of them coming out from Fayetteville to attend.

After school he went home and carried on the business of his own education. Robert Harris had an organ in his home and there was a piano at the Howard School. Charles took both organ and piano lessons and practiced an hour or two a day. He studied algebra and read a great deal of American history. He also read books on the theory and practice of teaching, and, for relaxation, reread the *Pickwick Papers* and *Uncle Tom's Cabin*.

When September came, Charles returned to Charlotte and spent another year teaching with Cicero Harris. During this year he was much interested in dramatics and formed a dramatics club with the pupils. They produced several plays—*The First Glass*, a temperance play; *East Lynne, or the Earl's Daughter; A Glorious Farce*, and several others. This venture into dramatics was delightful to Charles.

At the end of the school year, he again started out on his search for a summer school. He took a little one-ox railroad up to Jonesville, but when he interviewed the school committee he found that again there was no money for a teacher in the colored schools; he then was offered the white school with the advice that he would not be respected if he taught the colored school. He finally found a school in the country ten miles from Spartanburg, South Carolina, which to his homesick heart seemed a long distance from Charlotte, and from the girl he was interested in. During this summer he wrote faithfully in his journal:

July 10, 1875

I am in the woods again, ten miles from Spartanburg. I came up here yesterday afternoon; I am in a large old frame house. My room is upstairs. It is spacious, and tolerably pleasant. The people are very anxious to please.

I begin to feel a little Charlotte-sick, and to wish I could see J. If she were here I should be contented. I wish I could write to her without her mother's reading the letters. I would write nothing improper, of course, but I would pour out my heart. It is a shame for a fellow to be obliged to confine himself to such cold sentences as a mother would hold discreet. I love the girl and I hope she loves me and will continue to do so. Here is a lock of her hair! I kiss the lock of hair and press it to my bosom. Would it were she!

I wish I were about twenty-five years old and had about a thousand dollars or so, and she were a few years older, I'd marry her, if she'd have me, and I think she would.

It is a strange thing—a little strange why women have so much influence with men. They are the "weaker vessel," yet they often seem the stronger. I love a girl who is not, strictly speaking, any ways good-looking. To me, all her faults are nothing. I love her, and "as charity covereth a multitude of sins," love hides all defects. I would give anything for her photograph—Pshaw! What a fool I am, sitting here! I thought I was more of a man than that...!

> And O, my Eppie
> My jewel, my Eppie,
> Wha wadna' be happy
> Wi' Eppie Adair!...

During these eight weeks Charles experienced many emotions—enthusiasm, discouragement, boredom, homesickness, happiness at the success of his teaching, utter frustration at the pupils' inability to learn. He read Byron and Cowper in his leisure time, studied Latin and history, memorized many poems and songs which he never forgot, and wrote innumerable letters. His diary continues:

July 16

I had about 20 scholars today. This is Friday, and one week of my stay is past! It seems short. The first two or three days I was here, I was "awfully" lonesome. But now I have got to liking the place and the people very well. Life here is simple and pleasant. I rise at six, read till breakfast, if it is not ready; eat, read till school time, half past eight; go to school, let out about three o'clock, come home and read till dusk. Then I can sit and sing, and recite pieces I have learned; think over what I have read. This evening I went with Louis Bomar to get a load of oats, and had a jolly ride over the stones, and up and down the hills. I've been reading Byron and Cowper today. Cowper's *Task* is splendid. I will build a castle in the air. Cowper gives me the material in his *Task*. I don't wish my castle to be realized when I am old and worn out, but I would delight to lead a life like the one he describes in *The Garden*.

> Domestic happiness, thou only bliss
> Of Paradise which has survived the fall.

I would wish my life to be like that—rural retirement, plenty to occupy the mind and hands, a dear companion to share my joys, a happy family growing up around me, and when having had enough of the world, I pass away to a better, "my children shall rise up and call me blessed" and I be regretted and remembered with love and respect by all who knew me. This is enjoying life! I believe that life was given to us to enjoy, and if God will help me, I intend to enjoy mine.

July 22

Didn't write yesterday. Yesterday afternoon I came home from school, studied a while, and then went out and plowed about an hour. I've been away from home you may say, two years, and I think if nothing prevents it, when I am through with this school, that I shall go home. I would like to work on the farm a while. I can get employment up here, but I want to see the folks. I guess they'll consider me a "reprobate" and a "renegade" for not sending any money home. But when a fellow does the best he can, why he can't do any better.

July 30, Friday

Today will be the last day of the third week of my school. I wish 'twas the last day of the eighth week. Yesterday Louis went to town for me, and didn't get a letter. And I have written Pa one, Lewis one, Mr. Harris, Miss Vic, Mrs. Schenck, etc. and not one has written me.

Well, if nobody writes to me, I guess I can get along without.

> I'll be merry and free,
> I'll be sad for naebody,
> If naebody care for me,
> I'll care for naebody.
>   —Burns

I think my daddy might write and tell me how they are getting along. But I suppose I am considered as a prodigal, a reprobate, a spendthrift, and everything else evil. But I cannot help it. I'll try and send my dad just as much money as I can, and just as many good words. I'll confess he has some good little cause to be displeased with me, for thirty-seven dollars a month sounds pretty big. But I will explain all to him, and may the Lord soften his heart!

July 31, 1875 Saturday afternoon
About twelve o'clock, Louis and I set out for Colonel Coleman's or Capt. Coleman's for trunks. At Windmill Hill, about
five miles from here we had a fine view of the mountains. I intend
to go to them if possible, Saturday after next.

Twice today, or oftener, I have been taken for "white." At the
pond this morning one fellow said he'd "be damned if there was
any nigger blood in me." At Coleman's I passed. On the road an
old chap, seeing the trunks, took me for a student coming from
school. I believe I'll leave here and pass anyhow, for I am as white
as any of them. One old fellow said today, "Look here, Tom.
Here's a black as white as you are."

August 7, 1875
Today has been a happy day for me for I was at last enabled
to send Pa some money. I sent him fifteen dollars. I sent Lewis
two.

Mr. Turner gave me $37, and Richardson said that was a pretty
good salary for a third grade school.

I had a stormy time at meeting Wednesday night, but it's all
right now.

August 11, 1875
Last Saturday, I walked to Spartanburg and ate heartily there,
and then, contrary to the laws of nature and the laws of health,
set out immediately for home.

I suppose that my food was not well digested. I sweated a great
deal, and the wind blew very hard, and stopped the perspiration.
I also got wet a little. This combination of forces formed a re-
sultant bowel and lung sickness. Night before last I took a dose
of castor oil, but my stomach doesn't feel right yet. I hope and
pray that I won't be dyspeptic and consumptive.

Teaching school in the country is pretty rough for those who
are not used to it.

I began by taking too much exercise and eating too much, and
it is about to injure me. "All ye country school teachers, take care
of your health."

Today is Thursday. Tomorrow is the last day of the week.
Time "ske-daddles." Go ahead, old Time, but don't go too fast.
I think I'll go home after this school is completed "if I live and
nothing happens."

Honor thy father and thy mother, that thy days may be long
in the land which the Lord, thy God, giveth thee.

—*Bible*

Friday, August 13, 1875

I feel considerably better than I have been feeling for some
days. I hope I shall be well in a few days, but I cannot shut my
eyes to the fact that school teaching, directly or indirectly, has
ruined my health. I don't feel at all like a boy of seventeen
should.

Five weeks of school! Today closes my fifth week, and it is
either, one-half, or five-eighths of my school-term, and I don't
much care which. This week has passed very well. I have made
tremendous progress in algebra, almost finished Natural Philosophy, read *Universal Education,* and think it spendid, abounding
in plain representations of undisputed facts, and clear demonstra-
tions of excellent theories, many of which have been confirmed
by experiment.

When I finish that *Elementary Algebra,* I think I shall get a
University Algebra and try for a *Peck's Mechanics.* I would like
to get a *Bryant and Statton's Bookkeeping* but books cost a great
deal of money. I think when I finish my algebra, I shall take up
Latin grammar again, for if I have the remotest idea of studying
medicine, a knowledge of Latin is very essential.

When I received my salary, I bought Dickens' *Barnaby Rudge.*
It is splendid. In it I found Dolly Varden, after which character
I suppose the Dolly Varden dresses were named. Sweet Dolly!
Dear Emma! Faithful Joe! Honest Gabriel! Queer old Grip!

No one need tell me, that a school cannot be governed without
the administration of corporal punishment—unless it is a very
bad school indeed. I have taught five weeks without it, and can,
very probably teach five more; at any rate, I shall try. I have had
an enrollment for the month of but 38, but a good many more
will probably come. I want as large an enrollment, and as good
an average as possible. The "committee" said they were going
around to see about my board this week, but they "hain't" come
yet.

I don't want to pay Bomar anything, and won't if I can help
it. But I expect I shall have to. If I do, I'll be slim when I go
"ter hum. . . ."

Well! uneducated people are the most bigoted, superstitious,

hardest-headed people in the world! These folks downstairs believe in ghosts, luck, horse shoes, cloud-signs, witches, and all
other kinds of nonsense, and all the argument in the world
couldn't get it out of them.
  These people don't know words enough for a fellow to carry
on a conversation with them. He must reduce his phraseology
several degrees lower than that of the first reader, and then all
the reason and demonstration has no more effect than a drop of
water on a field of dry wheat! "Universal Education" is certainly
a much-to-be-wished-for but, at present, little-to-be-hoped-for
blessing.

Saturday, August 20, 1875
  This is the doggondest county I ever saw to teach in. They say
they'll pay your board, and then don't do it. They accuse you
indirectly of lying, almost of stealing, eavesdrop you, retail every
word you say. Eavesdrop you when you're talking to yourself,
twist up your words into all sorts of ambiguous meanings, refuse
to lend you their mules, etc. They are the most suspicious people
in the world, good-sized liars, hypocrites, inquisitive little
wenches, etc. I wouldn't teach here another year for fifty dollars
a month!

  Charles Chesnutt was not to teach in small country schools for
long. He soon succeeded Cicero Harris as principal of a public
school in Charlotte, and in 1877, he was appointed to a position
of considerable importance in the new Normal School in Fayetteville established in that year by the State of North Carolina to
train teachers for its colored schools. It received an annual ap-
propriation of $2,000 from the state and was housed in the upper
story of the Howard School on Gillespie Street, a building supplied free of rent by the colored people of Fayetteville. Robert
Harris, principal of the Howard School, was appointed the first
principal of the new Normal School, with Charles, now nineteen
years old, as first assistant and teacher of reading, writing, spelling, composition, and related subjects.
  Among the interesting and prosperous colored families in
Fayetteville at this time was the Perry family. Edwin Perry was
proprietor of the barber shop in the Fayetteville Hotel; he was
considered very well-to-do by the colored people and was highly
respected throughout the town. The Perrys lived in an interesting

old colonial house with white columns and open fireplaces, and with a great magnolia tree standing guard at each side of the house. The Perry girls were bright and lively and were the leaders among the young folk. Susan Perry was a teacher in the Howard School and Charles spent much of his spare time at the Perrys. On June 6, 1878, Charles and Susan were married and set up housekeeping in two rooms of the Perry home.

Charles, now twenty years old, a teacher in the most important school for colored people in North Carolina, head of a household, began to look forward to the future. He had no intention of spending all his life in Fayetteville. Life there was too circumscribed, and he was ambitious. He loved to study, but there were no teachers from whom he could learn. He had been studying by himself for years; he wanted more than that.

He began to learn stenography at this time, thinking that if he mastered stenography, he would have a means of earning his living in some other place. He studied entirely by himself, for there was no one in the town familiar with it. Meanwhile, he continued to write in his journal:

October 16, 1878

I do not think that I shall ever forget my Latin. The labor I spend in trying to understand it thoroughly, and the patience which I am compelled to exercise in clearing up the doubtful or difficult points furnish, it seems to me, as severe a course of mental discipline as a college course would afford. I would above all things like to enjoy the advantages of a good school, but must wait for a future opportunity. In some things I seem to be working in the dark. I have to feel my way along; like Edmond Dantes in Dumas' *Monte Cristo,* I have become accustomed to the darkness. As I have been thrown constantly on my own resources in my solitary studies, I have acquired some degree of self-reliance. As I have no learned professor or obliging classmate to construe the hard passages and work the difficult problems, I have persevered until I solved them myself.

I love music. I live in a town where there is some musical culture; I have studied and practised till I can understand and appreciate good music, but I never hear what little there is to be heard. I have studied German, and have no one to converse with but a few Jewish merchants who can talk nothing but business. As to procuring instruction in Latin, French, German, or music, that is entirely out of the question. First class teachers would not teach a "nigger," and I would have no other sort.

I will go to the North, where, although the prejudice sticks, like a foul blot on the fair scutcheon of American liberty, yet a man may enjoy these privileges if he has the money to pay for them. I will live down the prejudice, I will crush it out. If I can exalt my race, if I can gain the applause of the good, and approbation of God, the thoughts of the ignorant and prejudiced will not concern me.

April 23, 1879

I had the pleasure of a long conversation with Dr. Haigh, when he was waiting for the advent of my little Ethel into this "sinful world." He thinks I can succeed in the North, for there are more opportunities, and less prejudice. What they want there is ability, and this qualification, with energy and perseverance, will carry a man through. I told him that my object was to obtain my proper standing in the world, to be judged according to my merit; and he expressed the same belief that I have had for some time—that when a young man starts out in life with a purpose, and works for that purpose, he is more than apt to accomplish it.

I will go to the Metropolis or some other large city, and like Franklin, Greeley, and many others, there will I stick. I will live somehow, but live I will, and work. I can get employment in some literary avocation, or something leading in that direction. I shall depend principally upon my knowledge of stenography, which I hope will enable me to secure a position on the staff of some good newspaper, and then—work, work, work! I will trust in God and work. This work I shall undertake not for myself alone, but for my children, for the people with whom I am connected, for humanity!

3

"I Think I Must Write A Book"

DETERMINED TO SEEK employment as a stenographic reporter in a large city as soon as he should acquire sufficient skill, Charles worked incessantly at his shorthand—worried Susan, as he said, into a positive dislike for him by having her read to him for practice. At the close of the school year, he packed his valise and started out for Washington and New York. He was filled with high hopes of success, and with bright visions of the rights and privileges enjoyed by colored men in the blessed land toward which his steps were turned. He had, however, sufficient sense to engage himself for the next school year, although he intended to resign during the summer if he could better himself.

When he had been in Washington about two weeks he received a letter from Susan which made him very homesick. Having seen most of the city and realizing that there was little prospect of obtaining employment there, he decided to return to Fayetteville and enjoy the summer vacation with his little family. He wrote in his journal:

Well, I am home again, a poorer, but a wiser and happier man. This little experiment has taught me: first, that I did not understand phonography sufficiently well to become an official reporter; secondly, that if I had, it was difficult to get a position on account of the great competition. I have learned that to travel with comfort, and to live in a large city requires considerable money; that employment-seeking in a strange place even with the best of qualifications, is a weary work; that the advantages of city life can only be fully enjoyed by the wealthy, while the poor feel the full weight of the discomforts. Absence from home developed in me some of that old failing, homesickness, which I had thought myself clear of.

I think, however, that what I gained was well worth what it cost me. The change of scene, the survey of a large and beautiful city, my visits to Congress, the speeches of great men, actual contact with many things which are nice to read of and to see; the visits to the Art Gallery, studios, schools, museums, etc..., and the intercourse with my friends, have enlarged my experience and knowledge of the world; and by robbing it of some of the stage effects of distance and imagination, have made me better content to remain at home and work faithfully in my present sphere of usefulness. The fatigue of traveling has rendered home comforts more enjoyable.

I am home again. I shall follow my inclinations during the summer and devote myself to study. I have formed a general plan —one hour daily to Latin, one to German, and one to French, and one to literary composition. I shall continue to practice shorthand. An hour's work in the garden, miscellaneous reading and tending to the baby will occupy the remainder of my time. In this manner, I expect to pass a very pleasant summer.

March 14, 1880
Mr. Harris is very sick, and I do not notice any improvement in his condition. I sincerely hope that he will recover, but fear that he may not. I understand that some of his friends have been making calculations about the future management of the Normal School, in case of Mr. H's death; but he is not dead yet, and even if he should die, I am afraid his friends' hopes would be dashed.

March 16, 1880
Judge Tourgée has sold the *Fool's Errand*, I understand, for $20,000.* I suppose he had already received a large royalty on the

* Albion W. Tourgée, native of Ohio, judge of the Superior Court in North Carolina during the Reconstruction period.

sale of the first few editions. The work has gained an astonishing degree of popularity, and is to be translated into the French.

Now, Judge Tourgée's book is about the South—the manners, customs, modes of thoughts, etc., which are prevalent in this section of the country. Judge Tourgée is a northern man who has lived in the South since the war, until recently. He knows a great deal about the politics, history, and laws of the South. He is a close observer of men and things, and has exercised this faculty of observation upon the character of the southern people. Nearly all his stories are more or less about colored people, and this very feature is one source of their popularity. There is something romantic, to the northern mind, about the southern Negro. And there is a romantic side to the history of this people. Men are always more ready to extend their sympathy to those at a distance, than to the suffering ones in their midst. And the people of the North see in the colored people a race but recently emancipated from a cruel bondage, struggling for education, for a higher social and moral life, against wealth, intelligence, and racial prejudice, which are all united to keep them down. And they hear the cry of the oppressed and struggling ones, and extend a hand to help them; they lend a willing ear to all that is spoken or written concerning their character, habits, etc. And if Judge Tourgée, with his necessarily limited intercourse with colored people, and with his limited stay in the South, can write such interesting descriptions, such vivid pictures of southern life and character as to make himself rich and famous, why could not a colored man, who has lived among colored people all his life, who is familiar with their habits, their ruling passions, their prejudices, their whole moral and social condition, their public and private ambitions, their religious tendencies and habits;— why could not a colored man who knew all this, and who besides, had possessed such opportunities for observation and conversation with the better class of white men in the South, as to understand their modes of thinking; who was familiar with the political history of the country, and especially with all the phases of the slavery question—why could not such a man, if he possessed the same ability, write as good a book about the South as Judge Tourgée has written? But the man is yet to make his appearance; and if I can't be the man, I shall be the first to rejoice at his début, and give God speed to his work.

May 29, 1880

I think I must write a book. I am almost afraid to undertake a book so early and with so little experience in composition. But it has been my cherished dream, and I feel an influence that I cannot resist calling me to the task. Besides, I do not know but I am as well prepared as some successful writers. A fair knowledge of the classics, speaking acquaintance with the modern languages, an intimate friendship with literature, etc., seven years' experience in the school room, two years of married life, and a habit of studying character, have I think, left me not entirely unprepared to write even a book.

Fifteen years of life in the South, in one of the most eventful eras of its history, among a people whose life is rich in the elements of romance, under conditions calculated to stir one's soul to the very depths—I think there is here a fund of experience, a supply of material, which a skillful pen could work up with tremendous effect. Besides, if I do write, I shall write for a purpose, a high, holy purpose, and this will inspire me to greater effort. The object of my writings would be not so much the elevation of the colored people as the elevation of the whites—for I consider the unjust spirit of caste which is so insidious as to pervade a whole nation, and so powerful as to subject a whole race and all connected with it to scorn and social ostracism—I consider this a barrier to the moral progress of the American people; and I would be one of the first to head a determined, organized crusade against it. Not a fierce indiscriminate onset, not an appeal to force, for this is something that force can but slightly affect, but a moral revolution which must be brought about in a different manner. The subtle almost indefinable feeling of repulsion toward the Negro, which is common to most Americans— cannot be stormed and taken by assault; the garrison will not capitulate, so their position must be mined, and we will find ourselves in their midst before they think it.

This work is of a two-fold character. The Negro's part is to prepare himself for recognition and equality, and it is the province of literature to open the way for him to get it—to accustom the public mind to the idea; to lead people out, imperceptibly, unconsciously, step by step, to the desired state of feeling. If I can do anything to further this work, and can see any likelihood of obtaining success in it, I would gladly devote my life to it.

June 25, 1880
Our school closed on Thursday morning. Our exhibition was held on Wednesday afternoon, and was quite a success. I have heard no expression of dissatisfaction from any one who attended, and, a presumptive proof that the services were not uninteresting, very few indeed of the audience left during the exercises, though the program occupied upwards of three hours. Mr. Bryan, editor of the *Examiner,* and Mr. Cobb were there. We had invited about fifteen of the principal citizens, but only these two deigned to acknowledge our courtesy by their presence. Well, the state paid for the paper and postage.

I expected, quite confidently, to take private instruction in French and German from Mr. Neufeld, the German teacher, and I had not the slightest doubt that I should be able to take Greek from Mr. Cobb, but *Mann denkt; Gott lenkt.* Professor Neufeld's time is so fully occupied that at present he cannot possibly take another pupil. He says there have been some objections made on the part of some of his patrons, to his taking a colored pupil. He says, however, that nothing of that kind would influence him at all, as he is sufficiently independent to lose twenty scholars, if necessary, without experiencing any inconvenience. He lent me a German reader, and has promised to consider my request still further.

I shall continue my studies as best I can. I have made considerable progress by my unassisted efforts heretofore, and feel that I can make greater now. Mr. Cobb is going away and cannot give me Greek, so I have yet to decide whether I will take it or not. I shall read Latin, French, and German, with history, biography, and shorthand thrown in for lighter hours; composition and music shall not be forgotten; domestic economy, practically applied to housekeeping, will fill up another portion of my time, and with these friends and companions, silent but eloquent, I shall try to spend the summer pleasantly, and with profit.

June 28, 1880
Professor Neufeld has consented to give me instruction in French and German—three lessons a week—Tuesdays and Thursdays from twelve to one, and Saturdays in the morning. I am very happy to have this golden opportunity. I have succeeded tolerably well without any instruction heretofore, but now I will see what

I can do with it. I shall pay Mr. Neufeld five dollars per month, and I would willingly pay ten, if it were necessary.

I am trying to think of a subject for an essay—critical or biographical, and I also want subjects for a series of lectures which I purpose to deliver to the school, or to the literary society next session. I wish to inspire the young men with ambition—honorable ambition, and earnest desire for usefulness and I would point them to the heights of knowledge, and tell them how to attain them; to the temple of fame and how to reach it. It is true they cannot all be lawyers, doctors, and divines, but they will all be better men, if they cherish high aspirations. I shall write the lectures or essays and commit them to memory, so that I can deliver them with ease and effect.

July 5, 1880
I have had several lessons in French and German. I like my teacher very well; he is intelligent, polite, well-educated. He took the degrees in Philosophy at his University, and studied Chemistry in Paris, and Anatomy at Oxford, England, under Huxley, one of the leaders of the modern school of thought, i.e., a scientific infidel. He was elected, he says, to the Lower House of the Reichstag, I suppose, at the age of twenty-two. He has travelled much, having on one occasion accompanied an English geographical expedition through the United States and Mexico. He can teach Latin, Greek, French, German, and Italian.

The French accent is hard to learn. I am fortunate in getting a teacher who knows it correctly. I am now translating from English to German and French.

Wednesday, July 7, 1880
"A fellow feeling makes us wondrous kind." The people here, some of them at any rate, are prejudiced to Neufeld because he is a foreigner and a Jew. He says they are so much prejudiced that he would just like to hurt them real bad once. I wish he would. Some of these purse-proud aristocrats seem to think they own the whole world, and that other people live only because they graciously vouchsafe to permit them.

August 4, 1880
I am getting along finely with my German and French. One or two more lessons will take me through the first book, and then

after a rapid review, I will be ready for the second, which, as far as grammar is concerned, completes the course.

September 8, 1880

Mr. H. says that when a small boy, he was a Whig, although his father was a Democrat. He thinks his political opinions were influenced by a rhyme which was common in those days:

> Whigs
> Feed on pigs,
> And ride in gigs;
> Democrats
> Eat dead rats
> And ride on cats.

And as he always had an eye to the good things of this world, he was a Whig.

4

Principal of the State
Normal School at Fayetteville

IN THE FALL OF 1880 Robert Harris died, and the Local Board
of Managers of the Normal School, Dr. T. D. Haigh, the Honorable W. C. Troy, and J. D. Williams, Esq., three of Fayetteville's
leading citizens, insisted that Chesnutt go to the state capital
at Raleigh to apply for the position of principal. He took some
recommendations with him to give to the Superintendent of
Public Instruction. These recommendations were exceedingly
interesting. One of his sponsors wrote: "He is competent—he is
educated—and has the peculiar faculty of imparting information
to others. His morality is high-toned, and although colored, he
is a gentleman."

In anticipation of this appointment, the members of the Board
had held a meeting some days before, and had decided to ask
Governor Jarvis to increase the salary of the principal from
$62.50 to $75 per month, for they wanted Chesnutt to remain
in Fayetteville and be satisfied.

In November, 1880, Chesnutt at the age of twenty-two, became
principal of the Normal School at the then unusual salary of
$75 per month. At times he was content; more often he yearned
for wider fields; and he chafed constantly under the hampering
restrictions of life in the South.

Susan and he had moved from the Perry house into a home
of their own. The baby Ethel was growing into a fine little girl,
and another child, Helen Maria, was born in December. They
were in comfortable circumstances and Susan was able to have
a woman to help her with the housework. Charles bought an

organ which gave them both great pleasure. Susan and the two little girls spent the summer months up in the mountains (as they were then called) at Carthage, and Charles joined them when he was ready for his vacation. Charles's position made it necessary for them to entertain people from out of town—ministers, educators, teachers who came to visit the school—and as both he and Susan were extremely hospitable, this was a pleasure as well as a responsibility.

Chesnutt's ardent spirit, however, could not find enough to do. The school did not use up all of his energy, and he arranged to give some of the more ambitious young people of the town lessons in music. He taught both instrumental and vocal music at twenty-five cents a lesson. Soon he had ten pupils taking organ lessons and five, singing lessons.

Then he started a Latin class of ten young men and women. This class met twice a week in the evenings, for which he charged each member one dollar a month. These young colored people of Fayetteville, striving hard for a finer and fuller way of life, were learning how to appreciate beauty in its various forms: in music, in literature, in life; and they were willing to pay for it. Under Chesnutt's leadership they made rapid progress.

Chesnutt was also active in the Methodist Church as organist, choir-master, and superintendent of the Sunday School. Thus he was devoting himself intensively to the service of his community. But in addition to all these activities, he kept up his reading and study and worked endlessly at the practice of shorthand. He kept his notes in shorthand; he took down all the lectures he was able to attend. In October, 1880, he went to Raleigh to report a speech of Frederick Douglass for the Raleigh *Signal*. On Sundays he reported the minister's sermons. He had Susan reading to him late into the night. He woke her up before dawn to get more practice. And during these years in which he was mastering stenography, he met not one person who knew anything about it. He had determined to leave Fayetteville and to seek his fortune in the North, but he wanted to be sure that he could support his growing family in some other way than teaching before he gave up his position at the school. Stenography was a comparatively new profession, and he intended to get into it on the ground floor. Shorthand was to be the magic carpet to take him to the North, to the land of opportunity, to life! He wrote in his journal:

Jan. 15, 1881

I gave up my French and German lessons at the beginning of the year. I cannot afford to pay for them, and I think I have about used up my teacher. Not that I know a tithe of the German or French that he does; but I have got to the end of my method, and he doesn't seem to know much about oral instruction. As an offset to the loss of the German and French, I shall, during the remainder of the session take a thorough course in history and poetry. I have already read Goldsmith's *Rome,* Macaulay's *Life and Letters* and have begun Merivale's *Rome* which I shall read with the greatest minuteness. I want to be a scholar, and a scholar should be accurate in all he knows.

Jan. 21, 1881

I had a conversation with Robert Hill last night, about Southern affairs. He is very intelligent, uses good English, and understands what he talks about. He was once a slave, and was badly treated. His argument to the white man who tried to coax him to come over to the Democratic Party, and "Let them damn Yankees alone," was, "Take away all the laws in our favor that 'them damn Yankees' have made, and what would be left?" He believes that the local affairs of the South will be best administered by the property-owners, but he is a stalwart Republican in all National affairs—in all of which we agree.

He related a conversation he had with John McLaughlin—a poor white man, and a clerk in Williams' store.

"Bob," said McLaughlin, "what kind of a fellow is this here Chesnutt?"

"Well, sir, he's a perfect gentleman in every respect; I don't know his superior."

"Why! He's a nigger, ain't he?"

"Yes, but—"

"Well, what kind of an education has he?"

"He's not a college bred man, but he has been a hard student all his life. You can't ask him a question he cannot answer."

"He's this shorthand writer," musingly.

"Yes, sir."

"Does he think he's as good as a white man?"

"Every bit of it, sir."

Then Hill went on to argue about the equality of intelligence and so on, but McLaughlin wound up with this declaration,

which embodies the opinion of the South on the Negro Question—
"Well, he's a nigger; and with me a nigger is a nigger, and
nothing in the world can make him anything else but a nigger."

Saturday, March 12, 1881
I have just finished Merivale's *General History of Rome.* I like
it very much. It is calm and judicial in tone, and so far as my
knowledge of history will allow me to say, perfectly impartial.

I shall now take up Greeley's *American Conflict,* and read it
in connection with such other works on American history as I
can procure. I shall pay special attention to the political history,
and the governmental policy.

Thursday, March 17, 1881
I have skimmed *The Negro in the Rebellion* by Dr. Brown *
and it only strengthens me in my opinion that the Negro is yet
to become known who can write a good book. Dr. Brown's books
are mere compilations and if they were not written by a colored
man, they would not sell for enough to pay for the printing. I
read them merely for facts, but I could appreciate the facts better
if they were well presented. The book reminds me of a gentleman
in a dirty shirt. You are rather apt to doubt his gentility under
such circumstances. I am sometimes doubtful of the facts for
the same reason—they make but a shabby appearance.

I am reading Molière's *Le Mari Confondu,* or the *Cuckold.* It
is amusing.

I had a rough time in school today. I had to keep my men
in and lecture them about "wenching," as the *Spectator* hath it.
Then the girls got to fighting this afternoon. The young folks
seem to have spring fever. I suppose the weather affects them
somewhat like the other young animals. I am afraid they are told
very little at home about correct principles.

Sunday afternoon, April 10, 1881
Our Second Term Examination was over yesterday. I am quite
fagged out. Examinations are very useful and necessary, but they
are also very tiresome.

* William Wells Brown (1816-1884), Negro reformer and historian, author
of numerous books, among them, *The Negro in the American Rebellion, His
Heroism and His Fidelity* (1867).

Wednesday night, May 4, 1881

Several things have occurred lately which lead me to think that the colored man is moving upward very fast. The Prohibition movement has the effect of partly breaking down the color line, and will bring the white and colored people nearer together, to their mutual benefit. Some of the white teachers in the Graded School came down to visit our school a few weeks ago, and one of them gave us quite a puff in the *Examiner*. We are evidently in the good graces of the best people of the state.

The Colored Presbytery of Yadkin have been in session here for nearly a week. I invited them down to visit our school, and yesterday they made a "reconnaissance in force," and seemed to be very well pleased. We made a requisition on them for "gas," which they supplied in considerable quantity; their advice was excellent. A more intelligent body of colored men has never met in our town before.

July 21, 1881

I am reading a course of professional literature at present, Boot's *School Amusements,* and Wickersham's *School Economy.* I have already completed, and derived valuable information from both. I expect to devote the remainder of the vacation which I spend in Fayetteville to preparation for the next session.

Thursday, August 4, 1881

The question of Prohibition or free whiskey will be decided today. We had a large and enthusiastic Prohibition meeting at the market house last night. The anti's had their row at Liberty Point. I made a rather poor speech; Scurlock and Slocomb, very good ones. Our campaign has brought out a number of quiet men to the front.

Tomorrow I go up to Carthage with Elder Grange to see my wife and babies. They have been away for about a month, and my heart yearns for them. I will take Shakespeare and a Mental Philosophy, a Logic, and a few other books to amuse myself with. From Susie's account, the weather is much pleasanter there than here.

December 31, 1881

This is the last night of the old year—a fit time to take retrospect of the old, and to make good resolutions for the new. But

I am too lazy tonight to do either the one or the other—so I shall close my journal, and read *King Henry the Sixth*. I read *Henry the Fifth* the other night. Falstaff was a jolly old rogue, ancient Pistol a cowardly braggart, Fluellen an amusing character. I saw the play acted by Rignold some years ago, and in it the part of Fluellen and his "disciples of the Roman wars" was very well rendered indeed. Goodby, Old Year! Welcome, new! and as the poet would probably remark, "Do well by me, and I'll do the same by you."

Saturday, February 18, 1882

Last night I paid Mr. Hodges, my tutor, ten dollars, balance due for two months instruction in Greek. He is a very nice young man, a thorough Southerner, but also a gentleman. My intercourse with him was pleasant enough. He is a college graduate—Davidson College, and pretty well informed, but without much taste for literature, as I have scarcely seen a book in his room for four months except his medical books, which I suppose he has been studying diligently.

I have now spent four months in the study of Greek, and according to my plans for the session, I must now stop, and devote my time to phonography and composition in preparation for a different work from the one I am now engaged in. I hope to write two hundred words a minute in two months' time. My friend Hodges has paid me some high compliments; as he is a Southerner, I suppose I ought to feel highly gratified.

"Praise from Sir Hubert Stanley is praise indeed," but I have become so accustomed to it, and to the narrow prejudice which prevents it from bringing any substantial rewards, that I am afraid I don't appreciate it as I ought.

March 7, 1882

I am reading a memoir of Sydney Smith. It is interesting, but not so much so as Macaulay's *Life and Letters*. What a blessing is literature, and how grateful we should be to the publishers who have placed its treasures within reach of the poorest. Shut up in my study, without the companionship of one congenial mind, I can enjoy the society of the greatest wits and scholars of England, can revel in the genius of her poets and statesmen, and by a slight effort of imagination, find myself in the company of the greatest men of earth. Can work procure success? Then success is mine! My only fear is that I may spoil it all by working too much.

I hear colored men speak of their "white friends." I have no white friends. I could not degrade the sacred name of "friendship" by associating it with any man who feels himself too good to sit at a table with me, or to sleep at the same hotel. True friendship can only exist between men who have something in common—between equals in something, if not everything; and where there is respect as well as admiration. I hope yet to have a friend. If not in this world, then in some distant future eon, when men are emancipated from the grossness of the flesh, and mind can seek out mind; then shall I find some kindred spirit, who will sympathize with all that is purest and best in mine, and we will cement a friendship that shall endure throughout the ages.

I get more and more tired of the South. I pine for civilization and companionship. I sometimes hesitate about deciding to go, because I am engaged in a good work, and have been doing, I fondly hope, some little good. But many reasons urge me the other way; and I think I could serve my race better in some more congenial occupation. And I shudder to think of exposing my children to the social and intellectual proscription to which I have been a victim. Is not my duty to them paramount? And can I not find hundreds who will do gladly, and as well, the work which I am doing?

In May, 1883, Charles reached his goal—he could write two hundred words a minute. Now was the time for him to leave Fayetteville and to seek his fortune in the golden North. It needed courage to make this decision. None of the people dearest to him approved of his going. Susan, whose third baby was expected in September, and her parents thought him very foolish. What more, they asked, could a man in his position want? His father disapproved of his plans and tried to discourage him by telling him how glad he had been to get back to Fayetteville. His three sisters were heartbroken; his pupils would not believe that he could desert them; his friends urged him to reconsider his decision. But Charles, moved by some inner force, resisted all appeals and submitted his resignation to the Board of Managers.

FAYETTEVILLE, N. C.
May 12, 1883

To THE BOARD OF MANAGERS OF THE
STATE COLORED NORMAL SCHOOL
GENTLEMEN:

I hereby respectfully tender to you my resignation as principal
of the State Colored Normal School at this place, to take effect
at the close of the present session, June 22, 1883.

My motive in resigning the position is to enter into another
business which I have long contemplated following.

I take this opportunity to express to you my profound grati-
tude for the hearty cooperation you have given me in the
management of the school; for the implicit, and I trust, not ill-
deserved confidence which you have shown in my efforts to fill
the position satisfactorily; and for the uniformly kind and courteous treatment which I have received in all my intercourse with
you. I have endeavored to merit your confidence, and it is with
sincere regret that I sever the connection that has existed between us.

With the earnest wish that the school may long continue to
prosper under your management, I remain,

Very respectfully
Your obedient servant,
CHARLES W. CHESNUTT, PRINC.
STATE COLORED NORMAL SCHOOL

Then he set about the grim business of burning his bridges.
He arranged with his father-in-law to board Susan and the babies
until he could send for them. Susan's mother would be a strength
for her to cling to when the new baby was born. He sold most of
the household furniture, cleared out his desk at school, paid all
his accounts at the neighborhood stores, and packed his valises.
He began to have a conviction of guilt. Was it wrong of him to
want to leave? But he closed his mind to all doubts and fears
and kept on with his preparations.

The students in the Normal School gave him an autograph
album, which he cherished all his life. On the Sunday before
he left, he bade the Sunday School pupils farewell. With tears
in his eyes, he told them that he had to go, that some inner com-
pulsion made it necessary for him to leave them, and then, when
they were all in tears, too, he went to the organ and announced

the hymn—"Fierce and wild the storm is raging," which seemed
not inappropriate to the occasion.

The members of the school board and others wrote him splendid recommendations. The Fayetteville *Observer* of June 11,
1883 had a flattering editorial about him.

One of the leading merchants of the town, Mr. A. H. Slocomb,
invited Chesnutt into his office a day or two before he left, expressed his regret at his going away, and asked him his plans.
Chesnutt explained that he had learned the art of shorthand, and
hoped to earn a living by it in New York. Mr. Slocomb wished
him good luck; but added that if he found things harder than
he had anticipated, and needed financial aid, he was to go to
Mr. Slocomb's factor in New York, who would be instructed to
advance him money if he applied for it.

So, filled with courage and high hopes, armed with notebook
and pencil, followed by the tears and blessings of the community,
Chesnutt started northward on the great adventure.

5

Stenographer, Lawyer, Author

WHEN CHESNUTT reached New York he found that his stenographic skill secured him immediate employment. He became a reporter for Dow, Jones and Company, a Wall Street News agency, and contributed a daily column of Wall Street gossip to the *New York Mail and Express.*

In an essay entitled *Literary Reminiscences,* which he wrote many years later, he says: "I worked once for six months in a Wall Street news agency, in the shadow of the New York stock exchange, some twenty-seven years ago, when Jay Gould and William H. Vanderbilt were the money kings that dominated the financial world. And yet I never, to my knowledge, saw either of them, or sought to have them pointed out to me. I do not know that it could be called a literary reminiscence, but as one of my duties I supplied a daily column of Wall Street gossip to the *Mail and Express,* then the property of Cyrus W. Field, to provide which required me to interview various prominent brokers, and occasionally Mr. Field himself. One of my principal victims was Henry W. Clews, even then a prominent banker and broker, who has maintained a prominent place in the public eye on a shore which has been strewn with innumerable wrecks. I often wonder, when I read newspaper comments on stock market conditions and prospects, whether any of them were written by green young men from the country, with as little knowledge of finance as I had; and I am always suspicious of the man who foretells the course of the market."

He was thus able to carry out the plans that he had made before leaving Fayetteville. He could earn his living by this magic gift of stenography, and make a slight start into the field of literature via the gate of journalism. But, as time went on, he became homesick for Susan and longed to see his little son, born since he left. New York seemed a poor place in which to rear a family, and in November he resigned and went to Cleveland, the city of his birth. There he secured a good position in the accounting department of the Nickel Plate Railroad Company, writing letters and footing ledgers. At night, after his day's work was over, he would write down all the interesting incidents of the day, and thus stored up material for some of the humorous writings which were later published in *Puck* and *Tid-Bits*.

Susan, who was only twenty-two, was getting restless down in Fayetteville, but she kept as cheerful as she could and wrote frequently to Charles.

SUSAN TO CHARLES, NOVEMBER 20, 1883

Your letter informing me that you had secured a position in Cleveland has been received. You can't imagine what a load was taken off me when I read it. When I heard you had gone to Cleveland, not only my eyes were open, but my heart, for I saw you were not satisfied in New York, and I was afraid you couldn't get employment in Cleveland right away.

I have been very sick since I wrote last—have had a severe attack of rheumatism. I was taken in the night and suffered all night. Nothing relieved me, so I sent for the doctor. He gave me something to take and rub with, and said if I got no better to send him word. However, I am better now, and can use my right hand once more.

I tried to settle up with Pa the other night, but couldn't for the lack of money. . . . If you have the money, and can pay $15.00 for the time I have been here, do so. Write to him, and tell him just what you will do, as I would rather have no more to say about it. . . .

I would like to have some money myself, as I owe the doctor $2.00, $1.00 for medicine, and some for washing. Don't get out of heart—I am as economical as I can be.

I can't write any more for Edwin is crying as loud as he can, so I must stop and take him. Your Pa was glad you had gone to Cleveland and hoped you might get employment there, as he said you had friends there to associate with, etc. Take care of yourself and your money. I am very anxious to see you once more. Write soon and let me know how you are getting on. Much love to you.

SUSAN TO CHARLES, JANUARY 22, 1884

Your letter has been received. I had been thinking for several days you had forgotten us, as I had waited so long to hear from you. It seems as if you are all frozen up, so you can't write, but if you want me to stay here, you must write often, for I find it a very hard matter to stay here, and I tell you if you don't hurry up and send for me you will have to come to see us, and perhaps a sight of you will set me straight again.

Mrs. James R. McNeill gave a social entertainment the other night, Wednesday night, I think, for the benefit of the new school building. It was quite a pleasant gathering. Prof. Smith entertained us with select readings, and Miss Libbie Leary and Georgia Simmons played and sang. Miss Libbie sports a heavy black silk, so does Mrs. Smith. Now since I am compelled to stay here for several months longer, I find it necessary to purchase another dress. I know your eyes will open when I say I would like to have a black silk, if not that, something else you might suggest. I am wearing the same dress I wore all last winter, and 'twill never do for me to look worse than other folks, it might cause people to make unpleasant remarks, etc. Think over the matter, and send me some samples to look at, or some money to buy it, like a dear good fellow. I really think I deserve *something* since I have given you up for such a long time....

Now, my dear old Carl, think over my dress, for you know "fine feathers make fine birds," or that's the case in this instance, and you wouldn't have *your* wife looking different from other folks. All the folks join me in love to you. The little girls send many kisses to dear papa. I hope this may find you enjoying good health.

But poor Charles could not send Susan the money for a black silk dress—he simply did not have it to spare.

SUSAN TO CHARLES, FEB. 10, 1884

Little Edwin is a beauty. I would like for you to take a peep at him now. He is as fat and rosy as can be. I have a time trying to make a nurse of Ethel. She doesn't like to nurse one bit. Whenever she has to nurse her little brother, she wishes that Doctor hadn't brought him here.

I want one more opportunity of keeping house, and I will just show you how well I can have things arranged and what a capital manager I'll be. How about help out there? Would I find it expensive hiring a girl about fourteen or so to help do the work? How I long to be with you once more. I don't believe I ever looked forward to the coming of warm weather so eagerly before. I have found out since you left what you were to me. You were a companion, and you knew me better even than my father or mother, or at least you were more in sympathy with me than anybody else, and my failings were overlooked. No one can tell, my dearest husband, how I miss that companionship. God grant that we may not be separated much longer, for I cannot stand it, I am afraid. . . .

In April Chesnutt sent for his wife and children. He could not give Susan the kind of home she was accustomed to, and she would have to suffer many hardships; but they would be together and that was what they both wanted. While waiting for his family to come to Cleveland, Charles prepared a home for them. He rented a little house on Wilcutt Avenue, a street running south from Woodland Avenue across from Woodland Cemetery, for sixteen dollars a month. He went shopping for second-hand furniture, and had a delightful time buying the barest necessities—two beds and their equipment, a cradle, a bureau, a washstand, a stove, a kitchen table, two wooden chairs, two cane-seated chairs, a couple of lamps, a few dishes and pots and pans, two wash tubs, a wash board and two flatirons. Susan was shipping their good furniture from Fayetteville, but it would not get there for some time.

He hired a woman in the neighborhood to clean the house, and he arranged the furniture, but the result seemed very bleak. He bought a mirror, some matting, and bright material which he had made up into curtains. Then the little house looked more inviting and Charles was better satisfied. He bought groceries and coal and coal-oil. He made up the beds, built a fire in the stove, so that it could be lighted at once, locked the door, and set out to meet his little family. Susan had asked him to meet her in Richmond, Virginia.

SUSAN TO CHARLES, MAY 2, 1884

Yours of the 29th ult. received. This leaves me a good deal better, and if I continue to improve, I shall be able to meet your Uncle Dallas by the thirteenth. I am very anxious to go to you, and the reason I disappointed you before was for your good. I am not strong, by any means, and the doctor told me I needed building up before I started out West. Well, I am taking medicine now, and I owe him for four visits, and if you can let me have money enough to pay him and one or two other little debts, I am willing to undertake the journey (God willing) by the thirteenth. I will write to your Uncle Dallas and tell him when I shall leave here. If nothing prevents, I shall meet you on the 13th or at least I shall leave Wilmington for Richmond at that time. I hope I shall not have to wait in Richmond for you. If possible, be there when I get there. If I am able, I shall pack my things tomorrow, and try to get them off on Monday morning. . . .

I hear you have had a cyclone or an earthquake at Cleveland. I wish you were not so far from home.

Susan left Fayetteville for Wilmington as she had planned. Dallas Chesnutt, Charles's uncle, was a railway mail-clerk, running from Wilmington, North Carolina, to Richmond, Virginia. Susan had arranged to take the same mail-train, so that she would feel somewhat protected on her journey.

The people of Fayetteville were very kind to her. They gave her all sorts of parting gifts. Mrs. Willie McNeill, who was fond of the children, made all three of them little satin bonnets—Ethel's was pink, Nellie's, blue, and the baby's, white. Susan in her tan linen dress and linen duster, and her three babies in their little satin bonnets were very cheerful and happy as they started off to go to their new home in Cleveland.

Charles met them in Richmond, the end of the Southern Line. As he walked through the train looking for them, he must have looked like a young god to Susan, who was ill and exhausted. The three babies were grimy and tired, their little satin bonnets the only cheerful thing about them. Susan seemed so terribly young and frail that Charles had a pang of apprehension. Was he right to uproot her and bring her into a northern climate?

They stayed in Richmond a day or two, so that Susan could rest, and then went on to Cleveland. The weather was very cold for May, and Susan could not get warm. She became seriously ill, and Neddie, the baby, suffered with her. The little girls were hardy enough, but Susan and the baby did not thrive, and Charles was terribly worried. Susan was unhappy and wanted to return to Fayetteville. The doctor advised Charles to let her go back, and he finally consented on the condition that the older children should remain with him.

"The girls stay here," he told Susan. "I'll get someone to look after them until you return. You will be better off without them." But Susan would not leave the little girls. Her health began to improve as summer advanced, and she was glad that she had not gone back. She had good neighbors, most of them people of German descent, who did much to make life easier for the little home-sick mother.

Later on the Chesnutts moved into a much better house on Ashland Avenue. It was a white, one-story house in a wide, well-kept yard with a white picket fence around it. Susan was well now and began to enjoy life. Charles was transferred to the legal department of the Nickel Plate Railroad, into the office of Judge Samuel E. Williamson, where he remained for two years, earning his living as a stenographer and studying law. He spent all his spare time in writing. Essays, poems, short stories, sketches, he wrote and destroyed and wrote again. Never satisfied with what he was doing, but driven by an urge to create, he kept on writing.

In April, 1885, S. S. McClure, a young man of about Charles's age, organized the first newspaper syndicate in the United States. For this syndicate he needed three hundred short stories a year, averaging fifteen hundred words each. These stories were appearing in the *New Haven Register, Pittsburgh Chronicle, Pittsburgh Telegraph, Cleveland News and Herald, Chicago Inter-Ocean,* and occasionally in the *Boston Globe.*

McClure, who had no capital at all, was "nursing this little project along on about $30.00 a week," and he could not pay popular and established authors for their work. He needed to find young and ambitious writers to cooperate with him. So he offered a prize for the best short story written by a new and unknown author. Charles read of this contest in the newspaper. He was certainly new and unknown, and he at once entered "Uncle Peter's House" in the contest. Susan and he waited impatiently for an answer. When it came, it was written in purple ink on paper without a letterhead. It informed Charles that his story had not taken the prize, but that McClure could use it in his syndicate and would pay him $10 for it. In the same letter was a request for more sketches from his pen.

Chesnutt had really broken into print, and when the story appeared in the *Cleveland News and Herald* in December, 1885, Susan and he were elated. During the next three years he wrote the following stories for the McClure Syndicate: "A Tight Boot," "A Bad Night," "Two Wives," "Secret Ally," "A Midnight Adventure," "A Doubtful Success," and "Cartwright's Mistake." Some of these were so long that they ran through two issues of a paper. Several of them were Southern stories; others were drawn from his experiences in New York City. He received five or ten dollars for each story, and repeated requests for others.

Meanwhile he was spreading his wings. In 1885, he published several poems in a weekly publication called *The Cleveland Voice.* In 1886, he began writing for *Family Fiction, The Great International Weekly Story Paper,* published in Washington, D. C.: "Tom's Warm Welcome," in November, 1886; "The Fall of Adam," in December; "McDugald's Mule," in January, 1887; "How Dasdy Came Through," in February; "Wine and Water," in April; "A Grass Widow," in May. "A Fool's Paradise" was published in *Family Fiction* in November, 1888.

In 1886 also Chesnutt began writing for *Tid-Bits* and later for *Puck.* These pieces were humorous sketches in which the scene was usually laid in a downtown business office, and the incidents had to do with railroads and lawyers. He also published other stories in the *Chicago Ledger* and in a paper entitled *Household Realm.*

When Chesnutt had read law for two years in Judge Williamson's office, he went down to Columbus to take the bar examination. *The Cleveland Leader* for Friday morning, March 4, 1887, said in its column, entitled "State Capital Gossip":

"Following is a list of applicants admitted to practice law by the Supreme Court: ... Charles W. Chesnutt, Cleveland. ... Mr. Charles W. Chesnutt stood at the head of his class, having made the highest per cent in the thorough examination, which was one of the hardest to which a class of students was ever subjected."

The elation that Charles and Susan felt on reading this in the morning paper was shared by the little girls who had always thought their father was a great man and now were sure of it.

It was just after Chesnutt was admitted to the bar that Judge
Williamson called him into his office and asked him what his plans
for the future were. Chesnutt replied that he had often thought,
in view of the race prejudice in the United States, that if he had
the means, he would take his wife and his three children and go
to Europe, to London, perhaps, where with his art and his profession, he could earn a living and relieve his children of certain
disabilities inevitable in the United States.

Judge Williamson, who was a wealthy man, said that he thought
it a very wise plan, and he added that if Chesnutt upon further
reflection was still desirous of going to Europe, he would advance
him the money to take his family to England and to carry him
along until he could get a foothold there.

Charles thanked him warmly and went home to tell Susan of
Judge Williamson's offer. But Charles was an idealist, and after
much discussion with Susan, he decided that he would rather
"paddle his own canoe." He felt that success in his own country
against terrific odds would be worth more than success in a foreign
country. He would wait and see whether someday, perhaps, in the
city of his birth, the time would come when he would be treated
as a scholar and a gentleman. Having made his decision, he went
on with his writing, and three months later *The Atlantic Monthly*
accepted the first of his conjure stories, "The Goophered Grapevine."

Chesnutt had moved into the offices of Henderson, Kline, and
Tolles, one of Cleveland's great law firms, and was working at
stenography while waiting for legal business. The little house on
Ashland Avenue became too small for the family as the children
grew older; so they moved into a larger house on Florence Street,
where the neighbors were friendly people. On one side lived an
English family named Wiley. Mr. Wiley and his eldest son worked
for the Standard Oil Company. Nell Wiley was fond of the little
Chesnutt girls and enrolled them in the Sunday School of St. Mary's
Episcopal Church on Woodland Avenue near Kennard Street.
Susan wrote to Fayetteville for her letter, and became a member of St. Mary's congregation, and later Neddie was christened
there.

On the other side lived a German family, the Dauberts, who
had recently lost their two little children. The Dauberts had a
beautiful garden with a pergola covered with grapevines, and the
children were invited to play in the yard. Mrs. Daubert would

bring out the toys of her children and the little girls played with them by the hour.

Ethel went to Dike School, and later Nellie was enrolled there. Charles bought a piano, and began to give Ethel music lessons. Christmas was always a wonderful time. The children never had a tree, but hung up their stockings in the sitting-room and came down early in the morning to see what Santa Claus had brought them. One Christmas, Mr. Virgil P. Kline asked Charles, "How old are the children now, Chesnutt?" "Nine, seven, and four—the boy is four," replied Charles. "I want to send them presents, but you will have to buy them, as you know what they want." Charles started home with three two-dollar bills, one for each child.

On Christmas morning the children found in their stockings the two-dollar bills from Mr. Kline. Charles advised them to bank their money with him, draw interest on it, and save the capital. Then and there they had their first lesson in Money and Banking. These little accounts with papa were magical. Whenever they wanted money for any purpose, they drew on these, which paid dividends until they were ready for college. "Mr. Kline's two dollars" became a family byword, and always, as they grew older, produced shouts of laughter.

Later, in 1888, Lillie, Charles's youngest sister, came up from Fayetteville to live with them. Charles, who by this time had an office of his own, took her into his office and taught her shorthand and typewriting.

6

George W. Cable and the Open Letter Club

WHEN Thomas Bailey Aldrich, editor of *The Atlantic Monthly*, accepted "The Goophered Grapevine," Chesnutt realized that his dream of being a writer might really come true, for *The Atlantic Monthly* was considered the most distinguished of all the monthly magazines. The next year, in May, 1888, "Po' Sandy," another conjure story, appeared in the *Atlantic*, and, as a result, in the following year Chesnutt's association with George W. Cable began. It developed rapidly through the interest of both men in the race problem. For many months the magazines of the country and the press at large had been giving much space to the discussion of the Southern question. The *Forum* of October, 1888, carried an article on "Race Antagonism," by Senator James Eustis, which caused much discussion both South and North.

There was at this time an association of thoughtful Southern men of broad vision who were seriously trying to find some way to solve the race problem justly. The organization was called the Open Letter Club, with offices at Vanderbilt University in Nashville, Tennessee, and in New York City. Its object is here quoted: "The Open Letter Club does not make itself responsible for the sentiments or principles expressed in the papers it publishes, but simply offers a medium for the interchange of information of every sort, and from every direction, valuable to the moral, intellectual, and material interests of the South."

Following the publication of the article in the *Forum*, the *Independent* published on November 8, 1888 a reply to Senator

Eustis's article. This was written by Atticus Green Haygood, of
Georgia, a man who knew the Southern people and the Negro
problem as well as any man in the South. The Open Letter Club
reissued this reply in pamphlet form and sent it out over the
country. Some of the leading men of the South were invited by the
Independent to comment on Dr. Haygood's reply to Senator Eustis,
and these comments were published as a symposium in its issue of
February 21, 1889. The Open Letter Club reissued the symposium,
with the addition of several other letters, in pamphlet form and
mailed them out to representative men.

George W. Cable, a member of the Open Letter Club, had liked
Chesnutt's stories in the *Atlantic* and had written congratulating
him upon them. He also sent the Open Letter Club pamphlets to
Chesnutt with the request that he supply more names for the mail-
ing list, especially those of prominent North Carolinians.

Chesnutt became deeply interested in this plan to arouse the
thinking people of the country in matters so vital to himself and
his race, and offered Cable his help in collecting material for discussion, in typing manuscript, and so on. He also wrote an essay
entitled, "An Inside View of the Negro Question," and sent it off
to Cable for criticism.*

Early in 1889, Chesnutt wrote to Cable at Northampton,
Massachusetts:

MY DEAR SIR:

Permit me to trouble you long enough for you to read this letter
concerning a purely personal matter. I have been chiefly employed,
during the past two years, as a stenographic reporter in the Courts
of this county, intending to use this business as something to occupy my leisure time while awaiting the growth of a law practice.
But by a very natural process, the thing to which I have given most
time has hindered instead of helped the thing it was intended to
assist. As a consequence, I have built up a business mainly as a
stenographer, which brought me in last year an income of two
thousand dollars.

But there is a bill pending in the Legislature of this state for

---

* George Washington Cable was at the height of his fame. He had published *Old Creole Days* (1879), *The Grandissimes* (1884), *The Creoles of
Louisiana* (1884), *Dr. Sevier* (1885), *The Silent South* (1885), *Bonaventure*
(1888), and *True Stories of Louisiana* (1889). Most of his writing was first
published in *Scribner's Monthly*. His activity in reform movements was intense, and he was a highly controversial figure in the South.

the appointment of two official stenographers for this county. There are five or six men now engaged in a free-for-all for this work, and probably all of these will be applicants for the two positions. I have perhaps, more than a fighting chance—certainly that, for one of them. If I should secure it, it would pay a salary of $1500.00 a year with fees to the probable amount of $1,000.00 or $1,500.00 more; and it would in all probability fully occupy all of my time.

In the event of a failure on my part to secure one of these positions, I shall be compelled to turn my attention to other fields of effort. And my object in writing to you is to ask your opinion as to the wisdom, or rashness, of my adopting literature as a means of support.

I am aware that I am, perhaps, asking you a question an answer to which you have very meager data to base an opinion on. And I realize that I am, perhaps, presuming on a very slight acquaintance with a busy man. But I will risk the latter and say as to the former, that I can turn my hand to several kinds of literary work, can write a story, a funny skit, can turn a verse, and write a serious essay. I have even written a novel, though it has never seen the light, nor been offered to a publisher. I know German pretty well, French passably well, and could translate either into grammatical English, and I trust, for the sake of a long-suffering public, into better English than a great many of the translations that are dumped on the market.

I am impelled also, to this step, by a deep and growing interest in the discussion and settlement of the Southern question, and all other questions which affect the happiness of the millions of colored people in this country. But life is short, and anything that one can do in this matter ought to be begun, it seems to me, while something of the vigor and hopefulness of youth remains. I am 31, and time flies rapidly. It seems to me that there is a growing demand for literature dealing with the Negro, and for information concerning subjects with which he is in any manner connected— his progress in various parts of the world—in the United States, Brazil, in South America, and in other lands. It seems to me that these subjects would open up a vast field for literary work, and one in which a writer who was connected with these people by ties of blood and still stronger ties of sympathy, could be *facile princeps*, other things being equal, or in which such a writer could at least earn a livelihood.

If I could earn twelve or fifteen hundred dollars a year at literature, or in some work directly associated with it which would allow
me some time to devote to letters, I think I should be willing to
undertake it in any event; or at least in the event of my failure to
apply for or to secure one of the appointments above referred to.

If from your own experience and knowledge of the literary life,
you think it likely that I could make a success in it; or if you know
or hear of any such employment as I have suggested, and will take
the trouble to write to me on the subject, I will be under greater
obligations to you than I am already.

Very respectfully yours,
CHAS. W. CHESNUTT

Cable's reply to this letter was the suggestion that Chesnutt on
his next trip East come to Northampton and have a personal talk
with him. In the meantime, Chesnutt kept on working with Cable
on the material in which they were both so vitally interested.

In March, 1889, Chesnutt went East and visited Northampton.
The outcome of his visit was an invitation from Cable to become
his secretary and to assist him in "this noble work." Chesnutt took
some time to think over the situation, to consider all things carefully. It would be a delightful thing to work with a man like Cable
on a matter so dear to both their hearts. Then, too, the little girls
were growing fast; and in Northampton there was a college for
women, on the way to becoming one of the greatest of its kind in
the country. The beautiful town in the Connecticut River valley,
hemmed in by pine-clad mountains, would be an ideal home for
his little family. Finally, on May 3, he made his decision:

CLEVELAND, OHIO
May 3, 1889

MY DEAR MR. CABLE:

I regret to say that after mature deliberation, I have reached the
conclusion that I could not afford to come to Northampton for
any sum which, judging from the figures you have already mentioned, you would probably feel justified in offering me. The con-
tingency which immediately inspired my first letter to you did not
happen—that is, the appointment of official stenographers—so that
my business is not affected in that direction. My earnings for the
month just ended, as per memorandum lying before me, are just
$250.65. I have made a change in my business which will, I hope,

enable me to increase the income from it with less work on my part individually. So you will see that even $1200.00 or $1500.00 a year would, in comparison, be a sacrifice of half my income—a sacrifice which I, personally, would not hesitate to make, in view of the compensating advantages, but which my duty to my family, and other considerations which would perhaps not interest you, constrain me not to make.

I hope, however, to do what I can in the good cause of human rights, and am not likely to grow lukewarm in it, for if no nobler motive inspired me, my own interests and those of many who are dear to me are at stake. But I hope still to find opportunities, and I shall write, and speak, and act, as occasion may require.

I enclose you a list of names of gentlemen who will be valuable additions to the list of those to whom Open Letter Club pamphlets are sent.

My office arrangements are now such that I can give prompt attention to copying or other work, and as I have already said, you can command me for assistance in anything where distance will not be too great an obstacle.

Respectfully yours,
CHAS. W. CHESNUTT

On May 30, 1889, the *Independent* published an essay by Chesnutt entitled, "What is a White Man?" Thus he entered the arena of letters in behalf of the colored people. The desire to alleviate the condition of the colored people was one of the fundamental principles upon which Chesnutt's life had been planned, and so another of his aspirations was being fulfilled. During the next year or two he devoted a great deal of his time to this work. He would make extracts of material, analyze essays, look up statistics on North Carolina school funds and send them to Cable for use in the Open Letter Club.

In 1888 Chesnutt decided to buy a house of his own, for the rented one on Florence Street was now too small for his family. On Sunday afternoons, he and the little girls always took a long walk, and now their Sunday walk became an adventure—they went exploring for a house. The children were wild with excitement. "Will it have a bathroom?" "Will it have gas?" "Will it have a furnace?" These and other questions bombarded Charles's ears. One Sunday they walked out Cedar Avenue, an attractive street with green lawns and beautiful shade trees and an electric car with open trailer gliding down the center. They came to a large black-and-white sign at the corner of a street—"Cottage Neighborhood—for families with young children." It was a very attractive street. There were no fences; the lawns extended the length of the street, cut only by the sidewalks. Glimpses of flower gardens in the rear added to its charm. There was a vacant lot halfway between Cedar and Central, and here Charles decided to build his house. He had found one on Hilburn Street that he liked very much and had his house built on that plan. Unfortunately the cost seemed too great; so he economized by cutting off six feet from the width of the house. As the girls grew up they said that it looked consumptive—it was too narrow for the space around it. But the children thought it was a beautiful house. There were nine rooms, two stairways, three fireplaces, a furnace with hot air heat, and gas for lighting. The bathroom was the last word in luxury—the woodwork of rich mahogany, the tub of shining zinc encased in mahogany. The floor was painted dark red, and the window, which let down on a chain when one wanted to open it, had a border of red, yellow, blue, and green glass squares around it.

The Chesnutts moved into 64 Brenton Street, in May, 1889. Euclid School, a little square white brick structure of two floors on Euclid Avenue near Genesee Avenue, was the nearest school. The walk to it was long, but the children gathered up their schoolmates as they went, and the way was always pleasant.

Every night Charles listened to the story of the day's happenings. His evenings were devoted to the children. He read to them as they sat around the fireplace in the sitting-room. *Mother Goose, Alice in Wonderland, Gulliver's Travels, The Swiss Family Robinson, Tom Brown's School Days, Little Women, The Nonsense Book, David Copperfield, Uncle Remus, The Arabian Nights, Pilgrim's Progress, Nicholas Nickleby, Old Curiosity Shop, Oliver Twist, Aesop's Fables, Grimm's Fairy Tales,* and scores of other classics became the literary background of the children. Then at eight-thirty or nine o'clock, Charles would close the book and quote, "Now it's time to guzzle and swill." Susan would bring in nuts and raisins, or apples, or popcorn to be popped, or chestnuts to be roasted, and milk, and after eating supper, the children would go happily off to bed. Then Charles and Susan would shut up the house and go to the upstairs sitting-room, where Susan would sew for a while, and Charles would write until very late.

Among his writings at this time were three stories that were published before the year was finished. One of them, a story entitled "Dave's Neckliss" appeared in *The Atlantic Monthly* of October, 1889. It was a tragic story of plantation life in the days of slavery, as told by "Uncle Julius" to his Northern friends. It was not a conjure story and therefore did not appear later in *The Conjure Woman*.

"The Sheriff's Children" was published in the *Independent* of November 7, 1889, and later appeared in the color-line stories entitled *The Wife of His Youth*. "The Conjurer's Revenge" was published in the *Overland Monthly* of June, 1889, and later appeared in *The Conjure Woman*.

Susan had been trying out hired girls for several months. The house was too large for her to do the work alone. The girls were usually German or Bohemian, just over from the old country. It was hard to make them wear shoes or wash their hair. Susan would become very impatient when she saw Annie going about the house in her stocking-feet or caught the odor of Mary's unwashed hair, so that a steady stream of new girls kept trickling in and out of 64 Brenton Street.

Finally one of Susan's good neighbors, who was moving away, recommended her own servant girl, who was an excellent housekeeper and cook and was very fond of children. So Julia Bash came to the Chesnutts, and remained for several years. Her personality was remarkable. The children loved and obeyed her and she was devoted to them all.

When the family moved into the house on Brenton Street they were transferred from St. Mary's parish to Emmanuel Church out on Euclid Avenue near Bolton Avenue. Emmanuel was at that time a little frame building set on sloping ground, with the Sunday School rooms and the church parlors at the foot of the slope. The minister, the Reverend Albert Putnam, lived on Euclid Avenue next door to the church. Behind Emmanuel was a wood that extended back toward East Prospect Street. Through it ran a little stream, and violets and other spring flowers grew there. Behind the church was a home for orphaned children. The members of Emmanuel Church were among Cleveland's finest people. Susan joined the Women's Guild, and the children were enrolled in the Sunday School. The church in those days was a family affair, with picnics and parties to which the entire family went and enjoyed themselves thoroughly. When Susan finally persuaded Charles to join Emmanuel, her cup was full.

During this period Chesnutt was working on a short story called "Rena Walden." When this was finished, he sent it to Cable who had gradually become his literary adviser and sponsor. Cable read it carefully and criticized it very frankly. He told Chesnutt that he had just missed the chance of winning fame with this story, and begged him to rewrite it more dramatically.

In November, 1889, Cable came west on a lecture tour and stopped a day or two in Cleveland. Chesnutt brought him out one afternoon to the new home at 64 Brenton Street, to show him his books and manuscripts. It was a very great occasion for the family. Charles came tiptoeing out to the kitchen while Cable was reading the new version of "Rena Walden."

"Let's invite him to supper, Susan. It's getting late."

The little girls looked at Papa with wide eyes. He was glowing, his eyes were beaming, he was bubbling over with happiness.

"Let's do it, Mama," they begged, and Susan rose to the occasion, although it had been a hard day for her. She and Julia prepared the supper while Aunt Lillie and the little girls set the table. In a burst of zeal, they took out a brand new table cloth which had not been hemmed, much to Susan's consternation, but it was too late to change it when she noticed it.

Susan decided to send Neddie to bed as he was getting sleepy, but Charles said he wanted all the children to have this wonderful experience. They sat spellbound as they listened to the little bright-eyed man who seemed to be having such a delightful time with Papa.

The work for the Open Letter Club went on uninterruptedly as the following letters show.

CHESNUTT TO MISS A. M. MOFFAT, SEC., OPEN LETTER CLUB,
N. Y., Nov. 13, 1889

I thank you for the opportunity of reading ex-Congressman Waddell's letter.* His statement of the system of County Government is correct, though if given in greater detail its scope and effectiveness in nullifying the Negro majorities would be more readily understood.

I cannot, however, quite agree with his statements as to the de-

---

* Alfred Moore Waddell (1834-1912), of North Carolina, a leader in the White Supremacy Campaign of 1898.

gree of corruption which characterized the "Carpet Bag" county governments. Not all were corrupt, nor all equally corrupt, nor was their financial condition so bad as he states. In fact, Mr. Waddell's letter bears me out on this point in a very striking manner. On the second page of his letter, he says, in one sentence: "The result [of Carpet Bag Government] was that in a very short time, they [the Eastern counties] were overwhelmed with debt and ruined financially." On the same page in the following paragraph, he says that the result of the return to the old system "was wonderful, for those which had been bankrupted were in a very few years out of debt, paying dollar for dollar, and their securities at par." I submit that the two statements do not harmonize perfectly. The ruin which could be so easily repaired could not have been as complete as would seem to appear from Mr. Waddell's first statement, especially taking into consideration the fact that the recuperative power of the South was very small for many years after the war. It must also be taken into consideration that the Carpet Bag governments found the South bankrupt, and so deeply involved in debt that a generation at least would have been required to pay it off in the event that the Confederate Government had been successfully maintained. Though this debt was wiped out by the issue of the war, the country was impoverished, the local treasuries empty, and industries paralyzed. The reorganization of the State and County governments, the establishment of a common school system, were necessarily more or less expensive, and a public debt was certainly not an original invention of the Carpet-Baggers.

But the greatest mistake which Waddell, and indeed most Southerners who express themselves on this subject, make is in ascribing the corruption of Carpet-Bag rule to the Negroes. That it was mostly due to the rapacity of the corrupt and unscrupulous white men seems to be overlooked. Mr. Waddell will not say that Negroes engineered or profited to any great extent by the several jobs of considerable magnitude which confessedly disgraced Carpet-Bag rule in North Carolina. The Negroes had no competent leaders among themselves. The white people of the South, smarting from the sting of defeat, stood sullenly aloof and gave the Negro neither advice nor assistance—were indeed rather gratified at seeing him sink deeper and deeper into the slough of incompetency and misrule, for successful government by the Negro would have been a shock to all their preconceived notions about the Negro, which would have been infinitely harder to bear than even the worst mis-government.

And that is the root of the whole trouble. The white people of the South do not want to be governed by the Negro at all, whether well or ill; more than that, they do not want the Negroes to share with them the power which their numbers justly entitle them to. They prefer to curtail their own liberties very materially, as Mr. Waddell's letter admits, in order that they may entirely eliminate the Negro from political significance. I do not believe that this is necessary. One half of the time and ingenuity spent in conciliating the Negroes, in winning their friendship and confidence, that is now spent in subverting their rights, would enable the white people of the South to govern by the influence which superior wealth, station, intelligence, and experience in public affairs would naturally give them. This method of controlling the Negroes has never been tried. It would require a change of attitude on the part of the Southern white people toward the colored people. It would require such a recognition of their political and civil rights as would disarm the suspicions with which the Southern Negroes now naturally regard political overtures by the whites.

No one would deny that such a state of things, if possible, would be better for both races than the present system of suppressing the Negro, even under cover of law as is done by the County Government system of North Carolina, and the more subtle but equally effective election law recently enacted for the purpose of "clinching" the present system. Until the policy of conciliation has been tried, and has failed, there will not be in the minds of fair-minded people any sufficient excuse for a system which is avowedly based on a denial of the principle of "pure Democracy"—so highly lauded by Southern white men in the abstract, and so completely ignored by them when it conflicts with their idea of the sublime superiority of the so-called Anglo-Saxon race.

To say that the misgovernment and corruption of the Carpet-Bag County governments was unparalleled in history is a strong statement. The government of New York City under the Tweed ring, the chronic political trouble of Central and South American states, the notorious corruption of Russian local government, are instances which invite comparison. And the recent defalcations of the treasurers of Kentucky and Louisiana suggest that even if the whites of the South have all the political honesty, they very unfortunately, have not enough to go around.

Pardon the length of my letter. Your correspondent is an able attorney as well as a veteran politician, and has presented his side of the case to you in its strongest light. But in a saving clause of his letter where he foresees a possible future where the Negroes will not (to paraphrase his language in the slang of the day) regard public office as a private snap, there seems to speak the fair-minded man, rising above the advocate, and looking forward to a time when the laws will be employed to extend rather than to restrict the liberty of the citizen.

CHESNUTT TO CABLE, MARCH 28, 1890

Yours of the 21st received. I have not yet been able to elaborate as careful a paper as I should wish, but I send you herewith the result of my labors. It takes time and deliberation to do statistical work, and I have not been in a position to give this paper the necessary attention without neglecting something else. My paper is brief and by no means exhaustive. You can make use of it in its present shape under my name, if you think it worthy, or you can use it in any way you see fit.

I also send you by express today the rather meager memoranda from which I have prepared it, including the latest report of the Com. of Education. If you can use them in adding to what I have written, I shall be glad to have you do so. In any event, kindly return to me all except the Commissioners' report, which please keep, as by some chance my congressman has sent me two of them.

I received a copy of your address to the Massachusetts Club. It is a clear and able presentation of the Southern question in a new light—the hopeless struggle for pure government without free government.

I do not comprehend how a fair-minded opponent, however radically he might differ from you, could find anything harsh to say in reply to so fair and courteous an argument; if any one can lift the race question out of the mire of prejudice and partisanship into the clear light of reason and patriotism, I think you are the man. I don't agree with you, however, in the pleas for one more chance for the Southern Democrats to deal fairly with their political opponents. It is true that something would be gained by a delay of the federal interference, and if the delay were long enough continued, no federal interference would be necessary to protect the Negroes in their rights. It is easy enough to temporize with the bull when you are on the other side of the fence, but when you are in the pasture with him, as the colored people of the South are, the case is different. I take it that every citizen is entitled to such protection as the government can extend to him in the enjoyment of his rights, and that he is entitled to that protection now, and whenever his rights are invaded. I sincerely hope that the present Congress will pass a wise and practicable federal elections law, and the president will have brain enough and backbone enough to enforce it. The ever-lengthening record of Southern wrongs and insults, both lawless and under the form of law, calls for whatever there is of patriotism, of justice, of fair play in the American people, to cry "hands off" and give the Negro a show, not five years hence, or a generation hence, but now, while he is alive, and can appreciate it; posthumous fame is a glorious thing, even if it is only posthumous; posthumous liberty is not, in the homely language of the rural Southerner "wu'th shucks" ——

Early in 1890 Chesnutt's story "How Dasdy Came Through," published in *Family Fiction,* February, 1887, became the center of a little controversy. In February, 1890, *The Century Magazine* published a story entitled, "How Sal Came Through," written by Harry Stillwell Edwards. Chesnutt immediately wrote the following letter to his friend and literary adviser:

CLEVELAND, OHIO
February 4, 1890

MY DEAR MR. CABLE:

In my letter to you of yesterday, I forgot to mention something that strikes me as either a remarkable coincidence or a rather bold plagiarism. The February number of the *Century* contains a contribution by H. S. Edwards, entitled "How Sal Came Through."

About three years ago, I published in a Washington paper, called *Family Fiction,* a story entitled "How Dasdy Came Through." It was about a colored girl who had a sweetheart. Another girl with a new dress and hat cut her out, and caught the fickle swain, to Dasdy's great chagrin. There was a revival in progress at the colored church, and Dasdy's mother advised her to seek the consolation of religion. Dasdy went to the mourners' bench for several evenings, and one night managed to "come through" just at the time when her successful rival, clad in the new dress and hat, was standing near her. In the irresponsible frenzy of "coming through," Dasdy tore the new dress to shreds and made a wreck of the new hat. The remedy was efficacious, and when she came out in a new dress of her own the next Sunday, in all the odor of sanctity, the fickle 'Dolphus returned to his first love. If that isn't the story in the *Century,* then I haven't read it correctly. It is padded a good deal more than mine and told in a different style, but the substance is the same, even to the name. Of course, it may be only a coincidence, but it certainly is a curious one. I have a printed copy of my story, to which my name is signed.

I don't know just how editors look on such an adaption, but I mention this to you as a matter of curiosity.

It might be doing the author a service for somebody to give him a point to quit writing when he has used up his own stock of ideas.

Very respectfully yours,
Charles W. Chesnutt

Cable answered at once, asking for Chesnutt's story and promising to compare the two stories carefully. He added that plagiarism was such a futile vice and so dangerous that it was little short of insanity to attempt it; that one must have overwhelming proof that it was not a coincidence, but the deliberate intention to deceive, before imputing it.

Chesnutt wrote again to Cable:

Cleveland, Ohio
May 6, 1890

My dear Mr. Cable:

I enclose you a copy of a communication from the editor of *Family Fiction,* with a newspaper clipping attached, from which you will see that I am not the only person to whom the idea of plagiarism has occurred in connection with Mr. Edwards' story in the *Century.*

This editor asks me for my opinion in regard to it. My opinion is that it was a deliberate plagiarism. You did not tell me in your letter what you thought about it, but I gathered from reading between the lines that your opinion does not differ very much from mine; correct me if I am wrong. At the same time, for obvious reasons, I would not wish to write anything to this editor which would lead him to make an editorial utterance reflecting on the character of a *Century* contributor, if thereby, I would run the risk of offending or antagonizing the editor of the *Century.* Taking the worst view of this case, there is an implied compliment to me involved in the fact that my plot was considered worth plagiarizing.

If it is not trespassing too much upon your time and good nature, may I ask your advice as to whether I had better discourage this editor from any further action in the matter, or tell him my opinion of it, and let him take what course he likes. His paper has a wide circulation, and while comparatively obscure, the story of the mouse and the elephant might not be without application. . . .

Cable wrote to Richard Watson Gilder, editor of the *Century*, who replied by sending him a copy of Edwards' letter in which he admitted a remarkable resemblance between the stories. He said, however, that he had obtained his facts from his wife who knew Sal well. He added that the incident referred to had taken place on a family plantation. Edwards' explanation was accepted; and upon Cable's advice, Chesnutt wrote the following letter to the editors of *Family Fiction:*

CLEVELAND, OHIO
May 15, 1890

EDITOR, FAMILY FICTION, WASHINGTON, D. C.
DEAR SIR:

Your note with enclosed clipping, calling my attention to the story of Mr. Edwards in the *Century,* "How Sal Came Through," was duly received. I had noticed the resemblance of Mr. Edwards' story to my story, "How Dasdy Came Through," published in *Family Fiction,* February 12, 1887. I have since investigated the matter and do not wish to make the charge of plagiarism against Mr. Edwards, who has accounted for his story in a manner which I must accept as satisfactory.

Yours very truly,
CHAS. W. CHESNUTT

In the meantime Chesnutt had rewritten "Rena Walden" and sent it back to Cable, who sent it on to Richard Watson Gilder, editor of the *Century Magazine.*

Gilder read it with great care, and because he was very much interested in Chesnutt's work, in the new point of view offered to American literature, criticized it very freely and returned it to Cable. Cable sent the letter of Gilder's to Chesnutt with the statement that Gilder was "terribly rough with those whom he takes an interest in and he certainly has taken an interest in you."

Cable urged him to write a new draft of the story and return it to him as soon as possible.

Chesnutt to Cable, June 5, 1890

On my return to the city after an absence of several days, I find the MS. of my story, "Rena Walden" with your letter and Mr. Gilder's. I thank you very much for sending me Mr. Gilder's letter, which I accept as a "faithful, wise word of friendly counsel." Its sincerity is obvious, its wisdom I cannot dispute, though I shall have to study both the letter and the story to avail myself of it. There is "something wrong," though Mr. Gilder doesn't tell you what it is. He says that he can talk about it more clearly than he can write. When you meet him again, will you, if you have time, mention the matter and give me the benefit of what he says? The construction seems to be "well enough," a part of the writing is "excellent" (it is the part to which I gave most time and attention, and leads me to hope that equal care would improve the rest), but the sentiment is "amorphous." I very much fear that I can only improve the language without affecting the sentiment much. I suspect that my way of looking at these things is "amorphous" not in the sense of being unnatural, but unusual. There are a great many intelligent people who consider the class to which Rena and Wain belong as unnatural. I heard a gentleman with whom I had just dined, for whom I had been doing some difficult work, a man of high standing in his profession, of wide reading and as I had thought of great liberality, whom I had heard declaim enthusiastically about the doctrine of human equality which characterizes our institutions—I say this gentleman remarked to me in substance that he considered a mulatto an insult to nature, a kind of monster that he looked upon with infinite distaste; that a black Negro he looked upon with some respect, but any laws which tended in any way to bring the two races nearer together, were pernicious and in the highest degree reprehensible. I fear there is too much of the same sentiment for mulattoes to make good magazine characters, and I notice that all of the many Negroes (excepting your own) whose virtues have been given to the world in the magazine press recently, have been blacks, full-blooded, and their chief virtues have been their dog-like fidelity to their old master, for whom they have been willing to sacrifice almost life itself. Such characters exist; not six months ago a Negro in Raleigh, N. C., addressed a letter to the Governor of the State, offering to serve out a term of seven years' imprisonment in the penitentiary, for his old master, and those who are familiar with the convict lease system know what that is better than the Negro did. But I can't write about those people, or rather I won't write about them.

I am a little surprised at Mr. Gilder's suggestion of a want of humor in the writer. Almost everything I have written has been humorous, and I had thought that I had a rather keen sense of humor. But my position, my surroundings, are not such as to make me take a humorous view of life. They rather tend the other way.

Pardon my references to myself—they are not meant to be egotistical, but when I first began to think, circumstances tended to make me introspective, selfconscious; latterly, I fear they have tended to make me morbid. It may be weakness, but my mental health and equipoise require constant employment, either in working or in writing. If I should remain idle for two weeks, at the end of that time I should be ready to close out my affairs and move my family to Europe. The kind of stuff I could write, if I were not all the time oppressed by the fear that this line or this sentiment would offend somebody's prejudices, jar on somebody's American-trained sense of propriety, would, I believe, find a ready sale in England. I have read a number of English and French novels recently, in which Negroes, and "Coloured people" play either principal or subordinate parts. They figure as lawyers, as doctors, as musicians, as authors, as judges, as people of wealth and station. They love and they marry without reference to their race, or with only such reference to it as to other personal disabilities. They seem to find nothing extraordinary in a talented well-bred colored man, nothing amorphous in a pretty gentle-spirited colored girl.

But our American writers are different. Take Maurice Thompson, for instance. His characters are generally an old, vulgar master, who is usually, when not drunk or asleep, engaged in beating an old Negro. Thomas Nelson Page and Harry S. Edwards depict the sentimental and devoted Negro, who prefers kicks to half-pence. Judge Tourgée's cultivated white Negroes are always bewailing their fate and cursing the drop of black blood which "taints"—I hate the word, it implies corruption—their otherwise pure race. An English writer would not hesitate to call a spade a spade, to say that race prejudice was mean and narrow and unchristian. He would not be obliged to kill off his characters or immerse them in convents, as Tourgée does his latest heroine, to save them from a fate worse than death, i.e., the confession of inferiority by reason of color. On the other hand, an English writer will make his colored characters think no less of themselves because of their race, but infinitely less of those who despise them because of it.

Pardon my earnestness. I write *de plein coeur*—as I feel. Mr. Gilder finds that I either lack humor or that my characters have a "brutality, a lack of mellowness, lack of spontaneous imaginative life, lack of outlook that makes them uninteresting." I fear, alas, that those are exactly the things that do characterize them, and just about the things that might have been expected to characterize people of that kind, the only qualities which the government and society had for 300 years labored faithfully, zealously, and successfully to produce, the only qualities which would have rendered their life at all endurable in the 19th century. I suppose I shall have to drop the attempt at realism and try to make them like other folks.

I cannot find words to thank you for your expressions of kindness and confidence in my powers. I have felt the same thing obscurely. Self-confidence I believe as essential to success in literature as in acrobatics; and next to an accepted MS., there is nothing so encouraging as the recognition of those who have proved their mettle in the arena of letters.

I will go right to work at "Rena Walden," and send you a draft when completed. I would not personally send the same story twice to an editor, unless so requested by him. But I will follow your advice in regard to the disposition of this one. I am grateful to Mr. Gilder for his interest in me, which the letter sufficiently testifies—I dreaded the printed slip.

Chesnutt rewrote the story and sent it on with this letter:

CLEVELAND, OHIO
July 25, 1890

DEAR MR. CABLE:

I send you herewith a new draft of "Rena Walden." I have endeavored to obviate as far as I could see them the things complained of by Mr. Gilder. In the first place, I have given the mother more heart, I think to the improvement of the character.

I have also shaded Wain down so that he is not quite so melodramatic a villain, and Rena's speech and so forth so that she is not quite so superior a being, leaving her to depend for her

interest more on the element of common humanity. The inti-
mated attempt of the old woman to poison Rena is ascribed to
senile idiocy, so to speak.

I have tried to word the dialogue so as to give the people a
little more imagination, a little broader outlook. And I have
also taken pains to refer in terms to the narrowness of their lives,
and to ascribe it to the influence of their surroundings. I have
endeavored to have the mother realize, vaguely, her own terrible
speciousness (I think I have even got your word "speciousness"
in these pages).

I have put so much of my time and my heart into this story; it
has been so very well spoken of by all who have read it (some
half dozen people—the last was a cultivated gentleman who is
familiar with English and French literature, with whom I went
on a journey a few weeks ago) that I mean to have it published.
I send it to you with *carte blanche,* with only the request that you
kindly give it as early attention as your own business will permit.
I imagine you mean, if you think it sufficiently improved, to
offer it again to the *Century,* although as I said, before, I personally would not have the temerity to do so. If it is not accepted
by the people to whom you send it, I shall offer it to the *Atlantic,*
and if rejected there, shall either publish it in book form, with
some other stories, or rewrite it into a volume of about three
times its present length.*

With renewed thanks for your kindness and appreciation, I
remain, as ever,

Yours truly,
CHARLES W. CHESNUTT

* As told later, it became the novel *The House Behind the Cedars.*

7

Family Interlude

WHEN Charles and Susan had been in Cleveland for several years, they were invited to join the Cleveland Social Circle. This little club had been organized in 1869 by a group of young colored people who wanted to promote social intercourse and cultural activities among the better-educated people of color. This was a very exclusive organization—membership in it was the *sine qua non* of social standing. The men were business or professional men, or had good middle-class jobs. Most of the young women stayed at home and took lessons in music, embroidery, or elocution and helped their mothers with the housework. A few were employed as teachers, dressmakers, or milliners.

The Social Circle met every two weeks at the homes of the members. These homes were scattered throughout the city and were for the most part spacious and well furnished. At the meetings there was always a literary and musical program. *The Social Circle Journal* was distributed at the first meeting of the month— a little four-page pamphlet containing essays, stories, and poems of the more ambitious members, the local society news, the meeting places for the following month, and the program of the current meeting.

When the Chesnutts entertained the club for the first time, the children were wild with excitement. They had been put sternly to bed and told to remain there. But when the program began, the little girls crept out of bed and sat on the top step of the stairway to listen. There were songs, piano solos, and recitations.

The recitations delighted the children, especially "The Wreck of the Hesperus" and "The Bells."

When the program was over, the guests went into the dining room and sat around the sides of the room, with big napkins in their laps, and ate scalloped oysters and hot chocolate, and ice cream and cake, while the children crept down the back stairs and got terribly in the way of everybody in the kitchen, until Charles, with a twinkle in his eye, grabbed them and embarrassed them frightfully by taking them into the dining room and introducing them, in their night-drawers, to all the company. They were very glad to escape and scampered back to bed without a word of protest.

Every summer the Social Circle had a picnic. They invited some outsiders, chartered a special car, and went by rail to Cuyahoga Falls or Silver Lake or Rocky River. Then, indeed, excitement reigned in the Chesnutt household. Susan always prepared an enormous lunch—fried chicken, home-made rolls and cakes, sandwiches of all kinds, pickles, fruits, and jars of lemonade.

They were finally dressed—everybody ate breakfast. Susan saw that the house was ready to be left—windows and doors locked, faucets turned off, lights out. After that, the holiday was Susan's, and Charles took charge of the children. In a delightful whirl they all hurried down to the corner, caught the street car, and went down to the Union Depot where they boarded the train. On the train, Charles entertained them, bought them candy, and Yucatan chewing-gum, while Susan relaxed and visited with her friends.

When they arrived at the picnic grounds, Charles gave the children spending money, and many of the others did, too, for these were about the only young children in the crowd and they were spoiled by everybody. They enjoyed rides on the whirligig, boat-rides, races, bottles of pop *ad nauseam*, for Neddie invariably ended the day with a bilious spell, and Charles had to carry the poor little man to the train. He slept in Susan's lap all the way home. But it was worth all the excitement that went before, and all the irritation that followed, for inevitably everyone was very tired and more or less cross the next day. It was the culmination of a whole year's anticipation and the subject of many happy memories.

The 1890's were years of very hard work. All day Charles worked steadily at his profession, and at night, after the children were in bed, he wrote. Susan cared for the children and managed the house with the very efficient assistance of Julia. The children worked at their lessons and in the yard. Ethel and Nellie longed for a garden and spent all their spare time trying to raise flowers, but they were never very successful because of the poor soil. Neddie worked trying to raise chickens and sell eggs to his mother and a neighbor or two.

Ethel, Nellie, and Ned took piano lessons and had to practice every day. Ethel and Ned became fair performers, but Nellie always developed a headache when it was time to practice, and finally Susan stopped her lessons.

One day, when Nellie was on her way to Goodyear's store with her week's allowance, she met some boys with a tiny gray kitten. They said they were going to drown it, and Nellie, who was very tender-hearted, offered them her nickel for the kitten. Susan was not enthusiastic about the purchase, but Charles persuaded her to let the cat stay. Charles had been reading Lafcadio Hearn's *Two Years in the French West Indies* and had taught the children to sing a little French song from the book. The song was an admonition to a girl named Madeleine not to make so much noise; the children liked it immensely and sang it all the time. The kitten was named Madeleine. One day Mrs. Reason, a very wise old lady, came to call. She admired the kitten, but when told its name, she protested, and told the children that this kitten was a boy kitten, and that the name Madeleine would not do for it. Consternation followed, for the kitten had learned its name, and answered to the call "Here Madeleine, 'Lane, 'Lane!" But Charles was equal to the occasion and suggested Tamerlane instead. The name proved to be prophetic, for the gentle little kitten grew up to be a mighty warrior, the terror of the neighborhood.

One cold night in December, when Nellie was just ten years old, she heard her kitten crying. She jumped out of bed and ran into the hall which extended the length of the house. Papa was at the other end, walking up and down. Nellie called to him and asked why her kitten was crying. Papa wrapped her in a shawl and carried her to the basement where they found the kitten sound asleep. Reassured, Nellie went back to bed and Papa tucked her in and closed the door. The next morning an unfamiliar woman met the children at the door of Mama's room and there, beside Mama in the big bed, was a tiny sister, very red and very sleepy.

The children were devoted to her. Ned wanted her called Alice after a little girl in the first grade. The girls chose Madeleine, in order to perpetuate the kitten's former name; Mama wanted Charlotte, after Papa, but he thought the baby ought to be called Susan. They compromised on Dorothy—the Gift of God—and of course, she became Dollie, and Dottie, and Dottie Dimple. Nellie loved to push the baby carriage up and down the street, for Dollie was a dear baby and attracted a great deal of attention. Tamerlane came in for comment, too—he lay at the baby's feet in their afternoon promenades.

Susan took the children into the country for the month of August. For several years they went to Saybrook, a little crossroads country town, about fifty miles east of Cleveland. Saybrook House, the village hotel, was a farmhouse owned by Mr. Munson, where the children lived the wholesome and delightful life of country boys and girls.

Charles came down on the "Conneaut Accommodation" of the Lake Shore Railroad every Saturday afternoon, and remained until Monday morning. The children went with the hired man, George, to meet him and drive him home. Eager eyes scanned Charles as he stepped off the train and willing hands relieved him of the numerous packages with which he was laden. Such interesting packages they were: candy, for he always brought the children a box of Chandler and Rudd's candy every Saturday of their childhood; storybooks for the week's reading; some tidbits for Susan, a toy for Dollie. It was a happy time.

Then on Sunday morning, Charles and "Old Man Munson" and the hired man would go out to the chopping block to kill the chickens for dinner, while the children ran as fast as they could into the orchard beyond the barn to escape being parties to the slaughter.

There was one colored family in Saybrook, the Richardsons. They lived in a very nice house on the main street near the crossroads. They shared the life of the community, took part in all the town's activities—the church socials, the picnics, the sewing bees. The Richardsons had steered the Chesnutts to Saybrook, and they made the summers interesting and pleasant for Susan, who was very fond of Mame and Florence Richardson. In 1891 Charles took his vacation alone.

CHARLES TO SUSAN, JULY 20, 1891, POINT CHAUTAUQUA, N. Y.

This is a rainy day, and a good day to write. Rain is pretty in the country; the green grass just seems to drink it in; it seems to have some object, some purpose more important than merely to lay the dust.

After I had dropped my last letter in the mail, it occurred to me that I hadn't mentioned Dollie in it. Give her her papa's love, and tell her I expect to find her walking and talking when I get back. Tell the other children to be good until I get home, and they shall have their vacation. Vacation, and the providing for those who are pleasure-seeking, is the business of this locality, and there are so many places to go that you don't get tired. Yesterday, I went to Jamestown, which is quite a city, at the eastern end of the lake. I dined at the Sherman House, and had a splendid dinner—mock turtle soup, fish, spring chicken, peach fritters with brandy sauce, potatoes, peas, watermelon, nuts and raisins, coffee. I get plenty to eat up here, and would undoubtedly get fat if I stayed long enough.

The rest of yesterday I spent at Lakewood, and looked on at the hops at the hotel, last evening. When I see the cute and pretty and polite children, I want to send my own to dancing school, want to get rich and give them a chance to enjoy the brighter side of life.

Am going over to the assembly grounds today, and shall take in a concert and a lecture by McMasters, a prominent historian. Must pay Tourgée another visit, and return a MS. which he lent me. He is a very interesting fellow, and improves on acquaintance. Will probably get home towards the last of next week, as I would have to hurry too much to get back to the picnic. My next long vacation will be spent with my family. It is very pleasant, but it seems a little selfish to take it all alone. However, I will make it up when I get home.

In the summer of 1893, Charles asked Susan to leave the children for a few days and accompany him to the World's Fair in Chicago. Susan was persuaded to go, and off they went leaving the children in care of Auntie and Julia.

They had a delightful time, and arrived home early one morning to find the house blazing with light. Auntie, Julia, and the three older children were pale and wild-eyed and barely able to speak.

"What in the world is the matter?" said Charles.

"Has anything happened to the baby?" exclaimed Susan rushing to the stairway.

"The baby is all right," said Auntie, "but some one tried to break into this house last night, and we have nearly died of fright."

"We heard him at the back of the house, so we turned on the lights and sat up the rest of the night," said Julia in a shaking voice.

Charles was extremely annoyed. "You two girls ought to be ashamed to frighten these children to death. I never heard of anything so perfectly silly. Come right out back, and I'll prove to you that it was only a dog, prowling around looking for something to eat."

Out they all trooped. There, leaning against the back of the house, was a ladder, reaching to an open second-story window!

"Well," admitted Charles, "that was a pretty smart dog to handle that ladder."

Ethel and Helen entered Central High School in September, 1893, where they elected the classical course. They entered into the life of the school and were, with rare exceptions, completely happy.

One thing worried them at first—their clothes looked hopelessly home-made. Many of the girls wore dresses made by professional dressmakers, but Susan enjoyed sewing and made all their dresses and wraps herself.

One Sunday when Ethel and Helen went for a walk with their father they opened up their hearts to him.

"Our clothes look different, and haven't the style they ought to have," complained Ethel.

"The material is just as good—Mama always buys good material —but they show that they are home-made, and the rest of the girls look nicer than we do," added Helen.

"We are old enough to have a dressmaker make our clothes," continued Ethel.

Charles was amused at the sophistication of his young daughters —he had not realized that they were so mature—and promised to think about the matter.

The next time Susan began planning new garments for the

children he told her that she must lighten her work by employing a good dressmaker for the older children, and by buying their outdoor wraps ready-made.

"But dressmakers and ready-made clothes are very expensive," said Susan, "and I can make them much cheaper, and they look just as well."

"But when you've done all that work, you won't look just as well—you'll be worn out—so let's try this plan for a while."

So there came a procession of excellent dressmakers—Susan was nothing if not thorough—who sewed for the Chesnutts down through the years.

8

An Absorbing and Profitable Business

DURING the summer of 1891 Chesnutt wrote the following letter:

701 Society for Savings Building
CLEVELAND, OHIO

MESSRS. HOUGHTON, MIFFLIN & Co., Publishers
BOSTON, MASSACHUSETTS
DEAR SIRS:

I desire to be informed on what terms, if at all, you will publish the enclosed MS. volume of stories, containing in all something over 60,000 words. There are eight stories, three of which have been published in the *Atlantic Monthly,*[*] at the dates noted on the first page of each respectively. (These stories I hereby ask your permission to reproduce.) Of the remainder, one was published in the *Overland Monthly,* and one in the *Independent.* The others are new stories.

I would call the volume *Rena Walden and other Stories,* or simply *Rena Walden,* that being the story for the sake of which I wish to publish the volume. . . .

There is one fact which would give this volume distinction—though I must confess that I do not know whether it would help or hurt its reception by critics or the public. It is the first contribution by an American of acknowledged African descent to purely imaginative literature.[†]

---

[*] "The Goophered Grapevine," 1887; "Po' Sandy," 1888; "Dave's Neckliss," 1889.

[†] Chesnutt overlooked the little-known *Clotel,* by W. W. Brown. See Hugh M. Gloster, *Negro Voices in American Fiction* (Chapel Hill, N. C., 1948).

In this case, the infusion of African blood is very small—is not in fact a visible admixture—but it is enough, combined with the fact that the writer was practically brought up in the South, to give him a knowledge of the people whose description is attempted. These people have never been treated from a closely sympathetic standpoint; they have not had their day in court. Their friends have written of them, and their enemies; but this is, so far as I know, the first instance where a writer with any of their own blood has attempted a literary portrayal of them. If these stories have any merit, I think it is more owing to this new point of view than to any other thing.

I should not want this fact to be stated in the book, nor advertised, unless the publisher advised it; first, because I do not know whether it would affect its reception favorably or unfavorably, or at all; secondly, because I would not have the book judged by any standard lower than that set for other writers. If some of these stories have stood the test of admission into the *Atlantic* and other publications where they have appeared, I am willing to submit them all to the public on their merits.

I want, of course, the best terms you can offer, and unless I can better them elsewhere I would prefer that your house bring out the book; the author having been first recognized by you (so far as any high class publication is concerned) , and the imprint of your house having the value that it has. . . .

I would be quite willing to reduce the number of the stories and leave out any that might be suggested, always excepting the longer one, "Rena Walden," and some further slight revision will be needed.

Please advise me as early as convenient on what terms, if any, you will undertake the publication, and oblige.

> Yours very truly,
> CHAS. W. CHESNUTT

On October 27, 1891, Houghton, Mifflin and Company replied:

DEAR SIR:

Your letter and our relations with you in *The Atlantic Monthly* predisposed us to a favorable consideration of your proposal for a volume of stories, but an examination, both of your book and of our accounts with the several collections of stories which we have issued the past year, leads us to question the wisdom of our undertaking the book, and to say frankly to you that we doubt if your own interests will best be regarded by a publication at this time.

We like your stories—some more than others—but our experience leads us to the conclusion that a writer must have acquired a good deal of vogue through magazine publication before the issue of a collection of his stories in book form is advisable. The position you have won is an honorable one, yet good as your work is, we question if it has secured for you so general a recognition that a book would be at once welcomed by a large enough number to insure success.

In a word, if we may undertake to counsel you, we should say, continue to publish single stories—the *Atlantic* would be glad to have the first consideration—for a year or two more, and then you will not only have a more distinct place in the public eye, but you will have a larger number of stories from which to choose a book full.

Should this agree with your final judgment, we should be very glad indeed to have another opportunity to consider your book. If, on the other hand, you decide to publish now, we must with great regret decline to undertake the book. Will you kindly instruct us what disposition to make of the MS.?

Chesnutt was disappointed but not discouraged, and replied as follows:

DEAR SIRS:

I am in receipt of your favor in which you so gracefully decline to undertake at this time the volume of stories which I offered for publication. But the letter is so nicely worded that I was almost—not quite—as well pleased as if you had accepted it.

You say you doubt if my own interests would be best regarded by a publication at this time. If you meant merely my pecuniary interests, that was a secondary consideration with me.... But if you meant that unsuccess, which the conditions you mention would seem to point to at this time, would do me harm and injure my chances of future success, I, of course, recognize that your experience and standing as publishers gives your opinion unquestionable authority. If it is not asking too much, would you be kind enough to tell me on which of those two grounds your advice to me was based?....

As I feel at present, I shall probably accept your suggestion to publish more stories before putting forth a book. The only question with me is that the money returns from literature are so small and so uncertain, that I have not had the time to spare from an absorbing and profitable business to devote to it, and therefore, my stories are so few and far between that the reading public has forgotten my name before they see it again.

I thank you for your words of commendation. I think most of the stories in the MS. sent you have either been published by you or offered to you for publication. There is one, however, "A Victim of Circumstance," which has not been offered anywhere; it is not a particularly cheerful story, but I would be glad to have you accept it for the *Atlantic* if you think it suitable; if not, please return it with the rest of the MS. to me.

Again thanking you for your advice, which I feel disposed to follow, I remain

Yours very truly,
Chas. W. Chesnutt

Chesnutt went on working and writing. He had had some correspondence with Albion W. Tourgée over his stories in the *Atlantic* and his articles in the *Independent* and had renewed this acquaintance on a visit to Chautauqua. In this same year, he contributed an article entitled "A Multitude of Counselors" to the *Independent* of April 2, for a symposium on "The Condition of the Negro," and in March, 1892, "A Deep Sleeper" appeared in a little Boston publication called *Two Tales*.

In 1893 Tourgée proposed to establish a journal to promote the interests of colored people. He planned to call it *The National Citizen* and made an attempt to sell enough stock to finance the project. He wrote to Chesnutt in November, asking him to help finance this publication and to become associate editor.

Chesnutt to Tourgée, November 27, 1893

I am in receipt of your last letter. I did not respond by telegram, as I could not assume the responsibility of raising the sum of $2,500.00. As I said before, I cannot see my way to doing it myself; and it would take some time to communicate with others in reference to the matter.

A newspaper venture is always a speculation, and if this one did not succeed, there would be nothing whatever to show for the money, except the memory of an effort in a good cause. I am willing to risk something in so good a cause. But I would regard it as a risk, and would prefer to confine my investment to what I could afford to lose. You have infinitely better opportunities for feeling the public pulse than I have; yet in my intercourse with the best white people of one of the most advanced communities of the United States, with whom my business brings me in daily contact, I have never, to my recollection, heard the subject of the wrongs of the Negro brought up; and when I bring it up myself, which I have frequently done, it is dismissed as quickly as decency will permit. They admit that the thing is all wrong, but they do not regard it as their concern, and do not see how they can remedy it. They might subscribe to such a journal if personally solicited, a number of them, but I fear that a journal devoted entirely to a discussion of one topic, so to speak—even so important a one as citizenship—would have a tendency to repel the average white man, rather than attract. . . .

As to the associate editorship, it would be a tempting offer from a journal already established; but I fear that even if successful, it could not pay me for giving up my business at the end of a year. I have long looked forward to a literary career, but I had not expected to seek it in the direction of journalism, and to accept your offer, assuming the *National Citizen* to become all you hope for it, would interfere somewhat with the plan of life which I had heretofore mapped out.*

Regretting, dear sir, that I cannot immediately and fully accept the very flattering offer you make me—for I consider it an honor to be asked to cooperate with you so closely, and assuring you that I will do all I can, without assuming any burdensome responsibility, to forward your plan, I remain

Sincerely yours,
CHAS. W. CHESNUTT

In 1894, Chesnutt replied to a letter from Cable:

. . . I thank you for the kind suggestion that I again enter the literary field. I have never abandoned it in fact, though I have not published anything since a story that appeared a couple of years ago in *Two Tales,* a defunct Boston venture.

Several days before I received your letter I had taken up the MS of "Rena Walden" with a view to re-writing it. I found myself

---

* This enterprise was later dropped because an insufficient amount of stock was sold.

much better able to realize the force of some criticisms of it that were made four or five years ago, when you were good enough to interest yourself in it. I have re-cast the story, and in its present form it is a compact, well-balanced novelette of 25,000 to 28,000 words. With four or five years of added study of life and literature I was able to see, I think, the defects that existed in it, and I venture now to regard it, not only as an interesting story, but as a work of literary art. I shall offer it for publication in a magazine, and whether successful in that or not, shall publish it in book form. I hope to write many stories, and would like to make a worthy *début* with this one.

My years of silence have not been unfruitful. I believe I am much better qualified to write now than I was five years since; and I have not used up a fund of interesting material which I might have expended on 'prentice work. Furthermore, I have saved ten to fifteen thousand dollars since I was with you at Northampton, and have the feeling of security which even a little of this world's goods gives, so that I can now devote more time, and, if necessary, some money to securing a place in literature.

Thanking you again for your kindly and inspiring wish, I remain, as ever,

Yours very truly,
CHAS. W. CHESNUTT

9

Educating the Children

DURING THESE YEARS Chesnutt's business affairs were flourishing. His office was getting the cream of the court-reporting cases in Cleveland. He was an indefatigable worker and put into his business the artistry and enthusiasm that he longed to put into literary effort. But his family had to be supported and educated, and business came first. As his income increased the Chesnutts were able to indulge in more pleasures. Among these traveling held the chief place. Susan's travels at first consisted of trips to Washington to visit her sister Jane Tyson, who had moved to Washington shortly after Susan came to Cleveland, and to Fayetteville to visit her mother. Charles sought wider fields and traveled extensively over the United States, Canada, and Europe. In 1896 he took his first trip to Europe and returned home inspired with the beauty of the Old World and with the spirit of brotherhood which, it seemed to him, prevailed there.

When Ethel and Helen began their senior year at Central High School, the important question was what college they would attend. Chesnutt had already decided that his children should have the best education that he could afford to give them. The memory of his own circumscribed youth, of the many difficulties that he had experienced when as a young man in the South he had worked so tirelessly to get an education, had made him resolve that his children should have a good education no matter what sacrifices were involved.

Western Reserve University was first considered. It was a fine college; it was in Cleveland; the girls could live at home; the expense would be slight; most of their classmates were going there—such were the advantages set forth by their parents. But the girls objected. This last year at high school was a disappointment to them. They had not said anything about it because there was really nothing to be said. They were enjoying their lessons very much; they loved their teachers; their scholarship rating was high; yet they were not entirely happy. So, they said, they would rather go to Normal School and begin teaching as soon as possible, than to plod out to Reserve for another four years of drudgery.

This heresy was a shock to Charles. With the greatest delight he had watched his daughters studying at the dining room table under the green-shaded student lamp which he had bought for them. Absorbed in their studies and delighting in the solution of the difficult points in their homework, they had seemed to him a very happy pair; they literally had to be driven to bed if their work was not finished, for there was a rule that by nine-thirty the studying must be over, and by ten o'clock the children must be in bed. During the half hour between, they ate a little lunch, milk with crackers or cookies, and chattered with Susan and Charles about the events of the day. So this attitude on their part was a blow to both Charles and Susan. They wanted their children to live wholesome normal lives, and here were their young daughters, suffering disillusion and defeat before they were out of high school. They decided to find out what was wrong, and they very soon did.

The girls told them that when the Senior Class was organized, and its activities under way, they realized with shock and confusion that they were considered different from their classmates; they were being gently but firmly set apart, and had become self-conscious about it. They knew that if they went to Reserve this state of affairs would continue, and so they had made their decision.

Charles learned that one of their friends had explained the situation to them. "After all," she had said, "you are Negroes. We know that you are nice girls, and everybody thinks the world of you; but Mother says that while it was all right for us to go together when we were younger, now that we are growing up, we must consider Society, and we just can't go together anymore."

When this dear friend came a day or two later to study some homework with the girls, Susan told her not to come again because her mother might object. "O, no," replied the girl. "Mother does not mind my studying with Ethel and Helen; it is only in social relations that she objects." "Indeed!" replied Susan. "Well, I object very seriously to your coming here to study with my girls —so please don't come again."

Charles recalled his visit to Northampton several years before, and after discussing the matter with Susan, decided to send the girls to Smith College, where for four beautiful years they could breathe the air of New England, the cradle of democracy. When this decision was made, peace settled down upon the Chesnutt family. Charles's trip to Europe, short as it was, had been an inspiration to him, and during that winter he wrote a number of short stories and worked on a novel, which he called "Mandy Oxendine." Susan was already planning the girls' dresses for commencement, and their wardrobe for college. Ned was being graduated from the eighth grade, and would enter high school when the girls entered college. Dorothy had not yet started school.

Early that year the girls had told their parents that they wanted to learn to dance. So a dancing club was formed. It was a family affair, composed of the families of their most intimate friends. The Chesnutt children were the youngest members of the club, the others all being adults. They met at Mrs. M. A. Bradford's Dancing School, at Cozad's Hall out on Euclid Avenue near East Cleveland. The lessons lasted from eight to eleven and were delightful hours of relaxation for all concerned. Charles especially enjoyed the lessons; the entire family looked forward to the dancing class.

By February Chesnutt had written several stories and had made great progress on his novel. His shorthand business was very absorbing; his writing had to be done at night and on Sundays. He was making money and saving much of it, for he intended before very long to give up business and devote himself entirely to literature. His plans, however, must be postponed, for he realized that sending the girls to Smith would be far more expensive than sending them to Reserve.

In February Chesnutt took stock of his literary output, selected three stories that he considered of *Atlantic* caliber, and sent them on to Houghton, Mifflin and Company. Then suspense filled the air at 64 Brenton Street as the family waited for the verdict.

Editorial Office of
The Atlantic Monthly
Boston, Mass.
February 10, 1897

Dear Sir:

We have in hand three contributions by you, "The Wife of His Youth," "The March of Progress," and "Lonesome Ben."

The last we think we ought not to use, and we herewith return it. The other two we hope to publish at an early time, if not immediately; and we wish to ask you if you do not think they might be published together. They both illustrate interesting phases of the development of the Negro race, and it has occurred to us that if they be put together under a common heading, they would produce a better effect than if published separately. If this plan commends itself to you, could you not suggest a general head under which they might appear, each with its own head?

In answer to your question whether we would consider a story of about sixty thousand words—it will give us pleasure to read it, but we ought to say frankly in advance that our engagements of serials are likely to forbid its use. We do not mean this, however, as a definite or final word on the subject. If you have the manuscript ready, send it.

> Yours very truly,
> The Editors of the
> Atlantic
> by W. H. Page *

February 13, 1897

The Editors of the Atlantic
W. H. Page, Esq.
Boston, Mass.

Dear Sir:

I am in receipt of yours of the 10th inst., making the very gratifying announcement that you have accepted for the *Atlantic,* two of the three contributions sent you by me. "Po' Lonesome Ben" was left out, which makes his name only the more appro-

* Chesnutt did not learn until some time later that Walter Hines Page was a North Carolinian, reared not far from where Chesnutt had spent most of his boyhood. Page joined the staff of the *Atlantic Monthly* in 1895 after having been editor of the *Forum.* In his criticism of the South and in his desire to arouse it to constructive action, he had much in common with Chesnutt in addition to his literary interest.

priate. I fear, however, that he will have company before I get
through corresponding with you.

I am very willing to adopt your suggestion to publish "The
Wife of His Youth" and "The March of Progress" under a common heading. But if I had thought of that in advance, I should
have sent you a third story, which is equally illustrative of the
development of the colored race in this country, and which I take
the liberty of enclosing herewith, under the title "A Matter of
Principle." If it should be found available, and the exigencies of
magazine space permit, the three might be published under the
general head, "Forward, Back, and Cross Over," adopting one of
the figures in a quadrille—"The March of Progress" coming first,
"The Wife of His Youth" next, and "A Matter of Principle" for
the crossover.

Or, if "A Matter of Principle" could be used, it might be published with "The Wife of His Youth" under the general heading
"The Blue Veins."

Or, if "A Matter of Principle" is not accepted, or whether
accepted or not, if you wish to publish "The March of Progress"
and "The Wife of His Youth" together as proposed, I would
suggest the general head, "Forward and Back," or "The Warp
and the Woof," whichever may commend itself to you. And if
neither strikes your fancy, I can try again.

I send you under this same cover the MS. of the long story you
have kindly consented to read, entitled "Mandy Oxendine." I
suppose that it will run about 50,000 words instead of 60,000. If it
should be found available generally, but not up to the mark in
any particular respect, I should be glad to have the benefit of
advice or suggestion that would help to make it go. For I expect
to write many stories, and do not know of any better place to
make a literary reputation than the columns of the *Atlantic*.

If "Mandy Oxendine" is not available for magazine publication,
I would like to know, since it must be read anyway, whether
Messrs. Houghton, Mifflin and Company would consider bringing
it out in book form; and if they think it worth publishing,
whether they would advise doing so now or waiting for awhile?

I hope that you may not think my letter too long, or that I am
imposing on your patience by sending so much MS. along. I can
say, by way of extenuation, that I have not sent you all my MSS.

Yours very truly,

CHARLES W. CHESNUTT

The summer holiday of 1897 was spent at Linwood Park, Vermilion, Ohio, on Lake Erie, about thirty miles west of Cleveland. Susan had chosen the month of July for the vacation because she wanted to get the girls ready for college in August. There the children spent hours every day in the lake or on the beach. Ned loved to swim, but the girls found it difficult. They all learned to row in the Vermilion River. They enjoyed the fun and excitement of bonfires on the beach at night with the other young people of the resort, while some adult told thrilling stories to the group.

Charles, usually accompanied by a guest or two, came up for the week-ends. Susan had taken the hired girl with her, for she wanted to be thoroughly rested before August when she must start to work on the girls' wardrobes for college. Charles's letters during the week were a source of great amusement to Susan and the children.

After the holiday was over Susan began the delightful but arduous task of getting the girls ready for college. Two dressmakers were employed and the house hummed with activity during August. The girls helped considerably by sewing hooks and eyes on the waists and brush-braid on the skirts. When a garment was finished it was hung in Susan's wardrobe, which had been cleared for this purpose, and every day or two Charles was led to the wardrobe to see how they were progressing, and to admire the clothes.

Challis dressing-sacks with flutings of gay ribbon all around them; lounging-robes of French flannel and eider-down; dresses, the skirts of which were lined with silk and interlined with horse-hair, and edged with brush-braid to stand the wear as they swept along the sidewalks. Braids and buttons and bands for trimming; leg o' mutton sleeves, collars heavily boned to stand up straight behind the ears; these filled the wardrobe with beauty, and the hearts of the girls with joy.

Then, when the dearest friends and the neighbors had seen and admired the garments, the trunks were packed, and one fine day in September the girls started off with Charles, leaving home without Susan for the first time in their lives.

10

Chesnutt and Walter Hines Page

CHESNUTT established his daughters for the school year at Northampton in a very pleasant student boarding-house highly recommended by President Seelye. Then he went on to Boston to discuss
his literary aspirations and plans with Walter Hines Page, editor
of *The Atlantic Monthly,* and with the members of the firm of
Houghton, Mifflin and Company.

As the train sped on toward Boston, he hoped that now, for a
little while, he would be free from the intense pressure under
which he had lived for so many years. His house was paid for, and
Susan had all the pride and pleasure of owning a comfortable
and adequate home in a pleasant and friendly neighborhood.

Then the three older children were disposed of for four years
at least, for Edwin had entered Central High School the previous
week, and if the fates were propitious, there would not be much
cause for mental exertion in their behalf. As for Dorothy, the
baby, she had just been enrolled in the first grade, and there was
no immediate urgency in providing for her.

Chesnutt's spirit soared. Now, at last, perhaps, he could pass
out of the world of dreams and preparation into the world of
books and authorship.

The visit to Boston was inspiring. Both Mifflin and Page
were very much interested in his plans and encouraged him to
keep on at his writing. Page suggested that Chesnutt send him
any material he had on hand for criticism and comment. On his
return he selected two stories and sent them to Page.

Now came a period of very hard work for Chesnutt. His business was growing so rapidly that he had much more than he could do and had to enlarge his office force. Susan was a social being and missed the girls terribly; so the house was filled with company, and Charles found little time for writing except late at night. The girls at Smith were not at all backward in expressing their wants. Each letter meant more work for Susan and more money from Charles, for their parents were quite happy to satisfy their demands as far as they could afford to do so. Charles and Susan were both going to college along with their daughters. Everything in the Chesnutt family was a community affair; parents and children were very closely knit, unusually so.

CHARLES TO ETHEL, SEPTEMBER 24, 1897

I got home Thursday night. Had a nice time in Boston. One of my stories will come out in the December or January number of the *Atlantic,* so the editor assures me. I saw the Shaw Memorial and the new Public Library building, which are "out of sight."

I have read your letters to your mother. She is coming downtown today to get the stuff for the curtains. I think you had best buy a desk and sell it when you come away—unless you can buy one that some one else wants to sell. Let me know when your money runs out, for of course, I want to get you properly started off. I hope you are nicely settled and got properly registered and started on your work.

I was in time for the little dance Thursday night. It was rather tame; there was something missing; and I haven't got accustomed to the house yet, it is so quiet and tidy.

Write me all the interesting things, and take care of yourselves, and be economical. Love to Nellie.

CHARLES TO ETHEL, SEPTEMBER 30, 1897

I presume you received my letter containing $15.00 for desk, etc., and noted what I said about it. I am quite willing to see you properly started off, and have you keep up with the fair average standard of the place. Of course, you cannot compete in expenditures with the daughters of the rich, of whom I suppose there are at least a few there. The expense account you send me is not bad; I shall expect you to keep up the custom.

... I send you herewith P. O. order for $15.00 to get the gymnasium suits; you might as well get them early. If you will find out the

82 · CHARLES WADDELL CHESNUTT

cost of sittings in the Episcopal church, I will send the money along to hold up the church's "protecting and sheltering arms." I might have attended to these things when I was there, but it is just as well for you to learn to transact your own business.

These letters are to you and Helen jointly; be good girls, be economical; remember that you are there not only to have fun but to study and prepare yourselves for future usefulness. My regards to Miss King and her mother. Your mother, Dottie and Ned send love. I do not need to say let me hear from you often.

WALTER H. PAGE TO CHESNUTT, OCTOBER 2, 1897

It has given me great pleasure to read the two stories you sent after your return home, namely "The Dumb Witness" and "The Bouquet." I do not hesitate to say that I should keep one of them, most likely both, but for the reason that we have had such hard luck in making room for your other two stories which I value highly, I do not feel like keeping these when we may not be able to use them for so long a time. This field that you are working is a very profitable one I think, but we cannot give it undue attention, and I fear that the two stories that we now have are as many as we ought to commit ourselves to for the present. I shall watch with great interest, however, the continuance of your work if you will be good enough to permit me. When you get your long story done, I cannot help thinking that it will be a successful book if you write that as well as you write short stories, and I have thought, too, that a skillfully selected list of your short stories might make a book. Whenever you are in the humor to talk about these things, let me hear from you.

The two stories already in the hands of Houghton, Mifflin and Company were "The Wife of His Youth" and "The March of Progress."

CHARLES TO HELEN, OCTOBER 13, 1897

I guess I will write you a personal letter, to keep you from feeling slighted. But for fear I shall have to write too much in it, I shall gradually increase the size of my handwriting.

We are all glad to know that you and Ethel are enjoying yourselves, but I trust you will not forget the serious side of it all. My primary object in sending you up there, at some personal sacrifice on my part and your mother's I will assure you, was that you might seek the higher culture, both of mind and heart, though I have not the slightest objection to your having a very good time.

I think you labor under a misapprehension as to all the Cleveland girls there being the daughters of rich parents; some of them I know are the daughters of professional and business men who work as hard for what their daughters spend as I do. Most of them, though, are older men and are perhaps a bit farther ahead.

I make these suggestions because the letters I get seem to put so much stress on these external matters. Sometime or other, when you are thoroughly settled and all your wants are supplied for an hour or two, you might drop me a word about what you are studying, and what lectures you attend, and so on. By the way, I believe you have said something about the library—it is a lovely one—and Ethel in her last told us about the absence of honors and marks.

Am pleased to know you are invited to join the Cleveland Club, and hope you will enjoy it. You should, of course, join the athletic department, and learn how to play shinny and baseball and prizefighting and fencing, etc., by their fancy names. You might also incidentally learn the meaning of the double-jointed Greek terms on the map of the grounds indicating the orders of plants that grow there.

Love to Ethel, and share this good advice with her impartially. There is plenty more of the same sort—I mean advice, to be had from me.

PAGE TO CHESNUTT, OCTOBER 20, 1897

I am very glad to have your letter of October 18th, and I like the frankness and spontaneity with which you write and the full explanation that you give of the stories you have on hand. Let us at once put the matter in practical shape and see what can be done. The best way to get at it, then, is for you to send us all the short stories, both published and unpublished, that you have, leaving out the longer ones (by the longer ones, I mean the story that contains 54,000 words and the other one that contains 29,000.) Send us all the rest, and let our readers take the whole collection up and see whether by selecting judiciously from them a selection can be made which seems likely to make a book of sufficient unity to put upon the market. If you will bundle up this whole lot and send them here by express, it will give us pleasure to take the matter immediately in hand, and I hope we shall be able to make a favorable report to you.

This seems to me the practical way to proceed, and we shall do our best to serve you.

CHESNUTT TO HOUGHTON, MIFFLIN AND COMPANY, OCTOBER 22, 1897

In accordance with letter of October 20th from your Mr. Page, I enclose the following stories, either typewritten or printed, with a view to a selection of them for a book:

A Matter of Principle	Uncle Peter's House
Lonesome Ben	The Fall of Adam
Jim's Romance	A Tight Boot
The Bouquet	Tom's Warm Welcome
Aunt Mimy's Son	The Goophered Grapevine
The Fabric of a Vision	Dave's Neckliss
The Dumb Witness	Po' Sandy
Mr. Taylor's Funeral	The Conjurer's Revenge
The Shadow of my Past	The Sheriff's Children
Uncle Wellington's Wives	A Deep Sleeper

October 22, 1897

MR. WALTER H. PAGE
BOSTON, MASSACHUSETTS
DEAR MR. PAGE:

I was duly in receipt of your favor of October 20, and I do not know of any better time than the present to act upon it. I have today forwarded to Messrs. Houghton, Mifflin and Company, by express, copies of twenty stories, including published and unpublished stories, from which I trust your readers will be able to select enough to make a book.

I think these stories will fall naturally into two or three groups, which will, of course, suggest themselves at once to the reader. This list is by no means complete without the two stories which you have on hand for the *Atlantic,* as I consider them, two of the best I have written, and I presume their publication in the *Atlantic* will help any book that might subsequently reproduce them. If I had to choose between having them printed in a book, and having them appear in the *Atlantic,* I should prefer the latter, but I presume you would use them in both.

Among the stories I send a few earlier stories and sketches; I do not know that they have much value, but the longest of them,

"Uncle Peter's House," has some elements of strength, though it is not so well written as the later stories. It is quite likely, when a selection has been made, if such be the outcome of your examination, that I might want to retouch a few of the stories selected before they are put into type.

There is one little story in the number entitled, "The Fabric of a Vision," sort of a study in unconscious cerebration, if I use the term correctly, which I thought you might possibly find available for the *Atlantic*. It is entirely outside of the distinctive line of stories from which a selection will probably be made.

I am under the impression that for one of the stories sent you, "A Deep Sleeper," Mr. Arthur Ware of your city, the publisher of *Two Tales*, holds an assignment of the copyright. I presume it can be obtained from him without difficulty. I suppose also that courtesy would require me to request permission of the publishers of any other printed stories that might be selected; I do not know just what the law of the case is.

Thanking you for your promptness in answering my letter and for your personal interest in this matter, and trusting that a favorable report may be made, I remain,

Sincerely yours,
CHAS. W. CHESNUTT

1024 SOCIETY FOR SAVINGS BLDG.
CLEVELAND, OHIO
December 7, 1897

DEAR MR. PAGE:

I felt in a somewhat effusive mood the other day, and I sat down to write a long letter, in which I was going to tell you something about my literary plans, how long I had cherished them, the preparation I had made for them by study in our own language and other languages, by travel in our own country and in Europe; how I had in a measure restrained myself from writing until I should have something worth saying, and should be able to say it clearly and temperately, and until an opportune time should have come for saying it; how I had intended, for reasons which were obvious, and had in a measure paved the way financially, to make my literary debut on the other side of the Atlantic, and to follow it up immediately by devoting my whole time to the literary life, etc.

But it occurred to me that you were a busy man, and that any-

thing I might say to you as an editor might be better said by what
I should write for publication; that all my preparations and my
hopes would be of no use to me, and of no interest to you, unless
I followed them up with something like adequate performance;
and that it would be in better taste to reserve personal confidences
until I might have gained your friendship and your interest by
having accomplished some worthy thing. So I concluded that I
would write you a simple business letter, and say that I sincerely
hope your house will see its way to publish that volume of stories
for me. I feel confident that they have sufficient originality to
secure a hearing, and that their chance of doing so will be very
much enhanced if they are brought out by a concern of Houghton,
Mifflin and Company's standing. It is not difficult to find a publisher of some kind, on some terms—but there are publishers and
publishers.

I am prepared to follow up a volume of stories by a novel. I
have completed the first draft of a long story which I mentioned
to you when I saw you in Boston, and have started on the revision;
in a month or two I hope to have it completed. It deals with no
race problems, but mainly with a very noble order of human
nature, more or less modified by circumstances. I have also the raw
material, partly digested, of a story on the order of what you suggested might be written along the line of my shorter stories. When
I get this other out of the way, I shall attack it seriously.

You may remember that you said to me that you hoped to get
at least one of the two short stories you have for the *Atlantic,* in
either the December or the January number. If that is not feasible
for the January number, I am sure you will do the best you can
for them.

I write to you thus fully—for I see I have written a long letter,
in spite of my disclaimer—because I do not want you to forget
me. I know you have a great many people on the ground, near
at hand, and that distance puts me at a disadvantage with the
relays of people waiting in the outer room to see you. I wish to
secure your interest and your friendship in furtherance of my
literary aims, and I do not think you will find it amiss that I write
and tell you so, and tell you why.

Permit me to say in closing that I thought the book reviews in
the December *Atlantic* exceedingly good, and that I remain,

Sincerely yours,

CHARLES W. CHESNUTT

HOUGHTON, MIFFLIN AND CO.
BOSTON
December 15, 1897

MR. CHAS. W. CHESNUTT
CLEVELAND, OHIO
DEAR SIR:

It has given me an unusual pleasure to receive your cordial letter—more pleasure than I shall now undertake to tell you when I am working against time to clear my desk of pressing tasks. But I write now to say simply this much—that your stories are undergoing a rather unusual experience here; because they are being read, I believe, by our whole staff of readers, and I hope to have in a very little while definite word to send you. The practical trouble presented is the miscellaneous quality of these stories. During the preliminary stages of our discussion about it there has seemed a better possibility of making two or three books (were there only enough stories of each group) than of making a single book of heterogeneous matter. But you shall hear our final judgment, which will be the most favorable one that can possibly be reached, without much greater delay.

I am delighted to hear that you have got a long novel so far ahead, for, as I think I told you, this seems to me a much more promising publishing opportunity, and a much more important step in your literary career than the book publication of any short stories whatever.

Again I wish to express my very cordial appreciation of your friendly letter, and it will give me and everybody here very great pleasure if it turns out that we can meet all your wishes, as I hope it may.

Very sincerely yours,
WALTER H. PAGE

11

"The Wife of His Youth"

DURING THE EARLY months of 1898 Chesnutt worked very hard. His business as a stenographer and court reporter kept on expanding, and his office was in demand not only for important cases in court, but for the many conventions that met in Cleveland. This business used up most of his energy, but in the evenings he worked on the novel that he had started. His collection of conjure stories was in the hands of Houghton, Mifflin and Company, and he was waiting eagerly for their verdict. He realized, none better, that publishers hesitated to invest money in books that the public might not appreciate. No great publishing house in the country, as far as he knew, had ever published a volume of stories or a novel written by a colored man, although Paul Laurence Dunbar had published some poems. Many books about Negroes had been written by white authors, and had achieved success, but no book about colored people written by a colored man had won popular or critical attention. Chesnutt had much to say on the subject and wanted to say it under the best auspices, and he considered that Houghton, Mifflin led the field in publishing.

So Chesnutt, not yet forty years old, worked at his business in the daytime; worked at his writing late into the night, when the house was not filled with company; kept Neddie up to the mark in his studies; accompanied Susan to those social functions to which she refused to go alone; enjoyed the developing personality of his little daughter Dorothy, and wrote frequently to his other daughters.

Charles to Ethel and Helen, January 14, 1898

Your mother has gone out to Richardson's in Collinwood to play cards or something, Neddie has gone along, and Dorothy and I have concluded to write you a letter. I have been very busy for several weeks, and Dorothy has been very busy. She has been writing tonight and is now getting ready to go to bed. She is learning very fast, and will catch up with you in about eight years if you don't look out. She writes a very pretty hand. We enclose you a specimen. You had better look to your laurels. She writes in a copy book now.

Neddie is quite a dude and pays much attention to his personal appearance. Mama is making Dorothy a gored skirt with trimming on the edges. It is made out of Nell's old blue dress. (N.B. Keep this dark.)

We are all well. Will and the other young man called last evening. I was not at home, but Dorothy and Mama entertained them. Much love from us both.

Susan to Helen, January 31, 1898

We Brenton Street people are planning for a big jollification meeting to be held Wednesday night. We have rented the Bohemian Hall on Plymouth Street, hired an orchestra, and will give a dance and card-party combined. Only the residents of Brenton are invited; it is given in order that we may all get acquainted with our neighbors. It originated with a few ladies who have been interested in the sewer and paving tax. It seems the City Council wanted to rush the paving through without giving us a new sewer. It has been said that the present sewer is defective. So these ladies decided that we could wait awhile for the pavement and have the sewer first.

Quite a number went down to the City Hall last Monday and tackled the councilmen. They carried their point; hence the jollification meeting. I am one of the committee. We anticipate a fine time. Will tell you all about it later on.

Susan to Ethel and Helen, February 8, 1898

The Brenton Street party is over, and we had a fine time. Papa went with the intention of staying until ten o'clock but it was after twelve when we left. The orchestra played good music, and the man who called the figures knew his business. I did not lack partners as I danced every dance. Even Mr. and Mrs. Tello danced.

All their girls were there and you know how they enjoyed it. We had two-steps, waltzes, redowas, plain quadrilles, Dan Tucker, and we finished up with a cake-walk. It was more fun than a little. Mamie Tello and Mr. Dan Reynolds took one of the cakes, and Mr. Jackson and the German countess (I have forgotten her name) took the other. It was amusing to see these staid men on our street in a cake-walk. Everybody enjoyed it and there is talk of repeating it every three months. . . .

CHARLES TO DAUGHTERS, FEBRUARY 28, 1898

Helen's letter came on Saturday. I am glad to learn that you are working hard and enjoying yourselves. It pains me to learn that you haven't time to learn how to "skee." I haven't the faintest idea what "skeeing" is, but it is a keen disappointment to me that you don't learn everything in the curriculum. Can't you take up "skeeing" in your second or third year? Is it harder or easier than Latin? Perhaps you could drop mathematics and take it up.

Have been reporting the Student Volunteer Movement Convention this week. It just this minute occurred to me that I might have looked in on the New England delegation and have seen if there was a delegate from Smith; but I didn't think of it in time. . . .

CHARLES TO ETHEL, MARCH 14, 1898

. . . I gather from your letters that you are having a good time, which I am glad to learn. I hope that by your diligence and good sense it may be but a prelude to a happy and successful life. I am growing older every day, and have not yet realized my own ambitions, so that a happy and successful future may depend largely upon yourselves; hence the importance of making the best of your present opportunities.

March 15, 1898

MR. WALTER H. PAGE
BOSTON, MASSACHUSETTS
DEAR MR. PAGE:

I have written to you before about a long story I have been writing. I have finished it—at least, I am going to stop working on it for the time being—and take the liberty of sending it to you herewith. I have entitled it "A Business Career." I think it has some of the elements of a good story, and I should like to have your house consider it with that end in view. It would certainly strike a considerable class of people in large cities, if brought to their attention. I do not know whether in form or subject you would consider it suitable for the *Atlantic;* if so, I should be glad to see it there.

Any information as to my collection of stories that you have been considering or any intimation as to when you will probably be able to use the stories accepted for the *Atlantic* will be very much appreciated.

In the meantime, I remain

Cordially yours,
CHARLES W. CHESNUTT

HOUGHTON, MIFFLIN AND COMPANY
BOSTON
March 30, 1898

MR. CHAS. W. CHESNUTT
CLEVELAND, OHIO
DEAR MR. CHESNUTT:

The unpleasant task (for I assure you it is an unpleasant one) falls to my lot to write to you, saying that the firm is sorry that they do not see a way to make you an offer to publish either a book made up of your short stories or the longer story, "A Business Career," the manuscript of which you were kind enough to send at my suggestion a little while ago.

The novel, we have regretfully come to the conclusion, would be a doubtful venture on our list. It does not follow, of course, that it would not succeed on some other list, for it might very well do so; but it has been impossible for us to reach the conclusion, after very careful deliberation and discussion, that it would be a wise venture for this firm to undertake—especially when the field is so absolutely over-crowded with novels as to compel a greater degree of conservatism on the part of publishers than was ever before warranted. A novel in these days must have some much more striking characteristic of plot or style to make its publication a good venture than was required a dozen years ago or less.

Concerning your short stories, the same general proposition holds, with an additional disadvantage from a publisher's point of view, that books made up of short stories become harder and harder to market; for the public seems thoroughly to have made up its mind that the business of the short story is completely done when it appears in a magazine.

This is a hard message to send you, because I have cherished the hope, ever since I read the first of your stories that came under my eye, not only that you would start a successful literary career with the first novel that you should put out, but that you would put out a novel which would fall properly within the scope of this house's publications. Now the first of these propositions—that "A Business Career" may be a success—is not at all denied by Messrs. Houghton, Mifflin and Company's conservative attitude towards it. You will doubtless be able to find a publisher, and my advice to you is decidedly to keep trying till you do find one.

There is yet a possibility of Messrs. Houghton, Mifflin and Company's doing something for you along this line—if you had enough "conjure" stories to make a book, even a small book. I cannot help feeling that that would succeed. All the readers who have read your stories agree on this—that "The Goophered Grape-vine" and "Po' Sandy," and the one or two others that have the same original quality that these show, are stories that are sure to live—in fact, I know of nothing so good of their kind anywhere. For myself, I venture unhesitatingly the prediction of a notable and lasting success with them, but the trouble at present is there are only about three of these stories which have this quality unmixed with other qualities. If you could produce five or six more like these, I think I am safe in making you a double promise —first, of magazine publication, and then the collection, I think would make a successful book. This last opinion concerning the publication of them in a volume I make on my own responsibility, for the firm has not warranted me definitely to promise so much; but we are all so impressed with them that I think there would be no doubt about it.

You shall receive a proof of the two stories that the *Atlantic* has accepted from you now forthwith.

I need not tell you that I hoped quite as sincerely as you did that we should have a different answer to send you; and I need not say to you that this answer must not be interpreted in any sense as a discouragement.

I beg you to command me in any way that I can serve you.

Very truly yours,
WALTER H. PAGE

When Chesnutt finished reading this letter he was very much disappointed, but not at all discouraged. *The Atlantic Monthly* had already published three of his stories and had accepted two more for future publication; so he knew that he could really write. Very well, then, he would write some more conjure stories for that book that Page had practically guaranteed.

Chesnutt to Page, April 4, 1898

I have written you a business letter today, and sent it to you with some stories, under another cover. As this letter is of rather a personal nature, I enclose it separately.

A friend of yours, Mr. Keatings, of New York, with whom I have had more or less business for several years in connection with a railroad receivership out here, was in my office a few weeks ago. In the course of our conversation, the *Atlantic* was referred to, whereupon Mr. Keatings said that one of his best friends edited the magazine, and mentioned your name, also the fact that you were a North Carolinian by birth and breeding, and a member of the old Virginia family of the same name.

Of course, I ought to have known all this before, but when one lives far from literary centers, and is not in touch with literary people, there are lots of interesting things one doesn't learn. I had even read some of your papers on the South, and know of your editorial work in North Carolina, but when I met you in Boston I did not at the time connect you with them. I calmly assumed, as nine people out of ten would, off hand, that an editor of the *Atlantic* was, of course, a New Englander by birth and breeding. But when Keatings enlightened me on the subject, I immediately proceeded to correct my impressions by reference to a biographical dictionary. You may imagine my surprise, and it was an agreeable one, I assure you, to find that you were "bawn en raise'" within fifty or sixty miles of the town where I spent my own boyhood and early manhood, and where my own forebears have lived and died and laid their bones.

I hope you will find time to read my "conjah" stories, and that you may like them. They are made out of whole cloth, but are true, I think, to the general "doctrine" of conjuration, and do not stray very far beyond the borders of what an old Southern Negro *might* talk about.

I am going to work on the novel I have been speaking of; it is a North Carolina story. With your permission, I shall sometime soon write you a note briefly outlining the plot and general movement, and ask you whether there is anything in the subject that would make it unavailable for your house. I am not easily discouraged, and I am going to write some books, and I still cherish the hope that either with my conjure stories or something else, I may come up to your standard.

In the meantime, I remain,

Cordially yours,
CHAS. W. CHESNUTT

Toward the end of May, Chesnutt sent Page the collection of conjure stories and the following letter:

64 Brenton Street
CLEVELAND, OHIO
May 20, 1898

MR. WALTER H. PAGE
HOUGHTON, MIFFLIN AND COMPANY
BOSTON, MASSACHUSETTS
MY DEAR MR. PAGE:

I enclose you herewith the six "conjure" stories you suggested that I send with a view to magazine and book publication. They are entitled respectively: "A Victim of Heredity," "The Gray Wolf's Ha'nt," "Mars Jeems's Nightmare," "Sis' Becky's Pickaninny," "Tobe's Tribulations," and "Hot-foot Hannibal" or "The Long Road." In writing them, I have followed in general the lines of the conjure stories you have read already, and I imagine the tales in this batch are similar enough and yet unlike enough, to make a book.

In one of them, "Hot-foot Hannibal," the outside and inside stories are both strong, and I have given an alternative title, "The Long Road," so that there is room for editorial choice, one name being taken from the conjure story, and the other from the outside story.

In the case of "Mars Jeems's Nightmare" the transformation suggested is not an entirely novel one, but the treatment of it is, so far as I know. I have thought a good title for the story would be "De Noo Nigger," but I don't care to dignify a doubtful word quite so much; it is all right for Julius, but it might leave me under the suspicion of bad taste unless perchance the whole title's being in dialect should redeem it.

Speaking of dialect, it is almost a despairing task to write it. What to do with the troublesome *r*, and the obvious inconsistency of leaving it out where it would be in good English, and putting it in where correct speech would leave it out, how to express such words as "here" and "hear" and "year" and "other" and "another", "either" and "neither", and so on, is a " 'stractin' " task. The fact is, of course, that there is no such thing as a Negro dialect; that what we call by that name is the attempt to express, with such a degree of phonetic correctness as to suggest the sound, English pronounced as an ignorant old southern Negro would be supposed to speak it, and at the same time to preserve a sufficient approximation to the correct spelling to make it easy reading. I do not imagine I have got my dialect, even now, any more uniform than other writers of the same sort of matter. If you find these stories available, I shall be glad to receive any suggestions in the matter of the dialect or anything else.

I hope you will like the stories and that you may find it possible to use them, or some of them, for the magazine, as well as for book publication, within the current year, if possible.

Of the three conjure stories heretofore written by me and published, one, "The Conjurer's Revenge," which appeared in the *Overland Monthly,* the mule transformation story, has a good deal of extraneous matter in it, and is a trifle coarse here and there. I shall rewrite it at once, as I think it was checked by your house as suitable for book publication.

Hoping that these stories may meet with favorable consideration, which I know you will be glad to find them worthy of, I remain,

Sincerely yours,
Charles W. Chesnutt

Editorial Office of
The Atlantic Monthly
Boston
June 24, 1898

Mr. Charles W. Chesnutt
Cleveland, Ohio
Dear Mr. Chesnutt:

"The Wife of His Youth" as you have by this time found out, appears in the July *Atlantic* and does its full share, too, to make this number interesting. The other story shall follow very soon. Very soon, too, you shall hear about the "conjure" stories.

Very truly yours,
Walter H. Page

EDITORIAL OFFICE OF
THE ATLANTIC MONTHLY
BOSTON
June 28, 1898

MR. CHARLES W. CHESNUTT
CLEVELAND, OHIO
DEAR MR. CHESNUTT:

The enclosed letter will, I am sure, please you. I send it to you in confidence and with uncommon pleasure.

WALTER H. PAGE

The letter which Page sent Chesnutt was the following, which he had received from James Lane Allen:

120 MADISON AVENUE
NEW YORK, 27 June

DEAR PAGE,

Who—in the name of the Lord!—is Charles W. Chesnutt? Half an hour ago, or an hour, I came in from the steaming streets and before beginning my day's work, picked up your ever faithful Atlantic. I read at once Bliss Carman's poem, which is mighty true, and then turned to the wife of my youth—I beg your pardon —to "The Wife of His Youth." I went through it without drawing breath—except to laugh out two or three times. It is the freshest, finest, most admirably held in and wrought out little story that has gladdened—and moistened—my eyes in many months.

If it is worth while, in your opinion, send the man my thanks, and my blessings on his pathway. And thank *you!*

Heartily,
JAMES LANE ALLEN

June 29, 1898

MR. WALTER H. PAGE
THE ATLANTIC MONTHLY
BOSTON
DEAR MR. PAGE:

I had written the other letter that I send you herewith, and it was lying on my desk, when I received your favor, enclosing Mr. Allen's letter. It is needless for me to say that I experienced genuine emotion at so spontaneous and full an expression of approval from one who speaks with authority, as one of the scribes. If there is any quality that could be desired in such a story that

Mr. Allen has not found in it, I am unable to figure out what it is. His letter has given me unfeigned delight, for I have read his books and know how to value his opinion. If you will be good enough to let him know that his praise and his good wishes are both a joy and an inspiration to me, I shall be obliged to you. You don't say anything about my returning Mr. Allen's letter. Of course, I should like to keep it, but if you think it would not be right to let me do so, I will content myself with a copy, which you will doubtless permit me to retain, in confidence, of course. In the meantime, I will keep the original until I hear from you again.

Cordially yours,
CHARLES W. CHESNUTT

EDITORIAL OFFICE OF
THE ATLANTIC MONTHLY
BOSTON
July 6, 1898

MR. CHARLES W. CHESNUTT
CLEVELAND, OHIO
MY DEAR MR. CHESNUTT:

Keep Mr. Allen's letter. Do not say anything about it for the present, because I really had no clear right to give it to you, but I do not feel sufficiently guilty to ask you to return it. Keep it as long as you like—permanently, in fact, and if by accident it ever comes out that I took the liberty to give it away, I am sure Mr. Allen will forgive me; but I should prefer at present that he should not know it.

I hope to see him before very long, and when I do I shall simply repeat to him in conversation that you know of the compliment he paid you and appreciate it very highly indeed.

Very truly yours, with Tar-heel cordiality
WALTER H. PAGE

P. S. The other story comes out forthwith and the conjure stories are in our readers' hands.

"The Wife of His Youth," which appeared in the July *Atlantic*, was a story about a colored man, Mr. Ryder, who though free-born, had run away from the South to escape being enslaved, and had in the course of years, by work and effort, risen to a position of eminence and leadership among the colored people of Grove-land. The people of his immediate circle had certain definite standards of life. Mr. Ryder was the most conservative of the group, and the most insistent that these standards be maintained.

Mr. Ryder had not married; in fact, he had not even con-sidered marriage, until he met Mrs. Molly Dixon, a young widow, handsome, vivacious, well-educated, well-to-do. At last his heart was touched; he decided to give a ball in honor of this young woman, and at the end of the evening, to announce their engage-ment. He had no reason to fear a refusal.

But, *Dis aliter visum est,* for on the day of the ball a complica-tion arose which forced him to make a decision between love and duty, between honor and dishonor, between happiness and the consciousness of doing right. The story is ·as a whole "marvel-ously simple, touching and fascinating," as one reviewer stated.

Chesnutt subscribed to a clipping bureau, and the clippings on "The Wife of His Youth" began to come in. He was thrilled with the effect the little story had upon the literary world. It was called one of the best short stories of the year; one of the most remark-able productions recently appearing from the pen of any Amer-ican. Many of the critics believed that it was destined to take its place among the few classics in the short story line.

CHESNUTT TO PAGE, AUGUST 14, 1898

I have been hearing from my story every day since its publi-cation. Editors kindly send me marked copies of magazines and papers containing approving notices. I get compliments right and left from the best people of Cleveland on the ethics, the English, and the interest of "The Wife of His Youth." I have had letters from my friends and notices in all the local papers. My autograph has been called for from "down East"; and a local publisher wants to talk to me about a book; a clipping bureau would like to send me clippings; and taking it all in all, I have had a slight glimpse of what it means, I imagine, to be a successful author.

It has been very pleasant and might have turned a vain man's head. I thank you for the pleasure, and shall guard against the other myself. I know it is a long way from a successful story—its success being partly due to its novelty—to a successful literary life, based on an enduring popularity. I shall enjoy the one and hope for the other.

I am going to take a brief vacation within the next thirty days, and shall probably turn my footsteps eastward and be in Boston a few days, if I can hope to meet you there. There are some matters I should like to talk to you about, and if you will be good enough to let me know whether you will be in Boston from now on, or if not, during what time you will be absent, so that I may time my visit to catch you, I shall esteem it a very great favor.

I want to send along, a week or two in advance of my visit, a couple of stories I should like to have you read. I want you to read them as a friend, if you have the time, and tell me whether I have made the most of the longer one.

EDITORIAL OFFICE OF
THE ATLANTIC MONTHLY
BOSTON
August 17, 1898

MR. CHARLES W. CHESNUTT
CLEVELAND, OHIO
DEAR MR. CHESNUTT:

It is a great pleasure to receive your letter, and to learn that you are hearing so many good things from "The Wife of His Youth." It is pleasant, too, to know that you are soon coming to Boston. You will find me here whenever you arrive, but it would be best if you would send me a line a day or two before you come, so that I may be sure to be here. My absence will never be more than two or three days. Send the stories along about which you write, and I hope even before you come to have word for you about the "conjure" stories.

With congratulations and all good wishes,

Very truly yours,
WALTER H. PAGE

Ten days later Chesnutt went down to Boston as he had planned.

CHARLES TO SUSAN, AUGUST 31, 1898

This leaves me well. I saw Mr. Page today and had quite a long talk with him. I am to see him again tomorrow about my conjure stories. He told me that Booker T. Washington and John H. Durham had each been in his office within twenty-four hours.

I'll be here a few days until I get my matters with Page talked

over, and run down to New York a day or two and get home
sometime next week.

CHARLES TO SUSAN, SEPTEMBER 3, 1898

I am still here in Boston and getting along very nicely.

A New York editor called on me at the hotel yesterday and
invited me to lunch with him next Tuesday in New York, at his
club, to meet Mr. Allen and some other fellows of the Literary
Guild. They all seem wonderfully impressed with "The Wife of
His Youth"; they say it is performance, not promise, and that if I
never write anything else, I have still established my claim to
literary excellence and standing.

PAGE TO CHESNUTT, SEPTEMBER 6, 1898

I write this personal note to tell you that Messrs. H. M. and
Company will publish the book of Conjure stories for you. They
reached this decision unanimously today. A formal letter will
follow in a day or two.

BOSTON, MASS.
September 9, 1898

MR. CHARLES W. CHESNUTT
CLEVELAND, OHIO
DEAR SIR:

It gives us pleasure to report that after thorough consideration
we feel disposed to publish for you your collection of short stories
which we have nick-named "conjure" stories, (for we think that
a better title may possibly be found.)

Let us say first that it gives us unusual pleasure to add a book
by you to our list; and then we ought frankly to say that this particular book we cannot help regarding with some doubt as to any
great financial success. The workmanship is good—of some of the
stories, indeed, we think it is exceedingly good; but whether the
present interest in this side of the Negro character is sufficient to
carry the book to the success we hope for can be determined only
by experiment. We are willing to make the experiment, however,
and hope for the best results. We have felt disposed to express this
doubt, not as a discouragement, but simply to record our present
feeling as regards the financial outlook, so that you may have
documentary evidence, when the book shows unusual popularity,
of the lack of foresight on the part of your publishers!

We wish to bring out this book early on our spring list, and to do this we ought to have the manuscript ready at your earliest convenience. We return the whole lot of stories to you, so that you may make the changes that we suggest and any others that occur to you. Please return them as soon as practicable.

We shall be glad to pay you the customary royalty on a book of this sort of ten per cent on the retail price of all copies sold. If this be satisfactory to you, a contract in regular form will be sent to you forthwith and the transaction formally concluded.

With thanks and best wishes for the success towards which we shall do our utmost, we are

Very truly yours,
HOUGHTON, MIFFLIN AND CO.
W. H. P.

September 19, 1898

MESSRS. HOUGHTON, MIFFLIN AND COMPANY
BOSTON, MASS.
GENTLEMEN:

I was duly in receipt of your favor of the 9th instant, notifying me of your decision to publish the book of conjure stories for me. Permit me to assure you that I appreciate the privilege of "coming out" under the auspices of your House, and that I thank you for the complimentary terms in which you announce your decision.

With regard to the financial success of the book, I am only solicitous that you may not lose by the experiment, and I am sure we should all be glad to see it turn out a pronounced success. I return the manuscript herewith. I have slightly enlarged the introduction to the first story, have revised the introduction to the others so as to avoid unnecessary repetition, and have arranged the stories in what I think good order. "The Goophered Grapevine" cannot well be anything but the first story, "Po' Sandy" is a good second, and "Hot-foot Hannibal" winds them up well and leaves a good taste in the mouth. Barring the first one, however, and perhaps the second, the order is not essential. I have left out the two stories, "Tobe's Tribulations" and a "Victim of Heredity." They are not, I will admit, as good as the others, and unless you think the book too small without them, I am content to leave them out. I have no idea, of course, of the form in which you think of bringing out the book, but should like to have it as dignified as the quantity of matter and the outlay you contemplate will permit.

The customary royalty of ten per cent on the retail price of all copies sold will be quite satisfactory to me, and I shall be very glad to close the transaction formally by signing a contract in regular form.

With sincere thanks for the interest and confidence you manifest in my work, which could not be better shown than by your decision in the case of the book, and with the sincere hope that the outcome may be satisfactory to us both, and that this may be but the beginning of a connection which I am proud to have made, I remain,

Yours very sincerely,
CHARLES W. CHESNUTT

September 27, 1898

MR. WALTER H. PAGE
BOSTON, MASS.
DEAR MR. PAGE:

I wrote the *Overland Monthly,* asking permission to republish the story, "The Conjurer's Revenge," and received a reply waiving the copyright, which reply I attach hereto.

I am getting along swimmingly with the novel. The development along the lines we talked about has opened up new vistas of action, and emotion, and dramatic situation. This, of course, throws some other parts a little out of proportion. I hope to be able to complete it in a very few months, as I am figuring so as to get plenty of time to work at it.

I left "Her Virginia Mammy" with Mr. Gilder. He returned it with the statement that they didn't quite take to it, that he thinks "perhaps, somehow, it seems to lack something in the way of charm and mellowness, but it is not badly built either." He says further: "I read the *Atlantic* story that you asked me to read. It is certainly very striking, but somehow it seems as though that poor fellow was entitled to a compromise of some sort. I don't know just what it would be, but the precise outcome hardly seems humanly right." It is surprising what a number of people do not seem to imagine that the old woman was entitled to any consideration whatever, and yet I don't know that it is so astonishing either, in the light of history. I find, on looking over my memorandum book, that "The Wife of His Youth" was sent to the *Century* before it went to the *Atlantic,* so I do not, therefore, worry about the rejection of "Her Virginia Mammy." I hardly think it worthwhile to send it to *Harper's,* in view of a conversation I had with Mr. Alden. I shall probably have to send it back to you, but I'll try it at one place more. If it were located in New Orleans, fifty years ago, it would be more likely to have "mellowness," but I guess it is too nearly up-to-date to suit Mr. Alden or Mr. Gilder.

I hope you may see your way to get "The March of Progress" in the November number, as you thought you could when I saw you. The October number hasn't reached Cleveland yet, but I suppose will be out today. I know of several people who are looking for that story.

Sincerely yours,
CHARLES W. CHESNUTT

September 29, 1898

MR. CHARLES W. CHESNUTT
CLEVELAND, OHIO
DEAR MR. CHESNUTT:

I have received your letter of the 27th and read it with great pleasure. Especially am I glad to hear of the progress that you are making on the novel, and I look forward with great pleasure to seeing it. I have enjoyed very much what you write me about the *Century* and *Harper's*—well, it takes all sorts of magazines as well as all sorts of people to make a complete world.

This is written hastily to acknowledge your note and to wish you all good luck. The next story we have by you is still on deck, of course, but a story is one thing that can be pushed off a preliminary schedule more easily than any other form of literature—unfortunately—but it has got to go in pretty quickly at the worst.

Very truly yours,
WALTER H. PAGE

12

"The Conjure Woman"

THE DISGRACEFUL "massacre" or "revolution" (according to the
point of view) that occurred in Wilmington, North Carolina,
during the November elections of 1898, caused Chesnutt to
change his views about the Old North State, where he had spent
his youth. He had been happy to believe that North Carolina
was an exceptionally fair and liberal state, but this race riot
showed him how little advanced it really was.

CHESNUTT TO PAGE, NOVEMBER 10, 1898

I am deeply concerned and very much depressed at the condition of affairs in North Carolina during the recent campaign. I
have been for a long time praising the state for its superior
fairness and liberality in the treatment of race questions, but I
find myself obliged to revise some of my judgments. There is
absolutely no excuse for the state of things there, for the State has
a very large white majority. It is an outbreak of pure, malignant
and altogether indefensible race prejudice, which makes me feel
personally humiliated, and ashamed for the country and the
state. The United States Government is apparently powerless,
and the recent occurrences in Illinois in connection with the
miners' strike seem to emphasize its weakness.

EDITORIAL OFFICE OF
THE ATLANTIC MONTHLY
BOSTON, MASS.
November 22, 1898

MR. CHARLES W. CHESNUTT
CLEVELAND, OHIO
DEAR MR. CHESNUTT:

We are going to use right away, in the number that we are making up, one of the conjure stories that has not yet been published (the manuscript of all the conjure stories for the book, by the way, is now in the hands of the printer); and we are going to use the story that you carried away from here with you if you do not find somebody else eager to use it. Let me ask, therefore, if we may not trade off "The March of Progress," which we accepted a long time ago, for the conjure story? That will leave us with two stories of yours in hand for magazine use, both of which, to be frank, we prefer to "The March of Progress," because "The March of Progress" is rather a sketch than a story. If you have any objection to this, be frank to express it, because "The March of Progress" is not, you will understand, objectionable to us, but it simply is not so good as either of the other stories, for our particular use at least.

Very heartily yours,
WALTER H. PAGE

ETHEL TO CHARLES, THANKSGIVING DAY, 1898

We received the check and thank you very much for it. Dear Miss Jordan is as lovely as ever. In class the other day she was talking about suffrage and the scandalous proceedings in North and South Carolina and different places South and West, and she felt very, very strongly on the subject and said this country couldn't talk very much of justice and freedom and the "noble privilege of suffrage" (she did say that with *such* sarcasm) while such shameful injustice went on. And she went on to say that in the South Negroes were not only refused suffrage, but were kept from trades and getting into employment by Trades Unions and such things; and in Georgia now the people are clamoring for the reduction of the amount allowed for educational purposes to the Negroes; and then they blame the Negroes when they do not always succeed in getting along well and advancing toward the higher paths of life. She said a great many very true things; I think she is an admirable woman. She read one of my themes out in class the other day as a very good theme. I love college more and more each day, and Miss Jordan also.

"Hot-foot Hannibal," the story for which Page traded "The March of Progress," was published in *The Atlantic Monthly* of January, 1899, to promote interest in *The Conjure Woman*, which was scheduled for publication in March of that year. This story drew many comments from the press of the nation, and the forthcoming volume was anticipated with a great deal of interest.

The people of Cleveland were so interested that some of the members of the Rowfant Club suggested to Houghton, Mifflin and Company that they issue a special limited Large-Paper Edition of the book. Subscription forms were sent out, and the subscriptions justified the issue of a Large-Paper Edition of one hundred and fifty numbered copies at the same time as the trade edition was issued. This Large-Paper Edition was printed on hand-made linen paper, and bound in linen-colored buckram, while the trade edition was bound in brown cloth with a picture of Uncle Julius between two white rabbits on a red background at the top. Later on, when Chesnutt became a member of the Rowfant Club, he had his author's copy of the Large-Paper Edition rebound in blue morocco with hand-tooled designs at the Rowfant Bindery; this volume remains a family treasure.

SUSAN TO HER DAUGHTERS

I have other paper in the house, but it is upstairs, and I am too lame to go up and down very often, so I think you will not mind my writing on this. I was out yesterday for the first time in two weeks. Edwin's shoes had given out and I had to go downtown with him to get another pair, as his father is too busy now to think of things of that kind. His assistant, Mrs. Jones, is in very uncertain health and can't be depended on just now, so it keeps your father anxious and overworked. I am glad that he gets so much encouragement in his literary work, as that keeps his spirits up, and helps him to slave along without thinking too much about it. I am only sorry that he did not get this encouragement ten years ago.

This letter set the girls to worrying about their father. The fact that his expenses were so heavy that they kept him slaving

along, as Susan expressed it, convinced them that they had been
unfair to him in coming to Smith. So they wrote offering to leave
at the end of the year and continue their education at Western
Reserve University.

Charles answered at once telling them that it was very dutiful
and considerate of them to make such a proposal, but that he was
quite able to keep them at Smith and was in no sense over-
weighted by the burden.

March 22, 1899

MR. WALTER H. PAGE
BOSTON, MASS.
MY DEAR MR. PAGE:

I have been reading the March *Atlantic,* and haven't found a
dull line in it. The contrast between slavery struggling for existence in an essentially free democracy, and liberty struggling
vainly for life in a despotism, is strongly marked in Mrs. Howe's
Reminiscences and Prince Kropotkin's autobiography. The dialect story is one of the sort of Southern stories that make me feel
it my duty to write a different sort, and yet I did not lay it down
without a tear of genuine emotion. The advertising pages were
interesting for two reasons—because of the very handsome charac-
terization of my book, and the announcement that you are going
to write an essay on the race problem.

I have known for some days that you were in the South, and I
guessed that you had gone down there to see if you could help
pour oil on the troubled waters in North Carolina. I hope your
labors have not been in vain.

In a letter received yesterday, from Wilmington, the writer
characterizes the town as a place where no Negro can enjoy the
blessed privilege of free speech and a free press; and where every
organization, whether social, political, or industrial, undertaken
by our race, must needs meet with opposition from the whites,
incited by jealousy and envy.

It would be a great privilege for me to talk with you about
what you heard and saw there, and I hope to have it ere many
months. I know your views in general on these subjects and have
no doubt that you have heard both sides of the matter—if there
can be two sides to it.

Your house has turned down my novel Rena in great shape.
They have condemned the plot, its development, find the distinctions on which it is based unimportant, and have predicted for it

nothing but failure. I have not slept with that story for ten years without falling in love with it, and believing in it, and I should feel very unhappy about it if it came back without your having read it, if you have not already. The fact that it met with your approval in the rough, was my chief incentive in rewriting it. Whether I took the wrong track in my revision I don't know; perhaps I did; but if you find time, I should like you to read it —even if it is already disposed of—in order that I may be able to discuss it with you when I see you again. If the distinctions on which that story is based are so unimportant as to foredoom to failure any story based on them, then I have yet to find my *métier* as a story writer, for they are my strong cord, I firmly believe. . . .

EDITORIAL OFFICE OF
THE ATLANTIC MONTHLY
BOSTON, MASS.
March 31, 1899

MR. CHARLES W. CHESNUTT
CLEVELAND, OHIO
DEAR MR. CHESNUTT:

I am a long time in answering your letter because I did not get back home as soon as I hoped to come, and this is the first chance I have had in the few days since my return. I need not tell you that I had a very delightful time in my journey through Tennessee, Mississippi, Louisiana, and thence through all the states back to North Carolina, and I hope to have something to say about what I saw a little later.

I feel, I think, as badly as you do about Rena. I read it just before I went away, but the House declined its publication not on my reading—certainly not wholly on my reading (this I tell you in confidence), but their judgment was made up after the most thorough consideration of the whole problem from every point of view, and it was reached, you may be sure, with great regret by everybody concerned. While I had a feeling that the story would probably succeed, I could not throw away another feeling, that you had not by any means, even yet, done your best work on it, or had developed to the fullest extent the possibilities of the story. It has great possibilities, and while it has many attractive qualities as it stood, I believe that a year hence if you read it over again you will agree with me that it is not even yet sufficiently elaborated and filled in with relieving incidents—not sufficiently mellowed—there is not sufficient atmosphere poured round it somehow—to make it a full-fledged novel. The feeling here was, and to some extent at least I share it, that you had so long and so successfully accustomed yourself to the construction of short stories that you have not yet, so to speak, got away from the short story measurement and the short story habit. A novel is something of greater leisure, and different and more elaborate structure, not simply a longer thing. It must also be a much more elaborate thing. It might have been that the House would have thought it worthwhile to publish a story as good as this if it had come from a writer from whom they had less expectations than from you, but I cannot help having a suspicion that your best literary friends—those whom you have won by your short stories that have appeared in the magazines and that make up *The Conjure Woman*—would have had a feeling that your novel was not equal to them. I wonder if this all seems to you in the line of a right judgment, or simply a piece of cruelty and inappreciation! Of one thing you may be sure—that we have the same hearty good wishes for you, and earnest hope to serve you through your whole literary career that we have always had.

I am exceedingly glad to hear of your private good fortune in your business affairs, and I hope you will go forward with literary work with renewed energy because of this little incident, and that I shall have the pleasure in the future as heretofore of knowing and sharing your plans.

Very heartily yours,
WALTER H. PAGE

The Conjure Woman was published during the last week of March. This book of plantation tales as told by "Uncle Julius" in the dialect of the North Carolina Negro was quite different in point of view from the plantation stories of George W. Cable, Thomas Nelson Page, Harry Stillwell Edwards, and others of that school. There was no glossing over of the tragedy of slavery; there was no attempt to make the slave-master relationship anything but what it actually was.

So Chesnutt and his family had reason to be elated at the very favorable reviews in most of the papers and magazines. He had surmounted some serious handicaps. His business absorbed most of his time, for his expenses were great, and he needed to earn the money to bring up and educate his four children according to the standards of which he had dreamed during his own re-stricted youth down in North Carolina. In addition, he was col-ored, and no colored man except Paul Laurence Dunbar had won any laurels in the field of American literature.

Then Cleveland was far distant from literary circles, which at that time were centered in Boston and New York. It was essen-tially an industrial city whose people were more interested in amassing fortunes than in cultivating the Muses, and its atmos-phere was not especially inspiring to aspiring writers. But Ches-nutt's *The Conjure Woman* headed the list of the six best-sellers in Cleveland for the month of April.

In the reviews that poured into his office from the press of the nation he was hailed as a new force in the field of American letters, presenting in accurate yet picturesque literary form phases of a tragic period in our national life. One reviewer wrote that Chesnutt had made a notable gift to his time, the value of which would perhaps be realized only in far-off future years. His impartiality, his strict sense of justice, the perfect dialect, the absence of false sentiment, the certainty with which he spoke, his literary skill and genuine human feeling, his unfaltering artistic sense, were all stressed again and again in the reviews which kept appearing for several months.

With the publication of *The Conjure Woman* Chesnutt stepped into the first rank of American writers of the short story. Its liter-ary success had been by no means a foregone conclusion. Hough-ton, Mifflin and Company's hesitation and delay in deciding to publish a book of short stories by Chesnutt is proof enough of this.

After the publication of *The Conjure Woman* the Chesnutts were so happy that they had to celebrate in some way. Charles persuaded Susan and her three daughters to spend the Easter vacation in Washington with the Tysons, who had been urging them to come. The girls wrote glowing letters home to him tell-ing about all the wonderful experiences they were having sight-seeing and meeting interesting people. They thought Washington the most wonderful and beautiful city imaginable, a fit capital for their glorious country. Charles was delighted with their transports and hoped that disillusionment would not come too soon. Then they returned to Northampton and spent a delightful spring term reading the notices about the book that their father sent them, and pouring over the magazines in the Forbes Library which contained articles about him.

Susan on her return to Cleveland plunged enthusiastically into the annual orgy of spring cleaning, for she loved her home and spent tremendous energy in keeping it up.

ETHEL TO CHARLES, MAY 26, 1899

We received your nice letter and the newspaper with the article about you in it. Thank you very much; it was a very interesting account of your life and gave your own daughters new information about you and their grandmother. Cleveland is acting nicely, as it ought to, by you. We are very glad about the story the *Century* has accepted. *The Conjure Woman* is in the Forbes Library here; I do not know who asked for it. We thought we would, then decided it would be nicer if some one else did, because we were sure some one else would. Our own copy is being eagerly read; everyone admires the book greatly.

The clean house must be pleasant; I hear that you and Mother have controversies about grate fires these cool evenings. Aren't you ashamed to want to dirty her clean curtains? I hear also that you are going to have guests all summer. Tra-la-la! And that we have a new neighbor on Giddings. Love to all of you.

CHARLES TO DAUGHTERS, JUNE 1, 1899

I received your interesting letters and was glad to know you were well and happy. We are well, except me! *Ain't* that remarkable? I have had a horrible cold for a day or two, mostly in the head, but it is getting better.

I called on Dr. Thwing the other day. While at the house, I met your friend, Mary, who particularly requested that she be remembered to you.

If you have the *Bookman* in the library there, you will find in it this month about five columns devoted to me and *The Conjure Woman* with a portrait—two and more columns of personal notice and as much more of review. Look also in the *Book Buyer* for a good portrait of yours truly. Will have lots of pleasant things to tell you when you return.

Let me know when you need funds, and how much. We look forward with much pleasure to your approaching return.

Chesnutt spent his spare time during the early summer writing
some new color-line stories, so that he might have enough of
them to make a second book of short stories. The enthusiastic
reception of his short story, "The Wife of His Youth," by the
literary critics and the public, had made him believe that a book
of such stories would meet with the approval of Messrs. Houghton, Mifflin and Company. In July he sent the following letter to
Mr. Page:

July 15, 1899

MY DEAR MR. PAGE:

I am thinking of making a run down East in the near future,
and as one of the objects of my visit would be to see you and talk
with you, would you mind telling me whether you will be in
Boston or anywhere near it for the next month or thereabouts?
I see you are slated for some lectures at a Chautauqua, but I
suppose they will come later in the summer.

While I am writing to you, I will ask you, personally what you
think of the probability of Messrs. H. M. and Co.'s being willing
to bring out for me, at a suitable time from the appearance of
The Conjure Woman, a volume of stories along the line of "The
Wife of His Youth" ...

July 18, 1899

DEAR MR. CHESNUTT:

I thank you for your good letter, and I shall be glad to see
you when you come to Boston. My own plans are somewhat un-
settled, but the probability is that I shall be here when you come.
At any rate, let me know four or five days before you will arrive.

But if by any chance you should miss me, you will find the rest
of us here, every man of whom will be heartily glad to see you,
and to talk with you about the new book of stories which you
have in mind. Bring them along with you, and let us thoroughly
consider the project of their publication.

With hearty congratulations and all good wishes,

Very truly yours,
WALTER H. PAGE.

Chesnutt, while in the office of Houghton, Mifflin and Company, was introduced to M. A. DeWolfe Howe, who at that time
was associate editor of the *Youth's Companion,* and also editor
of the *Beacon Biographies of Eminent Americans,* which were
being published by Small, Maynard and Company of Boston.

Instantly the thought occurred to both of them that the biography of Frederick Douglass ought to be included in the series, and that Chesnutt was the man to write it.

That same evening Howe discussed the matter with Mr. Small, who thought that a biography of Douglass would be a desirable addition to the series. Chesnutt, on the following day, agreed to the commission and promised to have the material ready by October 15, which would give him about ten weeks to prepare it.

Page was glad to get the color-line stories and promised an answer about the possibility of their publication in a day or two. He then asked Chesnutt if he would be willing to substitute for him in a lecture course at Greenacre, a summer school in Elliot, Maine, if he could arrange it. Page suggested that this would be a good piece of advertising and would help him in his work.

Chesnutt in the meantime went down to New York to look up some literary people, and pull some strings, and waited for Page's answer about the new book.

Editorial Office of
The Atlantic Monthly
Boston
August 10, 1899

Mr. Chas. W. Chesnutt
New York City
My dear Mr. Chesnutt:

I didn't get Miss Farmer's telegram (from Greenacre) till this afternoon. I don't know why she didn't reply sooner, but she replied very cordially, as you will see. I at once telegraphed you.

I enclose a ticket that she sent me (R. R. ticket) from Boston. You'll need to leave New York tomorrow (Friday). The engagement is at 8:00 p.m. Saturday night. I have looked in vain for a pamphlet about the place and how to get there. But if you get to Boston tomorrow afternoon or evening, you can get to Elliot, Maine, on a train tomorrow night and you'd better come to Boston on the 10 o'clock fast train tomorrow (Friday) morning.

I thank you heartily, and you will have a good time, and do a good piece of work for yourself.

Yours very sincerely,
Walter H. Page

P.S. I hope to see you tomorrow. If I do not, ask at Elliot for the Greenacre meeting place, and there for Miss Farmer. She is the boss and she expects you.

In the same mail with Page's letter came an announcement from Messrs. Houghton, Mifflin and Company that "Mr. Walter H. Page has resigned the editorship of the *Atlantic Monthly* and has accepted an invitation to take a prominent post in the direction of the literary work of the allied houses of Harper and Brothers and the Doubleday and McClure Company. His successor in the editorship of the *Atlantic* is Mr. Bliss Perry...." With this announcement was a personal letter from Mr. Mifflin in which he assured Chesnutt that the fact that Page had left would make no difference at all in the firm's interest in his work.

August 15, 1899

MY DEAR MR. PAGE:

I reached Greenacre in good time; found Miss Farmer an amiable woman, with high but somewhat vague ideals that have in a measure obscured the practical side of things. I talked to quite an audience of highly intellectual people, or as I termed them in my remarks, "a choice band of enlightened spirits, seeking after truth in whatever guise," and some of the guises are queer ones. I had the close attention of the audience, and made a good impression, receiving quite as much applause as they could find any decent excuse for giving me. I frankly confessed my lack of skill as a platform speaker, but they were good enough to say I underestimated my effort, and that any lack of rhetorical graces was more than compensated for by my evident knowledge of the subject and the interesting nature of what I said. The subject was a little large, and I am afraid I dwelt more on the political and civil status of Negroes in the South and didn't have time to properly consider the remedies. I did suggest education, however, as the most obvious and immediate palliative, but maintained that race troubles would never cease until the Constitutional amendments were strictly observed, in the spirit in which they were meant, the color line entirely wiped out before the law, and equal justice and equal opportunity extended to every man in every relation of life. This sentiment was vigorously applauded.

Miss Farmer expressed herself as entirely satisfied, and I was satisfactorily entertained. She also insisted on paying my fare from New York to Boston, on my way to Greenacre.

I presume that she will write to you, and hope her report will relieve my mind of any fear of coming face to face with you in the future. I enjoyed the visit and the opportunity, got a number of

nice people interested in my work, (by the way, I read them a
story after the lecture,) and will be able, from the experience
gained, to handle the subject more effectively on another occasion. I have to thank you for all this, as another manifestation of
the friendship that has resulted in so many good things.

I hope that you may find your new work congenial, and am
sure that the world will be the gainer by enlargement of your
field of opportunity.

I am, as ever,

> Sincerely yours,
> CHARLES W. CHESNUTT

Later on, in commenting upon the Greenacre lectures, the
Boston Transcript gave a complete account of Chesnutt's talk,
and said that it had been one of the best features of the season.

Chesnutt went back to Cleveland a very happy man. Now he
had two publishers and had made a start on the lecture platform,
besides promising Howe some stories for the *Youth's Companion*.

On his return home he spent a short time working on the
manuscript of a collection of stories including "The Wife of His
Youth," which had been accepted by Houghton, Mifflin and Company, and then plunged into work on the Douglass biography.

August 23, 1899

Messrs. Houghton, Mifflin and Company
Boston, Massachusetts
Dear Sirs:

I have kept the MSS. of *The Wife of His Youth,* etc. a few days
with a view to selecting and arranging them most effectively. I
have made an arrangement, how effective I do not know, and if
any one there can suggest a better, I shall cheerfully acquiesce.
The total amount of matter is 65,000 to 70,000 words.

Mr. Page suggested as a good name for the volume, *The Wife
of His Youth, and Other Stories of the Color Line.* I have not
been able to think of any better title, and all the stories deal with
that subject directly, except one which treats it, I might say, col-
laterally. So unless there is some good reason to the contrary, I
rather think that name would very aptly characterize the volume;
and I should like to hope that the stories, while written to depict
life as it is, in certain aspects that no one has ever before attempted to adequately describe, may throw a light upon the great

problem on which the stories are strung; for the backbone of this volume is not a character, like Uncle Julius in *The Conjure Woman,* but a subject, as indicated in the title—*The Color Line.*

The story "The Sheriff's Children," was published in the *Independent,* and I have the permission of that paper to reproduce it. But they would like to have their courtesy acknowledged in the book, if feasible, and I suppose it is entirely so. Mr. Page left a note on his desk for Prof. Perry, suggesting that he look over the unpublished stories, and see if there is one suitable for the *Atlantic.* I have addressed a separate note to Mr. Perry, and have no doubt he will give the matter attention, and do whatever he finds best in the matter.

I enclose your copy of the contract, which is entirely satisfactory, with the change of name suggested above, if that is agreeable to you.

Sincerely yours,
CHAS. W. CHESNUTT

August 23, 1899

LEWIS H. DOUGLASS, ESQ.
WASHINGTON, D. C.
MY DEAR MR. DOUGLASS:

I have accepted a commission from Small, Maynard & Co. of Boston to write for their *Beacon Series of Biographies of Eminent Americans,* a volume on your illustrious father. It is to be a small book—really a sort of extended sketch; it would be presumptuous in me to undertake anything more important without long and careful preparation.

The subject is one that appeals to me, and there is abundance of material, that is, as to the public portion of his life; for the facts of his early life there is practically only one source—his various autobiographies. I hope with the material at hand to be able to construct in even the limited time at my disposal, a dignified and appreciative sketch—a birdseye view as it were—of the life of our most distinguished citizen of African descent.

The immediate object of my writing to you, however, is to ask if you can tell me where I can get the best photograph of your father, or two or three from which a choice can be made, and which I can procure permission to use, in the form of a small frontispiece. It seems to me I have heard somewhere that there is a particular photograph that the family prefer. I will very willingly pay for what I want, if the photograph is purchasable. I want a photograph, if possible, and not an engraving.

My little book will contain a chronology showing the principal events of Mr. Douglass's life. These are matters of history mainly, but I would particularly desire to get straight the various honors that were shown your father—the bust at Rochester, and subsequent monument, and things of that kind. I do not venture to intrude upon a busy man's time, but if you have any printed matter in the way of newspaper clippings that would give dates and names of participants in the meetings to honor Mr. Douglass, or with reference to his funeral and burial place, I would esteem it a favor to have the privilege of looking at them. It is my sincere desire to honor the memory, as adequately as the scope of this little work will permit, of one whom the world delighted to honor for so many years.

If you will kindly advise me about the photo, I shall be obliged. Mrs. Chesnutt has spoken to me of meeting you last spring, and has repeated some pleasant things you said about *The Conjure Woman,* for which I thank you.

Sincerely yours,
CHAS. W. CHESNUTT

13

Going into the Author Business

CHESNUTT HAD spent months trying to decide whether he could afford to give up his business and devote himself to literature. The income from his business was very good, but the Chesnutt standard of living was very good also. His two older daughters were half way through college and his son, still in high school, was preparing for Harvard. The income from his literary productions at that time could not possibly support the family, and this was always his first consideration. But many new openings in the literary world were being offered him and these he could not accept without giving up his business and devoting all his time to literary work. Susan and he talked it over evening after evening. They studied all their expenses, decided where they could reduce them, made a budget for the next two years, and finally decided that the business could go.

On September 30, 1899, Chesnutt gave up his business as attorney-at-law, court reporter, and stenographer, closed his office in the Society for Savings Building, and set up his literary office in his home at 64 Brenton Street.

CHARLES TO DAUGHTERS, OCTOBER 2, 1899

I received your letters the other day, and thank you for your congratulations. I am writing this letter at home 1 P.M. Have been writing on Douglass Biog. all the morning; it is going along swimmingly. Will read to a club at Willoughby next Friday and at Emmanuel, next Monday evening, Men's Club.

Am going to give a reading at Washington later. Glad you are having a nice time, making friends and getting an education. Ed Williams went away Sunday, I believe. Keep me posted as to bills, etc. and I will remit accordingly. Your mother sends love and says that if you don't need the new curtains send them home for the side room upstairs.

I will keep you posted as to my literary movements. Your mother says she will write when she gets time. Much love from your Daddy.

P. S. An elevator boy asked me the other day if it was true that I was going into the "author business." I told him "Yes."

SUSAN TO ETHEL, OCTOBER 12, 1899

...Your father is fairly started in his literary work. He has finished the Douglass biography, and is now busy reading the proof-sheets for his new book. So far he has had very little time to get lonesome, and I am hoping he will keep busy. I have given up the parlor to him; he has his desk and table and typewriter in there. By taking some of the chairs out he has plenty of room. I use the sitting-room for my friends. We have a telephone in the house. It was put in yesterday—in the dining-room....

About the middle of October Chesnutt began to realize that the "author business" involved a great deal more than the mere writing of a book. It was also the author's obligation to help sell the book. He received a letter from Herbert Small, of Small, Maynard and Company, asking for a list of names of persons who would be willing to handle the life of Douglass, with suggestions as to terms to be offered them. He was also asked for a list of special papers to which they might send copies for review—particularly, Afro-American papers—in order to promote the sale of the book among colored people. Small, Maynard and Company had recently published Booker T. Washington's *The Future of the American Negro* and was in search of new markets for both books. Chesnutt replied as follows:

64 BRENTON STREET
CLEVELAND, OHIO
October 26, 1899

MESSRS. SMALL, MAYNARD & CO.
BOSTON, MASS.
ATT: MR. HERBERT SMALL
MY DEAR MR. SMALL:

I have not answered your letter sooner, in which you acknowledged receipt of MS. of the Douglass biography, because I hoped to be in a position to answer it more fully by devoting a few days to looking up the information you asked for.

I have made some little effort to get together a list of representative Afro-American newspapers, and I am informed that the list I enclose, while including only a fraction of the several hundred that are published, will practically cover the country, and they include, I think, the best of them. . . .

I also enclose the names of a few individuals to whom the book might be sent with a reasonable hope of resulting publicity. I hope to be soon able to send you other names to be added to this list; I should like to be careful about it, so that you need not make too much outlay without hope of return. There is undoubtedly a large and growing reading class among the colored people, but as yet they are mostly poor, and I do not know how large buyers of books they are. My *Conjure Woman* I think has sold very well among them. I suspect the small size of the *Douglass* may work somewhat to its disadvantage, as compared, say, to the same matter put up in larger volume; this of course, would not apply to readers of taste and discrimination—which unfortunately all readers are not, as a publisher above all others probably knows. . . .

I presume you have already communicated with Mr. Washington, or with Emmett J. Scott, his private secretary. Scott is entirely *en rapport* with the matters you have asked me about— much more so, I imagine, than I am, for an exacting business in a western city has kept me out of touch with them in some degree. Anything you might get from Scott, who would know all about these school papers, for instance—would inure to the benefit of my book, and I am sure I hope that anything you get from me may help the Washington book; though of course, he is so much more widely known that the benefit would doubtless come from the other side. The *Douglass Biography* might possibly be available for use in some of those schools, if size and price can be harmonized.

I will write you again before long. I am going to give some public readings, one in Washington on November 17 and these will pave the way for my books; and after this season, I shall devote a good deal of time to platform work; I am told I read my stories very effectively. H. M. & Co. are booming me very nicely. They have out an *Atlantic* poster in which my name is prominently displayed—I have a story * in the November *Atlantic*—

* "The Bouquet."

and my new book of fiction will start things up lively in a few weeks.

I take pleasure in sending you today the large photograph which I promised to send you; you may perhaps find a place on the wall to nail it up.

With hopes for the entire success of our joint venture, and with assurance of my personal esteem, I remain

Cordially yours,
CHAS. W. CHESNUTT

Small was enthusiastic over Chesnutt's letter and among other things suggested that Chesnutt could easily write a remarkable series of essays, discussing from the point of view of the man of letters the many things in the literature and life of the colored people which could be treated in the essay form. "I do not mean," he wrote, "a serious heavy book at all. I mean just such a book as will be easy and delightful to read, and by its entertaining quality do more to influence the public than a whole ton of more serious works."

CHESNUTT TO EDWARD C. WILLIAMS,† NOVEMBER 2, 1899

I am glad you liked the photograph; also glad to know that you have a proper appreciation of the house of Houghton, Mifflin & Co. I have a rather good opinion of them myself.

I finished the proofs of *The Wife of His Youth* several days ago, and am sending off by this mail the last of the *Douglass* proofs. The editor has complimented me highly on this little book, and wrote the other day that the second reading impressed him no less favorably. I am pretty well satisfied with it myself, and I think I am rather hard to suit with my own work.

I gave a reading last night in a country lecture course in the historic town of Kirtland. I am going to read next week for a charitable club here, small gathering. Go to Washington, read there the 17th. Have an idea that I shall keep myself pretty fully occupied. "One" of my publishers has already suggested a line of writing which I may take up a little later. H. M. & Co. are certainly doing *The Wife of His Youth* up fine for me. I hope a pronounced success for it.

Have just received, while writing you, proofs of the illustrations. They do very well, only, as is always the case, they show

† Librarian at Western Reserve. Later Chesnutt's son-in-law.

that the artist hasn't read the stories carefully. They represent the wife of his youth, the lynching scene in "The Sheriff's Children," Uncle Wellington when he comes home and finds wife no. 2 gone, and Sophy standing with her bouquet outside the cemetery gate.

Hope you are doing well.

CHARLES TO ETHEL, NOVEMBER 12, 1899

I am going to Washington some time this week to give a reading there Friday night, and as I may not be back until the last of next week, I send you herewith N. Y. draft for, I believe, the usual amount.

Glad to know you had a pleasant time Hallowe'en. The characters, Simple Simon and Mother Goose, taken by you and Helen seem quite appropriate, and we are not surprised that you took the prize. Save the pictures.

My publishers are going to boom *The Wife of His Youth*. I mean they are going to give it every advantage, and do special work on it. It will be a beautiful book.

I am glad to know that the young ladies approve of "The Bouquet" and hope they will like the book. . . .

64 BRENTON STREET
CLEVELAND, OHIO
November 12, 1899

MESSRS. HOUGHTON, MIFFLIN & CO.
BOSTON, MASSACHUSETTS
GENTLEMEN:

Replying to yours of November 9, would say that I am pleased to know that you think of undertaking special work on behalf of *The Wife of His Youth,* and assure you that I shall be glad to cooperate in any possible way.

I have ordered a large negative made from the same photograph you have heretofore used, as it is generally regarded as a good one; I do this to save time, and will sit for another later. They will be mounted as you request, and I will forward some of them to you as soon as completed. I think I can get a good view or two of my library, and will have them made the first clear day.

As to old MSS. for use in windows, I had a great quantity of them—most of my things have been written several times—but they were mostly typewritten, and I burnt up a lot of them several weeks ago when I closed my business office. I have found a few, however, of which I send along by express several that are complete; they are not final copies but intermediate drafts. There are pages among them very effectively disfigured—I suppose those would be the most interesting, as the perfect ones being entirely typewritten would not reveal any of the author's individuality. This is a very dirty town, and the MSS. are somewhat soiled. I have a lot of incomplete copies, similar to those I send, and I can send them if you like.

It occurs to me that the drawings or oil sketches made for the illustrations to *The Wife of His Youth* would be good stuff for window displays. I have been promised one of the *The Wife of His Youth* scenes, but will cheerfully waive my claim until any possible good use can be made of it.

I have a set of proofs of *The Conjure Woman*, if they would be of any use in a window. Have you ever made up a window display showing a book in the various stages of production—the rough draft, the various revisions, the proof-sheets or revises, the unbound book, the completed book (with various editions), the portrait of the author, view of his study, and so on? I suppose you have.

I enclose another letter in reply to yours of the 10th.

Yours very truly,
Chas. W. Chesnutt

Houghton, Mifflin & Company
Boston
November 16, 1899

Mr. Charles W. Chesnutt
Cleveland, Ohio
Dear Sir:

We have received by express the manuscript pages which you mentioned in your letter and of which we shall be able to make excellent use. We await with interest the photographs which you will send us, and shall also be able to utilize these in the most effective way. In the same work we shall use the originals of the illustrations for *The Wife of His Youth*, but this will in no wise conflict with the "claim" which you have made upon one of them, which one we do not know.

In regard to the set of proofs for *The Conjure Woman* and your suggestion as to exhibiting in a window the process of book manufacture, the suggestion, we think, is a very excellent one and

will receive our attention. Meanwhile, please hold the proofs
subject to our subsequent requisition.

Yours very truly,

HOUGHTON, MIFFLIN & CO.

H.D.R.*

CHESNUTT TO EDWARD C. WILLIAMS, DECEMBER 5, 1899

Your letter of some days ago has been lying on my desk, but I
have only now found time to answer it. I had a very enjoyable
visit in Washington, was made much of, and came back home,
curiously enough, feeling smaller than when I went. Perhaps it
was merely the reaction; perhaps I had collided with the color
line—not personally but theoretically, for it is a very active and
controlling feature in that city.

I gave a reading at the Fifteenth Street Church, and *The Washington Times* said "there was not a dull moment in the whole
two hours." I addressed the Colored High School, and received
a regular ovation. Spoke to the students of Howard University,
and was invited to luncheon by the president. Addressed the
Bethel Literary and Historical Association on *The Relation of
Literature to Life*. Made a surprising reputation as a wit, and one
man told me that I left a marked impression on the community.
I was on the go all the time, met all the leading people, and was
fed all I could eat. I imagine my visit will result in the sale of my
books.

The Wife of His Youth is out. I am afraid it is a little late for
the best Christmas trade. The bookstores here are going to give
it a window display—portrait of the author, view of his study,
original paintings from which illustrations are made, etc. It is a
very handsome book, I think, and I am looking forward with
some interest to two things—how it will be reviewed, and how it
will sell!

I am writing something new, and think I shall try to get into
the lecture field on the edges, as it is late in the season. Have reviewed B.T.W.'s book, *The Future of the American Negro* for
the *Saturday Evening Post,* and have been requested to write a
signed article about it for the *Critic.* Saw a copy of the *Douglass*
at a bookstore last night, but I haven't received my copies yet. It
is quite a handsome little book; I believe the Beacon Biographies
already published, have sold up to four or five thousand.

* H. D. Robins.

I agree with you about Godkin; the paper has lost snap. I see the new editor whoops up Booker T. Washington. Dr. Washington has a great deal of ability, and I have no doubt will succeed in endowing Tuskegee handsomely; and his idea will doubtless spread and be fruitful of good. I see Georgia has defeated the disfranchising bill, for a wonder. I hope North Carolina will vote hers down next summer.

I feel a little at a loss since the *Post* let up on expansion. My views haven't changed a particle, but the case looks rather hopeless.

Glad to know you are working hard; it is no doubt a good thing for you. Understand you were up at Northampton, Thanksgiving, and that you were to lunch with seventeen girls at once. I presume you were equal to the occasion.

Hope this will find you well. All the family here are in good health and join me in regards to you.

CHARLES TO DAUGHTERS, DECEMBER 8, 1899

Received your letter the other day. Glad to know you had such a gay time while Williams was there.

I have sent you copies of the two books which I presume you have received. I had a pleasant visit in Washington. Met lots of people, was entertained handsomely, and all in all had a glorious time. Will give you more details when you come home; a number of people inquired about you.

The new books are beauties. The book stores here are making attractive window displays of them, with large portrait of the author, photo of his study and pages of his MS. Book is said to be selling well. People tell me it is fine—strong, interesting, dramatic, witty, heart-rending, etc. I really think myself that some of them are pretty fine stories.

I see you are to be home in a week or two. Send me a memorandum of the amount necessary to clean off the slate and bring you home for Christmas. I haven't begun to draw any considerable revenue from my writings yet, so do not touch me any harder than necessary.

HELEN TO CHARLES, DECEMBER 10, 1899

We received your books this week and they are fine. Henrietta Brown sat down and read *The Wife of His Youth* steadily until she finished it. She says that it is the first book that has caused

her to give up everything else for many a day. I don't care much
for the binding, but I suppose the publishers know what they are
doing. The illustrations are good, very good except the first one.
I never cared for that. I think it will be a grand success, and so do
the other girls that have read it.

The Douglass book is very sweet indeed; your style is perfect.
The preface is very nice. We take literature this year and are
capable of judging.

What are you doing now? Are you still working on Rena?

We shall be home in ten days. There are to be no cut rates.
You will receive a letter in a day or two on finances. Love to all.

> HOUGHTON, MIFFLIN AND CO.
> BOSTON, MASSACHUSETTS.
> December 8, 1899

MR. CHARLES W. CHESNUTT
64 BRENTON STREET
CLEVELAND, OHIO
DEAR SIR:

Your letter of recent date informing us of the displays now in
your city, and asking for circulars of the book, is at hand this
day. The circulars are being sent you.

We have in mind getting out a card such as we sent to Cleveland, but reading instead of *A Book of Short Novels,* in this wise:
Stories of the Color Line. With the recent coming forward of Mr.
Washington, the publication of his book, the growing interest in
Tuskegee, and the public notice attracted to the general subject
of the colored people, we believe it will be well worth while to
bring the book forward in a number of places in the way indicated; that is, as a book of stories treating of a subject, which
(as a Southerner I may say it gladly) is at last approaching a
possibility of enlightened and civilized treatment.

We have in mind special effort in Boston, Washington, New
York City, Baltimore, Philadelphia—perhaps in Atlanta, Louis-
ville, St. Louis. What do you think of the idea; and, besides passing on the list of towns above, what other ones could you suggest?

The writer is of the opinion that the books ought to find important places in the contemporary literature of this phase of our
modern life, and believes they can be brought into conspicuous
notice in this direction. In the matter indicated above, we shall

rely much upon your judgment; and shall, therefore, ask a very careful consideration of the proposal, on your part before replying to this communication.

We could hardly be persuaded that it would repay either you or ourselves to ask for reviews of the book from the body of Afro-American journals, or to advertise in them; and second, for the reason that the readers whom they reach are, unfortunately, not able to purchase many books. It is true, however, that a number of them are of a literate character, and that in greater number than is known to the writer. We know that a body of about one hundred Afro-American editors met in Denver last summer and that there is an Afro-American editorial association; but we do not know its headquarters or how many of the journals represented would conserve our mutual interests in the manner above indicated. Have you any information on these points? And could you let us have a list of carefully considered Afro-American journals which it would repay us to approach in this matter? Again, as we must rely greatly upon your judgment, we shall take the liberty of asking a very careful consideration of the matter and the papers themselves—that is, if you will take up the matter. The scheme may be found impracticable, but we shall be glad to take it up and utilize the idea if possible. So we shall await your reply with interest. We are,

Very truly yours,
HOUGHTON, MIFFLIN
AND COMPANY
H.D.R.

P.S. Please let us have a list of, say, half a dozen prominent Afro-Americans to whom copies of the book might be sent, who would be willing to give an "opinion" on it, and whose commendation (we anticipate no other sort of expression) would carry weight among all persons.

H.D.R.

December 12, 1899

MESSRS. HOUGHTON, MIFFLIN & CO.
BOSTON, MASSACHUSETTS
DEAR SIRS:

I am in receipt of your letter signed with the firm name and the initials of H. D. R., with reference to bringing *The Wife of His*

Youth forward along the line of the sub-title, as a contribution to the discussion of the color line.

I am entirely willing to have the book brought forward in any way that the greater experience of the house may deem wise, and I should welcome the thought that the book might be made to contribute in any degree to the "enlightened and civilized treatment" of a subject, the handling of which has shown tendencies to lapse into unspeakable barbarism....

I quite approve of your suggestion to make special effort in the cities named. I do not see why Cincinnati might not be added to the list of Northern cities, and perhaps Chicago, Detroit, and Columbus, Ohio, if it is not too small a town. I should think other New England cities wouldn't be a bad field; for instance, I have just received a splendid press notice from the Bridgeport, Connecticut, *Standard,* from which I quote as follows:

"No writer on kindred topics has made a greater impression on the discriminating public than has Mr. Chesnutt, and he fairly divides the honors of the literary situation with Thomas Nelson Page, Joel Chandler Harris, Paul Laurence Dunbar, and Booker T. Washington. In his stories Mr. Chesnutt not only manages to disclose the underlying facts and inevitable conditions of the race situation, but in so doing, he felicitously presents the Negro character in stories the literary merit of which is far above the average; and not one of all the writers upon 'the color line' has a truer sense of the picturesque and illustrative, or a greater charm of manner.... The stories of this collection have appeared in several high-class periodicals, the first, "The Wife of His Youth" being published in the *Atlantic Monthly* about a year ago, and their appearance in book form will be welcomed by a large number of appreciative admirers.

"The Stories are 'The Wife of His Youth'; 'Her Virginia Mammy'; 'The Sheriff's Children'; 'A Matter of Principle'; 'Cicely's Dream'; 'The Passing of Grandison'; 'Uncle Wellington's Wives'; 'The Bouquet'; 'The Web of Circumstance.' They possess a very great and peculiar charm and are full of careful studies from life, and to read and understand them is to know much about the heart of the important matter involved in the race issue, the settling of which will require almost limitless faith and patience, and be made only through sacrifice and suffering."

As to the Southern cities, I am afraid my suggestions would not be very valuable. I expect the book to receive some adverse criticism—any discussion of the race problem from any but the ultra Southern point of view naturally would.

One critic has already stamped me as an advocate of miscegenation, or at least desiring a relaxation of the rigid attitude of the white race in this particular, says that the theme is unsavory, that I do not understand the "subtle relations" existing between the two races in the South, and that I have some resentful feeling left over from the carpetbag era! I thought I had distinguished myself by Christian moderation. However, I anticipated such criticism, and imagine it is a healthy sign; it ought to help the book in its character as a study of the color line. It is quite likely that people will buy a book they disapprove of, if the disapproval be strong enough, just to see what it is like; and to the Northern mind, the fact that the South severely criticizes a thing, creates at least a suspicion that there may be something in it. . . .

The book was written with the distinct hope that it might have its influence in directing attention to certain aspects of the race question which are quite familiar to those on the unfortunate side of it; and I should be glad to have that view of it emphasized if in your opinion the book is strong enough to stand it; for a sermon that is labeled a sermon must be a good one to get a hearing. I have confidence in the book myself, but that might be an author's partiality.

The portion of your letter concerning Afro-American journals, I will answer in a day or two, under another cover.

I will also write again as to the half-dozen persons to whom a book might be sent for an opinion.

About Booker Washington, I don't know. Anything he might say would doubtless be valuable, if he would venture to express himself favorably on a book supposed from the Southern standpoint to preach heretical doctrine. Perhaps one ought not to ask him, however, until the Southern reviews come in. Though, as I have reviewed his book on *The Future of the American Negro* for the *Saturday Evening Post,* and have been asked to write a signed article on it for the *Critic,* one good turn ought to deserve another. . . .

Sincerely yours,
CHARLES W. CHESNUTT

64 BRENTON STREET
CLEVELAND, OHIO
December 14, 1899

MESSRS. HOUGHTON, MIFFLIN AND COMPANY
BOSTON, MASSACHUSETTS
GENTLEMEN:

Replying further to your letter of H.D.R. of December 8, I would say that I agree with him that it would not pay to ask for reviews from the body of Afro-American journals, or to advertise in them.

Several of the Afro-American newspapers, however, are well edited, intelligently conducted, and widely read. Messrs. Small, Maynard & Company asked me, when they brought out my little *Life of Frederick Douglass* in the *Beacon Biographies,* to furnish them with a list of newspapers for colored people, so that they might, if they desired to do so, send copies of the book for review, and I made up the list which I will give you here. I was informed by a colored editor here, to whom I applied for assistance in making it up, that it is a representative list and would reach all the different classes or readers that the colored press appeals to; though it embraces perhaps less than one-tenth of the entire number published. ...

If copies are sent to any of these papers for review, I imagine it would be worth the trouble to have a few carbon copies of passages from several notices such as the one I shall quote herein, and the one I quoted in my last letter, and send them along with the book, so as to sort of steer the reviewer's critical faculty in the right direction and appeal to his racial sympathies.

I have written to Major J. B. Pond recently, with reference to securing some lecture engagements through him. I have not yet received an answer from him, but ought to have one soon. As I was not quite ready for this kind of work at the beginning of the lecture season, I fear it may be late to do much through the regular agencies. If I do not hear from Pond soon I shall apply in another quarter, and shall probably have to go down to New York to work the matter up. If it is too late to do anything through the regular agencies, I shall endeavor to work out from this town as a center, and get in some preliminary work to prepare me for next season. I am told that my readings are very entertaining. I shall appreciate any advice or suggestions you can give me along that line. I want to reach the best class of hearers—those who read, appreciate, and buy books.

I am receiving some good reviews of *The Wife of His Youth* along the line on which you are thinking of pushing the book. I presume you have them, but I quote part of one from the *New York Mail and Express* (December 9, 1899):

"In *The Wife of His Youth and Other Stories of the Color Line* by Charles W. Chesnutt, we have a variation of most of the methods employed by American story-writers in handling the characterizations of our colored population, either before or since their emancipation, from a humorous or a pathetic point of view, and one that is so striking and so novel that it may fairly be called a new departure in Afro-American fiction, or a new and wise departure in art, since, instead of trying on the one hand to move our compassion for the Negro, because we have inflicted so much suffering on his race in the past, or on the other hand, to study and enjoy him, because he is such a comical, laughable creature, so childlike and irresponsible—it simply aims to interest us in him as an individual human being, without regard to the straightness or kinkiness of his hair, or the amount of nigritude in the color of his skin.

"The art of Mr. Chesnutt in these stories of his is so fine, so elusive, so shadowy, and yet so sincere and real, that one is compelled to feel it, and remember it, without quite understanding it. One can hardly read 'The Wife of His Youth,' or 'Her Virginia Mammy' without the consciousness of tears in his eyes, and tenderness in his heart, for the manhood and womanhood that he feels there—the pathos that no mere suffering could provoke, the subtle melancholy that has made Mr. Chesnutt its poet—the Laureate of the Color Line."

Very sincerely yours,
CHARLES W. CHESNUTT

The review in the *Boston Transcript* of December 16, 1899, was very appreciative:

"The simple art with which Chesnutt tells his tales is not unbefitting the primitive motives which make their pathetic interest. The color prejudices among themselves, the injustice from the white race to the black, the lengthening shadows of the long period of slavery, furnish his subjects. The narrator is never bitter, his experience and his observation force him to use his undoubted gift of expression in illustrating the facts which are brought before us more vividly in this way than in any other. In *The Web of Circumstance* we see that even Booker Washington's panacea for the condition of the Negro, 'proputty' and a good trade, is not a certain cure. Even though the stigma were removed which differentiates the black race in the estimation of the white, their own class distinctions, based on shades of color, will carry on the evils of the situation indefinitely. It is not the author's business to philosophize or to draw conclusions. In fact, he writes with an underlying hope and courage which accentuates the lesson which he is teaching and grasps manfully at the remote promise which the future holds out to faith:

" 'Some time, we are told, when the cycle of years has rolled around, there is to be another golden age, when all men will dwell together in love and harmony, and when peace and righteousness shall prevail for a thousand years. God speed the day, and let not the shining thread of hope become so enmeshed in the web of circumstance that we lose sight of it; but give us here and there, and now and then, some little foretaste of this golden age, that we may the more patiently and hopefully await its coming.'

"In saying, Amen, to this, we feel that the existence and character of Chesnutt himself are among the foretastes of the long-deferred golden age! The name-story is the most finished of these racial narratives, but the simplest of them all, 'The Bouquet' is the most perfect—a touching, homely idyl."

CHARLES TO DAUGHTERS, DECEMBER 15, 1899

Your interesting letters received. I thank you for your literary approval of my books, which I should value even if you didn't take literature and had to rely on your native instincts for your judgments. I will save up the press notices and reviews for you to read when you come home; they are very complimentary, most of them, on both *The Wife of His Youth* and the little *Douglass*. I enclose N. Y. draft to Ethel's order, which I hope will reach you in time for all your purposes. Use it economically, for at present, my income is small; I hope to increase it rapidly. Sorry the R.R. didn't make a rate, but suppose they think times are flush and everybody able to pay.

Weather is cold and snowy. Shall be glad to see you both when you come. Treasure up any remarks you hear about the books, as my literary reputation is now an important matter to me.

64 BRENTON STREET
CLEVELAND, OHIO
December 25, 1899

MESSRS. HOUGHTON, MIFFLIN AND COMPANY
H. D. ROBINS, ESQ.
BOSTON, MASSACHUSETTS
MY DEAR MR. ROBINS:

Your recent favor was received, and I am very glad to make your acquaintance, which I shall consummate in person when I am next in Boston, which will be sometime this winter. I quite agree with you as to the provincialism and backwardness of the South, and in your view that a new country—of course, not too new—is the place to look for the development of new men and new ideals.

I called on your friend, Mr. Blanchard, and spent a very pleasant half-hour with him. The question came up about what you were doing with H. M. and Co., and he said you were "selling Hopkinson Smith's books." I told him I thought you meant to take a whirl at mine before you got Smith's all sold.

I thank you for the proof of the very handsome ad, that appeared in the *Transcript*, where I also saw it, as I did the ad in the Cleveland papers. I cannot complain of being a prophet without honor in my own country, for the papers here give me much space. The *Transcript* has treated me very handsomely indeed; as you have undoubtedly noticed. There have been three notices of *The Wife of His Youth* since its appearance, all complimentary, and all finding something more in the book than mere reading for amusement; in fact, all the Boston papers that I have seen have commended the book. The little biography that Small, Maynard & Co. have brought out for me is received with an unanimity of appreciation that is very gratifying, and which will do its part, I hope, to swell the little stream that I am hoping may grow into a current of popularity.

If you have not sent a copy of *The Wife of His Youth* to T. Thomas Fortune, care the *New York Age*, 4 Cedar Street, New York, I should be glad to have you do so; he has written me that he will with pleasure write an "appreciation" of the book.

With reference to prominent colored men in Washington, of whom I wrote, I am informed that most of them have bought the book already, and that they will write something about it very willingly. My friend there who is attending to the matter is absent for the holidays, but will return on the 28th, when he will look after it.

I hope the house is encouraged by the reception *The Wife of His Youth* is receiving, and that they will do what they can to give it prominence. I am told it is selling well here in spite of the enormous Christmas trade in special gift books, etc. Burrows Bros. are going to give it another window display. I have had several favorable notices from St. Louis, which might be a good city to put on your list. I am also informed that Toledo, Ohio is a city where books dealing with the same general subject sell well.

Permit me to extend the greetings of the season, and to say that I remain,

Very cordially yours,
CHARLES W. CHESNUTT

The reviews of *The Wife of His Youth* kept coming in from all parts of the country. Chesnutt had opened up an entirely new field in American literature and was making a decided impression there. Two schools of thought were promptly developed. The first was that a new star had risen on the horizon of American literature and was shedding its clear cool light upon phases of American life hitherto untouched by American writers. Miss Alice Hanscom in Cleveland's *Town Topics* wrote:

"That author is indeed fortunate who stands alone in command of a field rich in material for ministering to human interest both intellectual and social, one who is by knowledge, sympathy and literary equipment pre-eminently qualified to bring the resources of his exclusive domain into effective and artistic presentation."

And another:

"A wholly new and hitherto unexplored field in literature has been opened up by Charles W. Chesnutt. The short stories of which the volume is made up are unique in that they present the negro simply as a human being, without the exaggerated pathos of the 'purpose novel,' or the equally exaggerated and sometimes fantastic humor of the 'negro story.' The book has found a place in contemporary letters, not only as novel and engaging fiction, but as a contribution to the literature of the race question—not the least serious problem before the American people for solution."

In the *Outlook* of February 24, 1900, appeared an article entitled "Two New Novelists" written by Hamilton Wright Mabie, in which he discusses Mary Johnston and Charles W. Chesnutt. The opening paragraph is as follows:

"The appearance of two new writers whose work has the quality which Miss Mary Johnston put into *Prisoners of Hope,* and *To Have and to Hold,* and Mr. Charles W. Chesnutt into *The Conjure Woman* and *The Wife of His Youth,* all with imprint of Messrs. Houghton, Mifflin and Company, is a matter of deep interest to all those who care for the expression of American life in art."

In speaking of Chesnutt he says:

"Mr. Chesnutt finds his field in the life of the negro, and writes as one who knows that life at first hand, and who is able to comprehend and interpret it both on the side of humor and of tragedy, because he has to a certain extent shared its fortune. . . .

"In this more recent volume, *The Wife of His Youth,* Mr. Chesnutt concerns himself largely with the negro of today under the new conditions under which he finds himself; and it is safe to say that no finer psychological study of the negro in his new life has been presented than that which is found in the story which gives its title to this volume—a story which in keenness of perception, in restraint and balance, in true feeling and artistic construction, must take its place among the best short stories in American literature. The two volumes taken together constitute an important addition, not only to our literature, but to our knowledge of the negro race; exhibiting as they do, the negro under two entirely different conditions. . . .

"It is in such work as that which Miss Johnston and Mr. Chesnutt have recently contributed to contemporary literature that the advancing movement of the American literary spirit is to be discerned. For this work has its roots in reality; its chief concern is the portrayal of life; it deals at first hand with original materials; it gives us new aspects of American life; it is the expression of what is going on in the spirit of man on this continent."

But the Southern reviewers and those of Southern sympathies spoke otherwise. Nancy Huston Banks in the February *Bookman* said:

"To Mr. Chesnutt, then, may perhaps be given the credit of the first publication of a subtle psychological study of the negro's spiritual nature, the first actual revelation of those secret depths of the dusky soul which no white writer might hope to approach through his own intuition. . . .

"All this and more may be said in praise of the first and shortest of the nine stories forming the volume. The others are hardly worthy of mention in comparison with the first. . . .

"As fiction it [the volume] has little if any claim to consideration, and a graver fault than its lack of literary quality is its careless approach to the all but unapproachable ground of sentimental relations between the black race and the white race. Touching this and still more dangerous and darker race problems, Mr. Chesnutt shows a lamentable lack of tact of a kindred sort, an incomprehensible want of the good taste and dignified reserve which characterizes his first beautiful story and the greater part of all his work. 'The Sheriff's Children' furnishes, perhaps, the most shocking instance of his reckless disregard of matters respected by more experienced writers. . . .'"

14

A Choice of Publishers

EARLY IN 1900 Chesnutt received the following letter from Walter Hines Page:

DOUBLEDAY & McCLURE CO.
PUBLISHERS
34 UNION SQUARE EAST
NEW YORK
January 24, 1900

MY DEAR MR. CHESNUTT:

I beg your pardon for so long a silence about *Rena*. One change has followed another so rapidly here and the work of getting my family settled has been so much more difficult than I anticipated, and my absences from my desk have been so numerous that I neglected the very things that I cared most to do. I do not know whether you have been informed of the definite shape that my work here has taken. I have become a book publisher on my own account, having cast my fortunes in with Mr. Doubleday who has built up the book publishing business of Doubleday & McClure Co. which now forthwith becomes Doubleday, Page and Co. I believe that we have already won some little reputation for the successful handling of good books, and the future certainly holds a very promising outlook. This much by way of personal explanation.

Now it has only been just lately that I have taken up *Rena* in her latest and finished form; and we have all read the manuscript with very great pleasure. My own judgment about it has been confirmed by the judgment of my partners, and I write to ask whether you care for it to be brought out by us. I ask this because

I do not have the slightest wish to draw you away from Houghton, Mifflin and Company who are my good friends as well as yours, but since you had this submitted there once and it was declined I do not know what your feeling is about re-submitting it; and so I put the question to you with directness and frankness.

If you are willing for us to publish it, I think the book will surely reach its maximum as well through our firm as if it were brought out by any other publishing house; and we shall put it through immediately on, let me say, the following business basis: 10% for the first 2000 copies, 12½% for the next 2000 copies, 15% on all over 4000 copies. I think that a graduated scale of royalties is the fairest, because under such an arrangement the author profits directly in proportion to the success of the book.

We all agree that the best title is *The House Behind the Cedars*. We are now getting ready all our spring books and we have about fifty very attractive and promising volumes on our list for Spring publication; and it is important, if we are going to bring this out, that an arrangement should be made at once. We should like to make a cover and a title page and to set up the first chapter at least, so that we may make a dummy to give to our traveling salesmen who are now just getting ready to start out to visit all the principal book sellers in the United States to place advance orders.

I will ask you, therefore, if you will not be kind enough to telegraph me as soon as you receive this letter.

I suppose you are wise in using old Judge Strange's name and old Mrs. McRae's name and all the familiar old family names and landmarks of Fayetteville, but some of our friends down there will be—well, I will say interested. I congratulate you on the local color and the accuracy of your descriptions of the town and the country. You seem to have caught the very spirit of the whole community. Then, too, the story of Rena herself is most admirably and dramatically unfolded.

With congratulations, as well as with apologies, and holding myself entirely at your service, I remain,

Yours very sincerely,
WALTER H. PAGE

P. S. The book ought to be similar in general manufacture to Kipling's *The Day's Work,* a copy of which I send you.

W. H. P.

SUSAN TO DAUGHTERS, JANUARY 26, 1900

Your father has just left for New York, so we are alone once more. He intended to go East the first of February, but received a letter from Mr. Page yesterday about publishing his novel *Rena,* and as Mr. Page wished to know at once, he concluded he had better go on so they could talk the matter over before deciding.

He is in a quandary about it. Mr. Page is no longer with Houghton Mifflin and Company, he is interested in the publishing firm of Doubleday, Page and Company, and as Houghton, Mifflin and Company have treated him so well, your father is not sure they will like this other firm to publish his next book. They have refused the story once, and predict failure for it, while Mr. Page thinks it a fine story and has made him a flattering offer; so, you see, an author has his trials and tribulations. I think he wants to talk it over with the other firm before deciding.

I think it is his intention to go on to Boston, but he left so hurriedly that he made no definite plans. He had a nice letter from the literary critic or editor of the *Boston Transcript,* with a cordial invitation to visit him at his home in Wrentham, Mass., when he next visited Boston, so I rather think he will do so. I hope he will enjoy his trip.

We went to hear Paderewski last night. We had to pay a good price for seats, but it was worth the price. He played at the Gray's Armory; all reserved seats were two dollars, general admission one dollar, and that immense place was simply packed. It was a fearful night, "it snowed and blowed", and was very cold, but that did not keep people away. Every note was as distinct and clear as a bell. He played over two hours, leaving the stage only once for a few minutes. It was fine playing, and it was a fine and appreciative audience that greeted him.

I have been out every evening this week except one. So I manage to lead quite a busy life. I daresay Papa told you about the reception which was tendered us at Dr. Jewett's on Cedar Avenue. Love to you both.

CHARLES TO SUSAN, JANUARY 27, 1900

Got here [New York] all right, and saw my man. They are real anxious to publish *Rena,* but I will not let them know until I have been to Boston where I think I shall go tomorrow afternoon. I don't need to worry about getting publishers at present.

Page is a fine fellow, wants my novel and wants it bad, but

doesn't want it unless I want him to have it. Leaves it all to me, and if I say so will publish spring or fall, as I say. This is between us—you and me, of course.

This Grand Union is a nice hotel; cheaper than the Waldorf.

Please send any future mail care Houghton, Mifflin and Company, 4 Park Street, Boston. Love to kids and more to you.

CHARLES TO SUSAN, FEBRUARY 3, 1900

Am in this village [New York] again. Had an interview with the famous Mr. Howells this morning. He is going to write me up for the *Atlantic*. Have got my name on the books of all the lecture bureaus, from Major Pond down. Made a speech in Boston yesterday.

I may stay over here until Monday, or may go home sometime tomorrow. Saw T. Thomas Fortune today, and some other folks, I may go by Northampton and see the girls, but as the chances are that I shall come back East in March, I may wait until then before seeing them. Will write you again. Hope you and children are well.

CHARLES TO ETHEL AND HELEN, FEBRUARY 4, 1900

It was my firm intention to visit you on this trip East, but you want me to make the best impression when I come, and I left home about ten days sooner than I expected, so that I didn't have time to get some "glad rags" that I intended to wear to impress my "distinguished personality" upon your under-graduate friends and to do you proper credit. Besides I have promised to send in the MS. of a certain novel in the shortest time possible, and in order to get it in on time, I must hustle it—and I wouldn't want to come to you unless I could stay at least a day.

Must hurry home for another reason—to send that tuition money. Will leave here for Cleveland in just one hour and will be there 9:30 tomorrow a.m. I want to visit you when I can take my time and enjoy it. I will let you know.

DOUBLEDAY & McCLURE CO.
PUBLISHERS
NEW YORK
February 17, 1900

MY DEAR MR. CHESNUTT:

I am now going actively ahead with my ambitious biographical plan. I enclose a little typewritten statement, which is yet confidential, outlining the scope of the series in a general way. Now I do not see why we should lose any time in coming to an understanding about Frederick Douglass. You can not only write the life of Douglass, but you can make a most interesting contribution to the history of the anti-slavery agitation. I take it for granted that you could not complete such a book, I will say roughly, within a year. It would be half a year, perhaps, after you finished it before it would actually be on the market, so that even if you should begin work now there would be no conflict between this book and your little book in the Beacon Series.

A biography is not going to sell, of course, to the same extent that fiction sells, but we expect to make a success of this series by keeping it alive over a long period of years. A fair business arrangement, it seems to me, would be about as follows: 10% on the first 2500 copies, and 15% thereafter (the book will sell for not less than $2.00). Then if we should issue a subscription edition the royalty would have to be less, because the expense of making and marketing a subscription edition is two or three times as great as the expense of selling the book through the trade, and the custom of putting smaller royalties on subscription editions is, I think, universal, since it is absolutely necessary from the publisher's point of view. If a good many years hence we should issue a subscription edition of this series, we would pay you on this special edition 15 cents a copy.

Why should we not come at once to an understanding in this matter and go ahead with it? Let me hear from you at your early convenience.

Very sincerely yours,
WALTER H. PAGE

EDITORIAL OFFICE OF
THE ATLANTIC MONTHLY
BOSTON
February 27, 1900

DEAR MR. CHESNUTT:

Mr. Perry and I have read "The Rainbow Chasers" and have liked it—in fact, we have liked some parts of it very much. The homely sincerity of it—its entire freedom from affectation and mere ornament of language gave us genuine satisfaction. The structure, however, of the story, and its leisurely rate of development, with the large element of reflection and meditation which your plan and purpose involve, seem to us on consideration to make it not readily adaptable for serial uses. You see, the magazine reader, getting a story in sections, demands a good deal of intensity, and a rather more than average rate of speed in the movement of the story to hold his attention. So we have very reluctantly come to the conclusion that it would not be wise for us to attempt to use "The Rainbow Chasers" serially in the *Atlantic*. I am very sure, however, that Messrs. Houghton, Mifflin & Company would be glad to consider the publication of it as a book, and we are keeping the manuscript here until we learn your wish in the matter.

With friendliest regards, I am

Yours sincerely,
W. B. PARKER

CHESNUTT TO EDWARD C. WILLIAMS, FEBRUARY 27, 1900

I am glad to hear you liked that valentine in the *Plain Dealer;* I did not kill the artist; the "ad" I thought sufficiently balanced the slander. I believe I told you that Mr. Howells had written me up for the *Atlantic* for early publication.

Page wants me to write a long life of Douglass for a new and ambitious series (this is confidential) making it a sort of history of the abolition movement—from that point of view. I haven't yet decided about *Rena;* but I think I shall write the *Douglass.* I think the Albany Library has a bibliography that would cover the subject thoroughly; if there is such a thing printed, will you tell me about it? I may have to come up there sometime and spend a week working on it.

I tried to make a speech the other night at Gray's Armory between the acts of "Thirty Years of Freedom." The audience happened to be taking "five minutes of freedom" at that time, which they deserved, for they had been bored more or less, and there was so much noise before and behind the curtain that my speech was not audible more than halfway; and those in the rear began to applaud so vigorously that I concluded to stop. One of the papers put it: "Somebody came out to make a speech, but when it became apparent that it was not audible beyond the first few rows, the audience began to applaud so vigorously that it gradually dawned on the speaker that they hoped he was through, and he did not go on." Thank the Lord my name wasn't mentioned! It was the first instance, to my knowledge, of a man being called

down by applause! It was a little discourteous, but it was good-
natured, and I bear no malice. It was a good speech, but the Angel
Gabriel couldn't have delivered it without his trumpet at that
hour and in that place. . . .

In the meantime two short stories by Chesnutt had been published; one of them, "Lonesome Ben," an "Uncle Julius" story
in the March issue of the *Southern Workman;* and the other,
"Aunt Mimy's Son," a pathetic little story about a devoted mother
and her ne'er-do-well son, in *The Youth's Companion* of March
first.

Charles to Daughters, March 3, 1900

Your letter received, and I enclose N. Y. draft endorsed to
Ethel's order. This leaves us all well.

I have been working downtown for the last ten days, in an old
matter, left over. It has not been an unpleasant diversion.

Did you see the piece in the *Outlook* of February 24 about me?
And did you read "Aunt Mimy's Son" in *The Youth's Companion* of this week? I have just received a letter from the *Atlantic*
saying they like my last book "The Rainbow Chasers" very much,
but don't think the action rapid enough for serial publication.
However, they would like to bring it out in book form. It seems
my star is rising—two months ago I did not know whether I could
write a novel; now two first-class publishing houses want to bring
out novels for me. One of the novels shall see the light reasonably soon.

I sent you a paper about the sleet storm. It was a bright day
yesterday, and the sun melted much of the ice, and today will do
much more. Hope you are well and happy.

Williams to Chesnutt, March 4, 1900

I have intended to answer your very interesting letter before
now, but have not been able to get to it.

I am very glad to hear that Mr. Howells is going to write you
up, for, with his appreciation of the aesthetics of style and diction,
he should be able to say something worth while, and his dictum
on any subject commands the respectful attention of the cultured
East. With their attention once at your command, I think you
can be trusted to do the rest.

These easterners are very ready to believe that nothing good
can "come out of Nazareth," and the West to them is a Nazareth.

They are distrustful of books published by Western houses, however good the book may be, and it takes a great deal of merit to overcome their prejudices.

I am hoping you will see fit to place *Rena* before long, as it surely is a good story, with all the elements of human interest. How is "The Rainbow Chasers" coming on? I am glad to hear about the Douglass book. It seems to me it would be a distinct contribution to American historical literature. In another letter, which perhaps I shall send you tomorrow I shall give a short bibliographical list. This library would be a very good place for such work. Oberlin College Library contains a great mass of original documents, etc., connected with the abolition movement. We have part of the file of the old *Ohio Observer* at Hatch library, containing contemporary accounts of the beginnings of the movement in northern Ohio. Harvard College library and the Boston Public Library would also have very fine collections. It always seemed to me a pity that Douglass himself did not attempt an ambitious history of that period.

Did you think of talking the matter over with Prof. Hart when he was in Cleveland? He is perhaps as high an authority as we have on American History, and as a bibliographer is surely second to none now in that field. Channing and Hart's *Guide to the Study of American History* is the most useful, for ordinary purposes, of any bibliography of American History.

I hope you will finally decide to undertake the work, and if I can be of any assistance in hunting up bibliographies or looking up quotations, etc., please command me. I shall try to send the bibliographical list tomorrow.

Chesnutt had arranged to return East early in March to give some readings and lectures in Boston and vicinity. When the girls at Smith learned of their father's plans they asked him to bring Dorothy and leave her with them for a little visit. Susan at first refused to allow her to go—she thought it utter nonsense for Charles to burden himself with the care of a little girl when he was going to be so busy about his own affairs, but Dorothy and Charles finally overcame her objections.

CHARLES TO SUSAN, MARCH 10, 1900

I arrived here on time today and read very successfully this afternoon to quite a large and appreciative audience.

I left Dorothy at Springfield. Helen was there to meet us, and took the little girl in tow. A young woman on the train relieved me of all trouble about Dorothy's toilet, etc.

I am invited to a breakfast tomorrow morning out in Cambridge, at which some of the speakers at the meeting today will be present.

A dear, delightful old lady in Worcester wants to have me come up there and lecture while I am here. I shall probably come, I shall also probably go up to Concord, Massachusetts to give a reading there, Tuesday night. Haven't just decided when I shall go to Northampton.

Please write or forward mail care Houghton, Mifflin and Company until further notice. The Touraine is a "swell" hotel, so l may not stay here long. . . .

CHARLES TO SUSAN, MARCH 14, 1900

. . . I expected to get a final decision on my "Rainbow Chasers" today, but one of the gentlemen was sick and the thing will go over until next week, but will be decided while I am here.

I was invited to dinner today; on Friday I dine at the Colonial Club, Cambridge, with Prof. Albert Bushnell Hart. Have two reading engagements for next Monday and one for Wednesday. Yesterday evening I went out to Wrentham, Massachusetts with my friend, Mr. Chamberlin,* of the *Boston Transcript,* and stayed all night. They meant to invite our girls to visit them during Easter, but the lady was taken down with the grippe yesterday, and received me in her bedroom, for she insisted on my coming up. Lovely people.

CHARLES TO DAUGHTERS, MARCH 15, 1900

I am thinking of coming up to Northampton Saturday morning and staying over Sunday, as I have some engagements here the first of next week. I suppose you are well, although your silence is equally compatible with death or disability.

I wired your mother to express me a certain pair of shoes to Northampton. Keep them for me—they are not for your wear—I want something for myself.

I hope the infant is enjoying herself. I may not be able to go home before the 28th and I expect the *mater* will become *dolorosa* before she sees her pickaninny again. Much love to my three girls.

* Joseph Edgar Chamberlin.

HOUGHTON, MIFFLIN AND COMPANY
BOSTON
March 24, 1900

CHAS. W. CHESNUTT, ESQ.,
CARE NEW YORK OFFICE.
DEAR MR. CHESNUTT:

We have decided to take *Rena* (under the title *The House Behind the Cedars*) in place of *The Rainbow Chasers,* and to publish it next fall on the same terms as *The Wife of his Youth,* with the understanding and agreement that this shall be the only book of yours published this year, and understanding that this will be agreeable to you, we shall forward the contracts to you at Cleveland early next week.

Yours very truly,
HOUGHTON, MIFFLIN & CO.
F. J. G.*

CHARLES TO DAUGHTERS, MARCH 24, 1900

Am writing this in the Springfield station while waiting for New York train. Thought I wouldn't take Dorothy to New York, as I might stay several days, but will either come to Springfield for her in a day or two or have you ship her to Albany. Will wire you from New York.

Rena will be published early next fall by Houghton, Mifflin and Co. I thought best to keep the three southern books together, and they asked the privilege of reconsidering *Rena.*

Read in Worcester last night to a good audience and very acceptably. Was entertained by a very nice elderly lady, and left her house early this A.M.

Hope you are all well, including D., for this is a family letter.

CHARLES TO HELEN, MARCH 25, 1900

Unless I telegraph you to the contrary, I should like to have you have Dorothy at Springfield Tuesday morning, so that I can take the westbound train leaving there at 8:35, which will bring us to Cleveland at 10:45 p.m. That saves putting Dorothy to bed and all that, though it is a long ride. You can leave Northampton at 6:55 and get to Springfield at 7:30, or you can leave Northamp-

* Francis J. Garrison.

ton at 7:50 and get to Springfield at 8:26; it might be safer to take the early train. I shall probably come up by an afternoon train and stay overnight at the Massasoit House. Much love.

Mr. Howells's article entitled "Mr. Charles W. Chesnutt's Stories" was published in the May issue of *The Atlantic Monthly*. The article gave the deepest satisfaction to Chesnutt, who felt that such recognition was added stimulus for greater effort. Howells's praise was almost unstinted. He spoke of Chesnutt's remarkable work; of the novelty of the material and the author's thorough mastery of it. He said in speaking of the name-story in *The Wife of His Youth*: "Any one accustomed to study methods in fiction, to distinguish between good and bad art, to feel the joy which the delicate skill possible only from a love of truth can give, must have known a high pleasure in the quiet self-restraint of the performance...."

In discussing the other stories in the volume he said: "It is not from their racial interest that we could first wish to speak of them, though that must have a very great and very just claim upon the critic. It is much more simply and directly, as works of art that they make their appeal, and we must allow the force of this quite independently of the other interest."

Howells went on to criticize occasional weaknesses in Chesnutt's work—times when the simplicity lapsed, when the impartial and aloof attitude became a little pompous, when the style was a little too ornate for beauty, or the diction too journalistic. He then continued: "But it is right to add that these are the exceptional times, and that for far the greater part Mr. Chesnutt seems to know quite as well what he wants to do in a given case as Maupassant, or Tourguénief, or Mr. James, or Miss Jewett, or Miss Wilkins, in other cases, and has done it with an art of kindred quiet and force.... They are new and fresh and strong as life always is and fable never is....

"Our own more universal interest in him arises from the more than promise he has given in a department of literature where Americans hold the foremost place. In this there is happily no color line; and if he has it in him to go forward on the way he has traced for himself, to be true to life as he has known it, to deny himself the glories of the cheap success which awaits the charlatan in fiction, one of the places at the top is open to him."

WILLIAMS TO CHESNUTT, APRIL 28, 1900

I have just finished Mr. Howells' criticism in the *Atlantic,* and cannot forbear sending you a hasty line of congratulation. I should think you might reasonably feel very much elated over such unqualified praise from the dean of American letters.

After reading such a criticism you must surely feel that it is good to have lived. I am sure no one enjoyed Mr. Howells' appreciation more than I did, except it be yourself.

SUSAN TO DAUGHTERS, APRIL 30, 1900

. . . I am quite convinced that I cannot stay in town this summer, so have decided to rent the house out near Willoughby. Ned and I went out the other day to look at it and were very much pleased with the house and surroundings, more especially the surroundings. We have two or three miles of beach all to ourselves and the man says plenty of shade all around when the leaves are out. Although the house is small, I think we can manage. Of course, our friends will have to be satisfied with spending the day with us, as we cannot offer them a bed.

The main difficulty will be in keeping enough to eat in the house. We can get plenty of milk, eggs, and chickens on the farm, and I think we can get to town often enough to get other things. I dare say your father will be in town every day. Ned says he is going out next Saturday to plant his garden. The McIntyres have given him an old boat which has been lying down at the D. & C. docks and he and George McIntyre are fixing it up in great shape. I forgot to say that Mr. Wellner is letting us have the place for $75.00. I told him we could not pay any more, so he says we can have it this year at that price. He is painting it on the outside and papering it also; I think it will be quite an attractive little place.

CHESNUTT TO WILLIAMS, MAY 12, 1900

I was busy last week, at vulgar toil, earning the money, in an old matter downtown, to pay the rent for our summer cottage, and I have not had time to answer your letter sooner. I am glad you liked Howells' article; it is quite appreciative and gave me much pleasure. I have lying before me a letter from Hamilton Wright Mabie in which he says: "You have captured the few who know and the many who feel. I hear continually the best things said of your work by such experts as Mr. Howells, Page,

James Lane Allen, and Mrs. Stuart;* things which ought to give you solid comfort. There is so much in your stories and it is of such quality that I am confident that you have come to stay."

These things are very encouraging. I have certainly won a welcome from my fellow-craftsmen, and if "the many who feel" will show their faith by their works and buy my books in large quantities, I shall be happy.

Glad to know you are working hard—a good thing for you at your age. I'm struggling with a careful revision of *Rena;* it shall be as good as I can write it.

The summer at Willoughby was delightful—a cottage in an apple orchard, a fine bathing beach on Lake Erie, a rowboat, an icecream freezer, blackberries in profusion. Charles insisted on blackberry or apple dumplings nearly every day and could not get enough of them. The farm supplied them with chickens, eggs, milk, cream, and butter. The town of Willoughby was a short distance away on the interurban, and it was a simple matter to go marketing there.

There was no chance to get lonesome. Cleveland friends came out often to spend the day, and Susan and the girls were kept busy at housework as well as at entertaining, for the hired girl they had taken out with them became discouraged at the amount of cooking that had to be done and returned to town. Edwin, after a couple of weeks of swimming and resting, got a job on a farm up the road and spent his days in healthful occupation and in saving money for the school year. Dorothy acquired two little kittens which her father promptly named Toussaint and Booker T. Chesnutt. When not supervising the making of the dumplings or playing with Dottie and the kittens or rowing the guests, Chesnutt spent his time at writing a series of sociological papers entitled "The Future American" which were published in three issues of the *Boston Transcript* in the late summer.

These essays in the *Transcript* were extremely controversial. The following editorial from the *Washington Times* of October 5, 1900, made some interesting comments on them: "Mr. Charles W. Chesnutt has been writing some articles on the race question for the *Boston Transcript* which will be worth the reading of anyone interested in that phase of the country's development. He faces the possibility of race amalgamation squarely, and speaks

* Ruth McEnery Stuart.

more frankly on the subject than most other writers have dared to do. He says in the third of these articles: 'The most powerful factor in achieving any result is the wish to bring it about. The only thing that ever succeeded in keeping two races apart when living on the same soil—the only true ground of caste—is religion, and, as has been alluded to in the case of the Jews, this is only superficially successful. The colored people are the same as the whites in religion; they have the same standards and methods of culture, the same ideals, and the presence of the successful white race as a constant incentive to their ambition. The ultimate result is not difficult to foresee. The races will be quite as effectively amalgamated by lightening the Negroes as they would be by darkening the whites.' "

The editorial in the *Washington Times* went on to say that it was only natural for fair colored people to pass over into the white ranks, and if it was made extremely advantageous for them to do so it was not only natural but inevitable. It said also that many cases of this kind had occurred, and warned the public that if they wanted to stop amalgamation they must give colored workmen and artists a chance to make the most of themselves, and not shut them out of everything, until those who could pass as white were compelled to do so.

15

"The House Behind the Cedars"

WHEN Houghton, Mifflin and Company asked Chesnutt's co-operation in getting some machinery ready for the proper ex-ploitation of *The House Behind the Cedars* he wrote the follow-ing letter:

64 BRENTON STREET
CLEVELAND, OHIO
September 27, 1900

MESSRS. HOUGHTON, MIFFLIN & CO.
BOSTON, MASS.
MY DEAR MR. ROBINS:

I am in receipt of your letter asking my cooperation in pre-senting my book *The House Behind the Cedars,* to the public who ought to be eagerly awaiting something from my pen—I only wish I knew they were! I will take up in their order the various points you suggest:

1st—I do not really know of any cities, except Cleveland, where I might hope to sell many books on the strength of my personal acquaintance. I have friends all over the country, and hope to have more, but they are more or less scattered, and many of them have been made through the medium of my writings. You could probably tell from your own order book where most books have been sold, which would be a better index than I could furnish of the number of my readers in such places. As to Cleveland, where the circulating libraries are well supplied with my books, I am told that neither of them stays upon the shelves, but that they remain constantly in circulation. That ought to be a good sign.

2nd—I do not know that I can specify any particular locality where the subject of the book, bluntly stated as a story of a colored girl who passed for white, would tend to cause any great rush for the book. I rather hope it will sell in spite of its subject, or rather, because of its dramatic value apart from the race problem involved. I was trying to write, primarily, an interesting and artistic story, rather than a contribution to polemical discussion.

I am inclined to think that perhaps a little judicious advertising in Ohio towns, suggesting that the author is an Ohio novelist, might be effective. I am quite sure of the hearty cooperation of the local book trade, and am going to ask their opinion about this Ohio advertising, and let you know about it immediately.

I have enclosed several notices along the line of what would seem to me a good way to advertise the book. These of course, you can use in any form you like, changing or combining them or cutting them as you like.

I hope the book may raise some commotion, I hardly care in what quarter, though whether, from the nature of the theme it will, I don't know. I published recently a series of articles in the *Boston Transcript* on the same general subject, which brought me a number of interesting letters from places as widely separated as Boston and Los Angeles. In the Washington, D. C. *Times* of August 18, 1900, was published a long editorial under the head of "The Yellow Peril in the United States," in which the writer said that the white race was becoming insidiously and to a large extent unknowingly corrupted with Negro blood, and cited a number of well-known Americans who are well-known, under the rose, to have remote Negro ancestry; of course, he did not mention names, but his descriptions were easily recognized by the well-informed. The question of "miscegenation" was brought up at the recent conference of leading white men of the South who met in May at Montgomery, Alabama, to discuss the race problem; and one of the solutions put forth involved the future amalgamation with the white race of at least a remnant of the black population. So that the subject I think may be regarded as generally opened up for discussion, and inferentially for literary treatment. I choose it because I understand it, and am deeply interested in it, but I hope to make it interesting to others because of the element of human interest involved.

I shall no doubt be in Boston during the fall or winter, I do not yet know just when, and shall probably give some readings in various towns, and if they can be utilized to promote the sale of my books, so much the better. I shall be glad to cooperate with you in any way I can in this matter, and shall write again in a few days, and will answer more promptly any other suggestions you may make....

CHARLES TO DAUGHTERS, SEPTEMBER 28, 1900

Your letters were received and read with much pleasure. We are glad to know you are comfortably settled, and that you met with a cordial reception from your friends of the faculty, etc. I don't know whether they had read my *Boston Transcript* articles or not, but shall give them opportunity to read various things from my pen. Am still reading proofs of *The House Behind the Cedars,* which is slated for publication, October 27. I hope it may make a favorable impression....

CHARLES TO DAUGHTERS, OCTOBER 12, 1900

Your interesting letters have been received from time to time. Am sincerely glad to know that you find the house life so pleasant, and that the young ladies are all so harmonious and agreeable. Have read with much interest the clipping sent, giving account of the 25th anniversary exercises, which were very interesting. Am pleased to know that you saw Mr. Chamberlin and Angel; she is a queer girl, but I imagine has quality; at least Chamberlin thinks so, and as I value his opinion concerning myself, why should I question it concerning his protégée? Hein?

We were invited to call on my friends, the Amblers several evenings ago, to meet a Mr. Caverno and wife, who were visiting there. One of their daughters is an instructor in Greek at Smith— I guess I have heard you speak of her—and another teaches in the Burnham School. They expressed their intention of looking you up or of hoping to see you at Northampton, whither they are bound by slow stages. I hope you may meet them, as they are very nice people. Mr. Caverno writes, along philosophic and similar lines, for the serious magazines, and is, I imagine, a retired minister.

We were pleased to learn from a recent letter, that Ethel and her young man had composed their differences; it is well enough not to have any. He has been around several times lately.

We have been having a Home Week celebration; I send you a newspaper. Your mother and I were down Tuesday evening to the theater, and took Dorothy down Wednesday evening, Carnival night. Lots of light and noise and people; nothing particularly elevating, but quite exhilarating.

I infer from looking at the calendar that you will soon be needing some money. Your mother has ordered me to send seven dollars extra for hats. I enclose N. Y. draft which I trust may cover the ground.

I have disposed of a couple of short stories since you left, and am just now putting the finishing touches on another very good one. Have also finished reading the proofs of *The House Behind the Cedars,* which has been improved by the process. I see it advertised as containing "a bold plot, developed with much force, and elaborating a sociological problem of great significance." I hope the book may "catch on." I should like to have it make a success, both critical and popular, though I hardly expect it to do more than fairly well.

This is a long letter, though it covers only a small piece of paper. We are all well. Schools have a Home Week holiday today. Hope this may find you well.

CHARLES TO DAUGHTERS, OCTOBER 29, 1900

I am writing letters this morning and drop a line to say that we are all well—except your mother is under the weather slightly. I received yesterday an advance copy of *The House Behind the Cedars,* which has a very handsome dress. I will today write the publishers to send you a copy which will get there, I suppose, in a few days. I read the *Century* proof the other day for "The March of Progress," and have had requests from two of the biggest publishers in the United States for my next novel. They want a strong race problem novel, and somebody shall have it! . . .

CHARLES TO HELEN, NOVEMBER 6, 1900

Your interesting letter came duly to hand; I also saw the one written to your mother, giving an account of certain "high jinks" on which I forbear to speak, with a silence more eloquent than words.

The reviews of the new book are coming in, and are very favorable. I mailed you a copy of the *Plain Dealer* yesterday, with the first review I had seen, although I have received several since, all favorable. Mr. Chamberlin has an excellent one in last Wednesday's *Transcript*. The *P. D.* says I have written a "story of absorbing interest and treated a perplexing problem with masterly ability". If this keeps up, the book will be a genuine success, and my next book a howling success. Several big houses have been after it already. This book ought to make an impression, and I have no sort of doubt it will.

I do not, however, expect to get rich out of it, and I therefore, have not sent a great deal extra in the check I enclose herewith. I'm afraid you are "spread"-ing too much. I guess you can worry along with this awhile.

One of my stories, "Tobe's Tribulations," a bullfrog conjure story, came out in the *Southern Workman* this last week, and the *Outlook Magazine* for November 3 has "The Sway-backed House." *The Youth's Companion* has paid for "A Limb of Satan," and the *Century* announces me as a contributor to its year of romance. I shall try to worry along at lit. until I get started good, unless I am forced into obscurity by my expenses—see to it that I am not. . . .

Chesnutt's first novel, *The House Behind the Cedars,* the name under which *Rena* was published, came out at the end of October and was widely reviewed throughout the country.

The novel presented another phase of the problem of the color line in America, that of intermarriage between the white and Negro races. It is the story of two young people, John and Rena Walden, the children of a colored woman, Mis' Molly Walden, and a wealthy and cultured white man of Patesville in North Carolina. The father was interested in these children of his and really loved them. He had planned to provide for their future, but had died suddenly without having made a will. So his wealth went to distant relatives and his children were left penniless.

John and Rena were both handsome children without the faintest appearance of Negro blood. Young John decided to be white and confided this decision to a friend of his father's, old Judge Straight. Judge Straight took John into his office as office boy, and John spent all his spare time studying law there. Later on, he moved away from Patesville into South Carolina, passed the state law examinations, and in time married a girl of good family and considerable wealth, and became one of the pillars of society in that community. Mis' Molly had encouraged him in his plans, for she had Rena who would be her mainstay as she grew older.

About ten years after he had left home, John returned to Patesville on business, and drawn by a natural desire to see his mother and sister, visited them secretly. He found that Rena had grown into a beautiful and lovely young woman and urged Mis' Molly to let him take her to his home in order to give her the advantages that he had gained for himself. Mis' Molly, after much mental anguish, finally made the sacrifice.

Rena became a charming addition to her brother's circle of friends. A young man fell deeply in love with her, and won her heart. Rena was now torn between her love for George Tryon and her conscience, which urged her to tell him of her antecedents. But, on the other hand, had she any right to undermine her brother's position by making known their Negro ancestry?

From this point, the story worked out to its inevitable end. It was a romantic and tragic story and was hailed by the critics as "one of the most vitally interesting books touching upon racial relations in the South we have ever read." The reviews were highly favorable. *The House Behind the Cedars* was called "a brilliant performance—clear, to the point, keen in its interests, penetrating in its presentation of character . . . so uniform in its construction, so strong in its treatment, so vital in its interest, that one will sit up far into the night to read it through, oblivious of the fact that he is not a part of it, so potent are the touches of local color." It was said to be "of absorbing interest, . . . easily the most notable novel of the month."

Chesnutt's days were busy now as he answered letters that poured in from all parts of the country, "fan mail" they would be called today. People sent him anecdotes and plots, begging him to make use of them in future stories. Literary clubs of every sort wrote to him to make engagements for readings or lectures. Several of the great publishing houses wrote asking for the privilege of publishing his next novel. Friends and acquaintances wrote congratulations and praises, and Chesnutt was a happy man for a while; but he began to realize that the sale of four books and occasional magazine articles, and engagements on the lecture platform would not go far toward the support of his family. Most writers did not expect to live on the proceeds from their writings alone; they had incomes from other sources, from positions in the field of literature, or education, or in some other field which left them time and energy for their writing.

Now and then a best seller reached the market and sold hundreds of thousands of copies, but his work was controversial, and controversial themes, especially those referring to the Negro, could not become very popular. Chesnutt's colored characters were striving to rise from their lowly position and to become an acknowledged and accepted part of the American scene. This point of view did not take hold of the imagination of the average American, and although the book had gone into its fourth printing by April, Chesnutt was not satisfied; he had hoped for a much larger sale.

16

Living at High Tension

CHESNUTT started the year 1901 in a somewhat pessimistic frame of mind, for the condition of the Negro in the South was becoming intolerable. By amending their state constitutions, Mississippi, South Carolina, Louisiana, and North Carolina had already robbed the Negro of his suffrage and consequently of his rights. Through these amendments a poll tax was required, the ill-famed "grandfather clause" invented, and certain literacy qualifications established. Had these amendments affected the whites as well as the Negroes, there might have been less objection to them, but they served the purpose for which they were intended—to disfranchise the Negro completely without seriously affecting the white vote. By this disfranchisement the colored people were left utterly defenseless, without any representation in the government or in the courts, and with no voice in electing the people who might be fair and just to them.

Chesnutt had been very much affected by the savage race riot that had broken out in Wilmington, North Carolina, in the November elections of 1898. He had friends and relatives in Wilmington and had received many reports of the trouble there. Feeling was very strong, and in the riot Alexander L. Manly, the editor of the Negro newspaper, the *Record,* who had cast some criticism on white women in connection with alleged rape and lynching, was driven out of the city; his printing office was destroyed, and much Negro property was damaged. A number of colored people were killed or died later of their wounds.

After the publication of *The House Behind the Cedars,* late in 1900, Chesnutt began to write a new novel based on the Wilmington riot. He thought that by this book he might stir up the thinking people of the country to a realization of what was taking place in the South. In February, 1901, he made a tour of the Southern states, reading and lecturing at some of the leading schools and colleges for colored people. He spoke at his old school in Fayetteville and renewed the friendships of his youth. From there he went to Wilmington and collected a great deal of material for the new novel. The people there were eager to tell him all the details of the riot, for they felt that his book might do much for the colored people of the South.

From Wilmington he went to Tuskegee as the guest of Dr. and Mrs. Booker T. Washington. Chesnutt was very much impressed with Tuskegee and with the people whom Washington had gathered about him. The annual Tuskegee Conference, which was held in February of each year for the benefit of the Negro farmers of the district, was in session, and he realized for the first time what a really great work Washington was doing for the Negroes of the black belt. This conference was among Booker T. Washington's most important projects at Tuskegee. Then and in years to come Chesnutt criticised Washington's philosophy very strongly, but he never underestimated the greatness of the work he was doing for the Negroes in the South.

From Tuskegee he went to Birmingham and then on to Atlanta University, lecturing in both places. On his trip northward he gave readings at Charlotte, North Carolina, where he had taught for several years, at Concord, at Livingstone College in Salisbury, and at the Agricultural and Mechanical College in Greensboro. A letter from Hampton Institute, asking him to stop over there and talk to them, followed him about, but never caught up with him until he had returned to Cleveland.

Chesnutt reached home very much depressed about race relations in the South, and with a serious cold that lasted for months. Several articles came out of this trip: "A Visit to Tuskegee," published in the *Cleveland Leader* of March 31, 1901, and "The White and the Black," an article on Atlanta University and the higher education of the Negro, with some reflections on the laws providing for the separation of the races in the Southern states, published in the *Boston Transcript* of March 20, 1901.

Another thing that added to his depression was the publica-

tion by the Macmillan Company early in the year, of a book
entitled *The American Negro*. This book was so defamatory, so
condemnatory of the Negro race that Chesnutt and some of his
friends decided to learn something about the author, a Negro
named William Hannibal Thomas, who seemed to be quite
unknown.

The *Boston Transcript* had reviewed the book rather favorably
and Chesnutt immediately wrote to express his views on the subject and to ask who could have written such a review.

His friend, Joseph Edgar Chamberlin, replied that he had
written the review, on the assumption that a book put out by the
house of Macmillan must be genuine and was therefore entitled
to a full review. He went on to say that if Thomas was a fraud he
should be fully exposed and the house of Macmillan should be
riddled for giving him a hearing. If he was not a fraud, he was
entitled to a hearing.

Chamberlin had then gone on to ask Chesnutt to write some
letters from the South for the *Transcript* and to cover the annual
conference at Tuskegee on February 22, as special correspondent.
He added that the *Transcript* was open to anything he might
write in reply to Thomas's book.

While on the Southern tour, Chesnutt received a telegram
from Jeannette Gilder asking for an article of fifteen hundred
words scathing the Thomas book. This was published in the
Critic of April, 1901, under the title, "A Defamer of His Race."

After his return to Cleveland, Chesnutt made a summary of the
data about Thomas that he had gathered from court records in
the various cities where the man had lived, and from the several
institutions in which he had studied or taught, and sent it with
the following letter to the Macmillan Company:

April 20, 1901

DEAR SIRS:

Several months ago your house published a volume entitled
The American Negro by one William Hannibal Thomas. I do
not know how fully the responsible heads of your firm were
informed of the contents of this volume, but I quote a few choice
morsels: ... [There followed a list from the book.]

When it is borne in mind that the term "freedman" or the
word "Negro" as used in this book, is taken as meaning the whole
colored race in the United States, who number some eight or

nine millions, the publication in cold blood of a book, the general tenor of which is indicated by the above extracts becomes, unless the book be truthful, nothing less than a crime, from which immunity is secured only by the fact that to libel a whole race is not an offense indictable in any court except that of public opinion. . . .

I have taken it for granted that if the Macmillan Company knew in advance of its publication that any book, the value of which rests upon the character of the writer, was written by a man notoriously untruthful, without character or standing anywhere, and with a long record in the criminal courts and on the threshold of them, they would not put the sanction of their imprint upon such a publication. I can scarcely believe that your house would be a party, and the principal party—for only your name gave the book any title to consideration—to so grave an attack upon a class, merely because they are supposed to be poor and ignorant and defenseless. . . .

I do not know whether the ethics of publishing ever require the withdrawal of a book from circulation or from sale, but if there was ever a case where decency and fair play demanded it, this seems to me to be one of them. . . .

The Macmillan Company replied immediately by asking for the numbers of the pages of the book from which the extracts sent to them had been taken. They stated that they relied upon their "readers" in books of this kind, and that the book in question had passed their readers with very considerable praise.

Chesnutt answered at once:

April 26, 1901

DEAR SIRS:

Replying to your very prompt acknowledgment of my letter of the 20th, I here repeat the passages quoted in my former letter, with some additional ones, citing the pages of *The American Negro* where they may be found: . . .

As I said before, the only possible excuse for making such statements . . . even if that should be a sufficient excuse—would be their truthfulness. In putting your imprint upon such a book, your house makes itself sponsor for their truthfulness, or at least for the man who wrote them, upon whose candor and means of knowledge their truthfulness must finally rest.

If such a book dealt with the manners and customs of the Fiji Islanders, and were equally false and illfounded, it might do no great harm. But gravely put forward, under the imprint of a great publishing house concerning neighbors and fellow-citizens, who have already a heavy handicap of race prejudice to carry, it might easily have a far-reaching and disastrous effect. The Negro in the United States stands at present in a critical position: his status as a slave is ended; his position as a freeman has not yet been made secure. The least that could be asked, in view of these facts, is absolute fairness in any discussion which involves his position in society. . . .

Referring to the question of responsibility mentioned in your letter, of course, the only kind of responsibility involved here is a moral one. I should imagine from reading the book, together with what I have learned about the author's life, that he might fairly be classed as morally irresponsible. . . . But in any event, the chief onus would rest upon your house, for the author was a man absolutely obscure, who had never done anything towards the world's work which would entitle him to a hearing as a spokesman representing a people, so obscure, indeed, that he must have imagined that his past could be concealed, or he never would have risked the inevitable exposure.

The fact of the matter is that the Macmillan Company has been grossly imposed upon, and has permitted itself to be made the tool of a corrupt and conscienceless seeker-after-notoriety. If I can convince the Macmillan Company of this fact, I shall have accomplished the purpose of this correspondence. What steps they will take, or can take, I do not know. I am quite aware that if I were addressing a publisher of a different class, I might run the risk of still further increasing the circulation of this infamous book; in the case of your house, I will take the chance.

The Macmillan Company stood by its guns and replied to this letter that Chesnutt's criticisms were somewhat unfair to both the author and the firm; that it was not the part of publishers to inquire into the private or moral life of an author whose manuscript was published by them; and that they had full confidence in the opinion of their readers who were "men of very considerable learning in this direction, and were connected with two of the highest and best educational institutions in the country."

Some time later, however, Chesnutt heard that the Macmillan

Company had withdrawn the book from sale and had endeavored as far as possible to withdraw it from circulation.

But Chesnutt could not devote all his time and interest to the Negro problem. Family matters were also causing him some concern. His two daughters at Smith were now in their senior year and had developed a great deal of initiative and independence. They were looking out for their own future and had written to both Tuskegee and Washington, D. C., about teaching positions for the following year.

This was not at all what he had planned for them. Ethel was engaged to be married to Edward C. Williams, Librarian of Western Reserve University, and the wedding was to take place after her graduation from Smith. Charles's dearest hope was to have Helen teach in one of the Cleveland high schools, Central High if possible. He was therefore very much surprised when he found that both girls wanted to leave Cleveland and teach in the South. He promptly went down to the Board of Education to see what chance Helen would have to teach in the high schools, and sent the following letter to her:

January 29, 1901

Your interesting, vivacious and business-like note came duly to hand, and it gives me much pleasure to note the energy and foresight with which you are looking out for the future. I trust you and Ethel have passed your examinations with satisfaction to yourselves and to your teachers.

I have paid a visit to Superintendent Jones, apropos of your future employment. The case seems to stand about like this:

You can get into the grammar schools in Cleveland by going through the Normal School for two terms of thirty weeks, after which you will probably be able to substitute for the remainder of the year. If you then wish to teach in the grammar schools, you can start on a salary of $475.00 a year, being $50.00 more than the mere high and normal graduate gets; in other words, your college education will enable you to start at $50.00 per year more.

For the High School, the rule is, four or five years experience before one can get in the high schools. If one does not care to go through Normal, this experience is best acquired in high schools in small towns, which counts in qualifying for high school positions here. I am told that the best time to apply for such positions is in March or April. If they were applied for now, the applica-

tions might be forgotten or mislaid. These high schools are glad
to get college graduates; they pay $40.00 or $50.00 a month.

Of course, all these rules are more or less subject to modification in case of great ability or demonstrated success. But success
can be demonstrated only through experience somewhere.

I mean to visit Tuskegee in a couple of weeks; shall leave here
sometime next week. I shall also visit Washington, and will look
around in your behalf. I am afraid we can't get you definitely
disposed of for a month or so yet, but you have so many lines
out that we may be able to land something.

As to Ethel's case, I don't quite understand its status; but the
same principles apply, if she should wish to teach.

While Charles was in the South, Helen became ill at Smith and
went home for a three weeks' rest cure; her eyes were affected and
she was unable to do her work.

SUSAN TO CHARLES

We had a surprise this morning. Helen walked in at breakfast
time. Says the doctor advised her to come home and take absolute
rest for at least three weeks on account of her eyes. That means
a lengthy bill at Dr. Baker's.

I am afraid she has strained her eyes severely studying astron-
omy which she ought never to have taken up. I fear they are in
a bad way now, but we have decided to say that she is run down
and has been advised to stop for a while. She will find it hard
work to get a position if it is known that she is having so much
trouble with her eyes.

After three weeks' rest Helen returned to college, and a few
days later received a letter from her father telling her that he
wanted her to teach in Cleveland; that he would be very much
disappointed if she did not give up her idea of going to Washington. He wanted her to attend the Cleveland Normal School and
ultimately to teach at Central High School. Mr. Harris had
promised to give her substitute work and to help her get into
Central at the earliest opportunity.

HELEN TO CHARLES, MARCH 17, 1901

I don't understand your attitude in this school-teaching business at all. We have counted on freeing you from the burden of
our support as soon as we left college, so this idea on your part

comes as a shock. You and Mama are always talking about the need of saving money and economizing; therefore I do not see the sense of your undertaking to support me for another year. The actual outlay for my board etc. would be very little, but by being in Washington I might be earning $600 or $700. . . .

As for your position in Cleveland, it has never had the slightest influence on my situation, and has never been of any advantage to me. . . .

I am not comfortable in Cleveland and never was, and I have always vowed that I would not settle down in that city. . . . And now you ask me to return and go to Normal School! I can't imagine anything more distasteful. I tell you all this because I want you to know exactly where I stand in this matter.

But since you do not wish me to go South and become independent, and since your heart is set on my going to Normal School, I will return to Cleveland and go to Normal School. But it will be on your own head if I don't get all these golden positions that are standing around waiting for me, according to Professor Harris. As for his advice about the South—he is a snob and always has been, and I don't care a snap about him and his advice.

Will you please write to Uncle Clay and tell him that you have arranged that I am to stay in Cleveland next year, and thank him for the trouble he has taken about the position in Washington. I think that you ought to explain to him that *I* am not backing out. I suppose every one will call me shiftless and worthless because after "this expensive education," as they say, I come back home and tag out to Normal.

Ethel will write to you herself. She, of course, would not dream of going to Normal School, and teaching in Cleveland; so as you say "it seems to be up to me" to do it. Well, I have stood a lot more than people give me credit for, and a few more blows won't materially affect my ultimate good. You will of course write to Uncle Clay.

I suppose that I shall be happier about this when I get settled at Normal, but now it seems very dreary. Much love to you.

CHARLES TO HELEN

Your letter came this morning. I am sorry my letter should have given you a shock. I trust it has not affected you seriously.

Perhaps in my thoughts about the matter, I did not place

stress enough upon the question of your situation in Cleveland, which you have stated tersely, vigorously, and I must admit, correctly, so far as I can see. I do not see, either, that time will materially modify the situation.

True, here you would have steady employment, and I might, if proper pressure were brought to bear upon me, find a more commodious house to live in. But I do not see how you could avoid the Normal School. If you have always meant never to settle down here, it would of course be wasting time to go through so distasteful a mill. My heart is not at all set on the matter. I am quite willing you should be independent; I have no objection to your living where you can see some young people, and possibly meet some young man whom you would like well enough to marry.

I rather expected that you would have written to Washington by this time and filed your application. Go on and do so if you prefer, as I imagine you do. I do not pin any faith to Mr. Harris, in view of what Mr. Jones said, and there is no doubt about your having to enter the graded school before you can get into the High School, and if you should change your mind about Cleveland, your Washington experience would count. If you should not like it at Washington, a year will roll by quickly enough, and you will have money in your purse. You won't be part of *the* people in Washington, but you will be part of *a* people, which is more than you would be here.

So you had better file your application, and file it right away, as there may be others ahead. If you don't get an appointment you still have Cleveland to fall back upon. We shall see you several times a year, and in summer anyway.

As to Ethel the affair is not so urgent, and I will write her, or wait until she writes me. I don't say she can't go to Tuskegee—but we will write about it.

Your mother agrees with me that we are solely animated by a desire for your happiness, and that in this respect your feelings are a very important matter to be considered, if not the controlling matter. We are quite willing that you should do as you like. All are well and send love.

ETHEL TO HER FATHER

Helen is in a frightful state; she has had headaches nearly every day lately, and today she is in despair. If you want your

Helen a total nervous wreck, just keep on in the way you are going. She is too proud, too ambitious, to act sensibly. She cannot keep on with the work; every time she does anything of any consequence she collapses with one of these headaches. It is criminal for her to try it; Baker ought never to have let her come back, with her eyes in the condition they are. She has got to stop and that immediately. She has got to rest, for a year or more. And Normal School, Washington, study or teaching of any kind are out of the question. She is so young that there is no need of her rushing any more, and a total cessation of all eye work is absolutely necessary. I don't think she had much rest at home. The girl is on the verge of nervous prostration and no one seems to realize it. At home you are all under a fearful nervous strain all the time; you do too many unnecessary things and you talk and discuss too much, and Helen has got to have rest somewhere. She has got to stop, and future questions can be settled at future times; if she comes home she must not be troubled with questions as to what she shall do in the future. She is not fit to do anything now. If the house at home is to be filled with company all summer, it is no place for Helen. I know you told her she ought to stay out and come back next year but she hadn't wisdom enough to do it. Please try to realize these things. She cannot keep on at college at present. Helen Chesnutt needs complete rest of mind and eyes for a long time and I propose to step in now, and see that she gets it. Pride and ambition are all right within certain limits but I don't want them to kill or ruin Helen. I should imagine from all I hear of you that you had better call a halt on yourself, too, or you will collapse. No matter how much will, ambition, pride you have, you can't strain Nature very long; something will smash somewhere and you are living too strenuously. We all need a little more practical sense about us, and less emotion and feeling. I hope you are recovering from your Southern trip. Much love to you.

CHARLES TO ETHEL, MARCH 25, 1901

Your very positive and commanding letter of several days since sent cold chills up and down my spine, and paralyzed me so that I have only just recovered. I am deeply concerned to hear of Helen's terrible plight, but hope it may prove to be not quite so bad as it seemed to you at last writing. I understand your mother has written you. I called on Dr. Baker on Saturday, the day after receiving your letter, and after waiting two hours had a talk with him. He has an idea that by taking it easy and not worrying, Helen ought to be able, so far as he can see, to pull through the school year. Possibly by the time she comes back from Boston, where she ought to try to be moderately quiet and take care of herself, she may feel in better shape. If not, it will be time enough then to take up the question of her immediate future. All dangers are not death. I think I have heard you speak of a girl who is almost blind who has taken her course right along. This momentary affliction of Helen's might give you an opportunity for a little self-sacrifice in the way of helping her; it might work for your own soul's good.

I quite agree with you that we all lead too strenuous a life, and that we ought to let up a little. It is not at all necessary for either of you to worry yourselves to death about what you shall do next year, which I suspect is the source of most of Helen's troubles. If she chooses to file that Washington application she would not be bound by it—she could resign in advance, if necessary; there will be plenty of others ready to take her place. Or, if her health requires it, she can stay out as long as necessary. I imagine I can support her a while without eleemosynary aid. What she would have to expect in either place you both know; but we have lived quite a while, and with a little philosophy, and a little less strenuousness, we can worry along almost anywhere.

With regard to your going to Tuskegee, you had better write me your views. I see the South with the chastened eye of experience; it may look very different, through the rosy spectacles of youth, to one who has never seen it. You are young too, and have, I trust, a long life before you, of which a year or two, here or there, under conditions at all tolerable, would not be missed. I should like to see you happily married, had indeed rather expected it, but that is a thing which I cannot control. It is natural, perhaps, that you would like a little liberty before being tied down.

Write to me again, some more strong, vigorous letters, and we will work all these things out. You have a couple of weeks' vacation, which ought to have a good effect if employed judiciously. All are well.

Helen returned home after the Easter vacation which the girls had spent in Boston and vicinity, visiting their college mates and other friends. She had been granted permission to be graduated with her class, but would have to return in March of the following year to complete her work and receive her degree.

Ned, now a senior at Central, was preparing for the Harvard examinations in whatever spare time he had from his duties as editor-in-chief of the *Central High School Monthly,* making trips here and there on Central's debating team, and preparing his speech as Class Humorist for the Class Night Ceremonies.

17

"The Marrow of Tradition"

CHESNUTT spent the spring and summer writing *The Marrow of Tradition*. He was appalled at the situation in the South, and through this novel expressed that feeling. In it he depicted the conditions in the town of Wilmington, North Carolina, at the time of the 1898 riot, and brought into the clear light of day the motives underlying the treatment meted out to the Negro by the South. It was not a pleasant picture and he realized that it would antagonize a large part of the reading public, especially in the South, but he was by nature a crusader and was burning with anger.

During the early part of 1901 several articles by Chesnutt, in addition to those already mentioned, appeared in the magazines. In the January *Century* a little story called "The March of Progress" was published. It was a touching story of an aging schoolteacher from the North who had devoted her life to the education of a generation of Negro children and to the uplift of the older people, only to find that she had outlived her usefulness. In the *Southern Workman* for May a sociological paper entitled "The Free Colored People of North Carolina" was published, and in the May *Modern Culture* appeared "Superstitions and Folk-Lore of the South."

In the summer of 1901 Chesnutt received a welcome letter from Horace E. Scudder, former editor of *The Atlantic Monthly*.

17 BUCKINGHAM STREET
CAMBRIDGE
June 2, 1901

MY DEAR MR. CHESNUTT:

I have been ill this past five months, and am only slowly recovering my usual vigor. I had many thoughts as I lay on my bed, and among others I thought of you and your work, and remembered that I had never written to tell you how much I admired your skill in making the change in the plot of the *House Behind the Cedars*. I found fault with the earlier version, but in this I think you have retained the magic element which marked the book in its first form and have given a more reasonable and far less irritating dénouement. As a work of art, the book seems to me to have gained distinctly, and as I said I admire greatly the literary skill which could so remodel the book. This faculty of seeing one's work from another's point of view is not common and argues well certainly for your power to do things in more than one way!

I am, with great respect,
Sincerely yours,
H. E. SCUDDER

In June, Susan, Charles, and Dorothy went to Northampton to see the girls graduated. They returned in time for Edwin's graduation from Central High School. On the trip East, Chesnutt went to New York and Boston to get in touch with his literary friends and to talk about his new novel. After his return to Cleveland, he wrote the following letter:

CLEVELAND, O.,
July 1, 1901

THE MACMILLAN COMPANY
GEORGE P. BRETT, ESQ.,
NEW YORK.

MY DEAR MR. BRETT:-

I was sorry that I missed seeing you while in New York, though it was my own fault in not calling at a different hour. I am sorry, too, that I did not return home via New York, that I might have responded in person to your letter which reached me in Boston.

As to my book, I appreciate the compliment you pay me in asking to look at it. It is not yet quite completed, and there is a bare possibility that I may seek another publisher than my present one, though the chances at present seem the other way. It may be a pleasure to you to know that Dr. H. W. Mabie and Mr. James Lane Allen, both of whom I met during my hurried trip East, strongly recommended me to send to you any manuscript which I might wish to inflict upon a wide public. I shall bear in mind your kind offer, and meanwhile remain,

Yours very truly,

CHARLES W. CHESNUTT

P. S. I am still of the same opinion regarding the Thomas book.

The summer was hurrying along. Guests from North Carolina, Washington, and Boston began to arrive. Chesnutt buried himself in his manuscript in order to complete it as soon as possible. Toward the end of July *The Marrow of Tradition,* was finished and sent on to Mr. Mifflin with the following letter:

CLEVELAND, O.,
64 BRENTON ST.,
July 25, 1901.

MY DEAR MR. MIFFLIN:

I send on today, under another cover, the manuscript of the novel upon which I have been working for the past eight months. Recurring to our conversation in Boston, I should like to have you put it at once in the hands of your readers—and decide whether or not it is a novel for which, so far as experience can predict or conjecture, a good sale can be reasonably expected,—by which I mean a sale much better than that of *The House Behind the Cedars.* I have put a great deal of work into it; it is entirely sincere, and it is certainly a much better book than any I have heretofore written. If you decide that there are possibilities for it, I shall be glad, as I said, to have you publish it.

Kindly let me know as soon as may be your verdict, and believe me,

Yours sincerely,

CHARLES W. CHESNUTT

A few days later an answer came from Houghton, Mifflin and Company, over Francis J. Garrison's initials:

BOSTON, July 31, 1901

DEAR MR. CHESNUTT:

We have read the manuscript of your "Marrow of Tradition"

with great interest, and are much impressed by its power and intensity. We need not say that we shall take great pleasure in publishing it, and we are adding it to our fall announcements.

While we are not in sympathy with the booming and hothouse methods of advertising which have been somewhat prevalent of late, but which we think are already growing in disfavor, you may be sure that we shall use every effort by what we regard as wise and legitimate means to secure wide publicity and sale for the work. We trust that the result will be gratifying to all of us.

Yours faithfully,

HOUGHTON, MIFFLIN & COMPANY

P. S. I add my congratulations. Am just called away for a few days—hence cannot write personally.

F. J. G.

And in August, in answer to a letter from Chesnutt, came a letter from W. B. Parker of Houghton, Mifflin and Company:

BOSTON, August 17, 1901

MY DEAR MR. CHESNUTT:

I have your letter of August 14th, and thank you for the friendly expressions which it contains, but am sorry to say I fear I can offer you scarcely one suggestion likely to be of service in reading the proofs of your novel. In reading the book I was swept along by so strong an interest that I paid little attention to details, and in fact for much of the time had my critical faculties thoroughly inhibited. I am afraid this argues a certain recreancy on my part, and I can only hope that all the readers of your book will become as absorbed in the story as I did. In that case they will have no opportunity to criticize.

Yours sincerely,

W. B. PARKER

After sending off his manuscript Chesnutt hoped to relax for a while. He felt drained of energy, for the story was very intense, and his ardent spirit had burned itself out. But he had accepted the chairmanship of the Committee on Colored Troops, for the 35th National Encampment of the Grand Army of the Republic scheduled to meet in Cleveland in the early part of September, and he found that this entailed more work and effort than he had anticipated.

Then, too, the house was humming with activity. Ethel had finally accepted the position at Tuskegee; Edwin, who had failed in the Harvard entrance examinations, owing to all his extracurricular duties at Central, was going to enter Dummer Academy in South Byfield, Massachusetts, to be prepared to enter the Sophomore class at Harvard the following year; and Susan was trying to get them both ready for the winter, as well as to entertain her guests and run her household. Helen, whose health had greatly improved, was considering her father's suggestion that she enter the Normal School, just for fun, to kill time until she should return to Smith in March to complete her unfinished work. So life at 64 Brenton Street was very strenuous and Charles had little chance for rest.

An appreciative review of Chesnutt's writings appeared in the *Book Buyer* for August under the title "A New Element in Fiction," in which Chesnutt and Paul Laurence Dunbar were compared and evaluated.

The Negro's situation in the South was becoming steadily more difficult and caused great resentment and apprehension among the colored people of the nation.

Then on September 6 President McKinley was shot at the Pan-American Exposition at Buffalo, just before he was scheduled to make a speech at the G.A.R. encampment in Cleveland. He died a week later and Vice-President Theodore Roosevelt became president of the United States.

The plans of Houghton, Mifflin and Company for the publication in October of *The Marrow of Tradition* went rapidly forward. They were sparing no expense in promoting its sale.

Every effort was made to get exactly the right cover for the book—a bright yellow with black lettering and silver decorations.

HOUGHTON, MIFFLIN AND COMPANY TO CHESNUTT

We are very glad to learn, through your letters of October 1st and 2nd, your satisfaction with the cover of *The Marrow of Tradition*, and with the efforts which we are making to launch the book on the market this fall.

First as to the cover. It seems to us that the design is simple and effective and that the color is telling. Of course, any light shade will become smooched and blackened in certain places, but we always provide printed jackets with the books, which will guard them against this in most places, and the fact that a few volumes may be injured cannot counteract the value which the color and general design will have on drawing book buyers toward the volumes.

[And from another letter] There is to be a splendid production of *Uncle Tom's Cabin* at the Boston Theatre for the next two weeks and beside the regular advertising, we are taking a page in their programme connecting your book with *Uncle Tom's Cabin* in such a way as to encourage the sale of it, we hope.

[And from another] Perhaps you will be interested to note the page in the November *Atlantic* devoted to *The Marrow of Tradition*.

[And again] We have engaged the large display windows at the "Old Corner Book Store" here in Boston for a week for the display of your book, and write to ask whether you could furnish us at once with a large size photograph of yourself, to be used in this connection. This store, you know, sent us an order last week for 600 copies of the book. With its striking cover, it ought to make a very good window display.

One of the first acts of President Theodore Roosevelt was to invite Booker T. Washington to dinner at the White House so that in a leisurely and informal way they might discuss the "Negro problem" and its bearing on the political situation. This simple act of the President aroused great Southern indignation and resulted in an unprecedented avalanche of bitter condemnation of Roosevelt and his policy of "social equality," and an equally violent denunciation of Booker T. Washington and the whole Negro race. While this fury was at its height Houghton Mifflin announced the publication of *The Marrow of Tradition*.

CHARLES TO ETHEL, OCTOBER 29, 1901

. . . The book is out and is taking quite a start. I suspect the Southerners will pitch into it. Several recent events will tend to bear out its probability, and ought to widen its circulation.

I have been bothered for a week with a touch of rheumatism in my right knee. Yes, I have been resting after my G.A.R. labors. Between the book, my Southern trip, our numerous visitors, and the G.A.R., I have had a slight revulsion from it all, from which I must recover. I think my publishers believe in the book, and we all hope it may do well.

You will see from the heading of this letter that I have moved from the Rose to the Williamson Building. I shall probably do some business this winter, as unless my book does very well indeed I shall need the money. Also need the pressure to keep me straight and make me work.

You must join me in hopes for the success of my book, for upon its reception will depend in some measure whether I shall write, for the present, any more "Afro-American" novels; for a man must live and consider his family. All the rest are well.

The story of *The Marrow of Tradition* concerned a young Negro surgeon who had taken high honors in medicine at the University of Vienna and had returned to the South to devote his life to the welfare of his own people. The leading white people of the town resented Dr. Miller's success. They were jealous of the new hospital which he had established, and begrudged him the financial security that he was rapidly gaining. Bitter feeling between the two races was augmented by editorials in the leading newspaper and when the inevitable explosion finally occurred, the results were disastrous.

The Marrow of Tradition was widely acclaimed as the most important book on the Negro question since *Uncle Tom's Cabin*. The critics called it a great book, one of the best of the season; they said that no book of the year could compare with it in dramatic power. Reviews came from all parts of the country and from Canada and England. The great dailies, the weeklies, the foreign language periodicals, the magazines devoted to literary criticism, all reviewed it at great length. The Northern papers expressed unqualified praise for it, stressing the fact that it was the first novel in American literature to depict the collision between the whites and the educated, cultivated colored people of the South.

Chesnutt had written a book of stark realism, presenting this conflict with unflinching earnestness, with extraordinary skill and with absolute fairness to white and black alike. But from the South there came a storm of resentment and unfavorable criticism. One paper attacked Chesnutt bitterly for writing a book of lies and slander about the South and condemned Houghton, Mifflin and Company for publishing it. Another characterized the book as utterly repellent to Southern sentiment and one calculated to do infinite harm to the South if widely read. Another called it "ridiculous silly rot." A leading Washington paper questioned the "wisdom of such a book as it arouses bitter resentments in politics and personal relations."

Unfortunately few people in the United States were really interested in any kind of colored people, least of all, people like Dr. Miller and his wife Janet. They felt that it was a wonderful and touching thing for a European peasant to come from intolerable conditions in his homeland to this great land of promise and in a generation or two to raise himself out of his ignorance and degradation to a level with other Americans less handicapped. But they wondered what right a Negro had to such aspirations. Let him stay where he belonged; let him be thankful to be alive, to be allowed to live; and let him cease whining for any status above that of serf. As one reviewer expressed it: "Mr. Chesnutt has made a most powerful argument in favor of social recognition; but it seems a waste of time and energy in the present state of American civilization."

Chesnutt was accused of bitterness by some of his critics, not the least of whom was William Dean Howells in an article entitled "A Psychological Counter-Current in Recent Fiction," which appeared in the *North American Review of* December, 1901. In this article Howells discussed some recently published books by leading authors. About Chesnutt he wrote: *"The Marrow of Tradition,* like every thing else he has written, has to do with the relations of the blacks and whites, and in that republic of letters where all men are free and equal he stands up for his own people with a courage which has more justice than mercy in it. The book is, in fact, bitter, bitter. There is no reason in history why it should not be so, if wrong is to be repaid with hate, and yet it would be better if it was not so bitter. I am not saying that he is so inartistic as to play the advocate; whatever his minor foibles may be, he is an artist whom his step-brother Americans may well be proud of. . . . No one who reads the book can deny that the case is presented with great power; or fail to recognize in the writer a portent of the sort of negro equality against which no series of hangings and burnings will finally avail."

In a letter to a friend of his Howells stated that Chesnutt had written of the black and white situation with an "awful bitterness," and went on to say that he was an artist of almost the first quality "and promised things thereafter that would scarcely be equalled in American fiction."

The book did much to increase Chesnutt's fame as a pioneer writer who had opened up an unexplored field in American literature. His characters were new figures in fiction—and his readers were made aware, for the first time, of the mental agony, the soul-maiming suffering of the intelligent, well-educated, aspiring colored people in the South.

Although *The Marrow of Tradition* was an acknowledged literary success—it had been accepted by the Booklovers Library, and was classed by the *Outlook* among the twenty-five books of literature of the year—as a financial venture it did not come up to the expectations of Chesnutt and his publishers. Houghton, Mifflin and Company had been so sure of its reception by the public that they had spent a great deal of money in advertising it. Both they and Chesnutt had expected it to secure a rapid and distinct financial success and they were all terribly disappointed.

CHESNUTT TO HIS PUBLISHERS, DECEMBER 28, 1901

I am beginning to suspect that the public as a rule does not care for books in which the principal characters are colored people, or written with a striking sympathy with that race as contrasted with the white race. .... If a novel which is generally acknowledged to be interesting, dramatic, well constructed, well written—which qualities have been pretty generally ascribed to *The Marrow of Tradition,* of which in addition, both the author and publishers have good hopes—cannot sell 5,000 copies within two months after its publication, there must be something radically wrong somewhere, and I do not know where it is unless it be in the subject. My friend, Mr. Howells, who has said many nice things about my writings—although his review of *The Marrow of Tradition* in the *North American Review* for December was not a favorable one as I look at it— has remarked several times that there is no color line in literature. On that point I take issue with him. I am pretty fairly convinced that the color line runs everywhere so far as the United States is concerned.

The reviews kept coming in—the book was so controversial that the critics could not drop it. Early in the spring the *Independent* published a review that was surprisingly virulent considering its source. Its nature is made clear in the following letter from Chesnutt to his publisher:

Cleveland, O.
March 20, 1902

Mr. George H. Mifflin
Boston, Mass.
My dear Mr. Mifflin:

I was duly in receipt of your favor of March 14, in which you enclosed a letter from Dr. DuBois, and some correspondence between yourself and Mr. Bowen * of the *Independent,* with reference to the review of *The Marrow of Tradition* which appeared in that magazine. Permit me to thank you for taking the matter up. The notice was not only unjust, I felt, to the book, and to my motives, but was personal to the point of offensiveness.

I had suspected what Mr. Bowen's explanation reveals, that some Southerner had reviewed the book. I think your last letter to Mr. Bowen in which you express the hope that in some way justice may be done to us in the columns of the *Independent,* was precisely the way to get back at him. An apology in private for an injury in public is poor compensation. The *Independent,* however, is so cocksure about all its views and opinions, that I shall be curious to see what form anything they may say will take, if they say anything at all upon the subject.

I thank you also for the letter of Dr. DuBois; it does not say a great deal, but what it does say is intended, I presume, by way of compliment. . . .

Yours very truly,
Charles W. Chesnutt

The *Independent,* however, did not retract its criticism of Chesnutt's book. Its literary editor, Paul Elmer More, read the book at the request of Bowen, and approved the previous review, stating that "Chesnutt had done what he could to humiliate the whites" and saying that the last chapter was "utterly revolting" to him.

Chesnutt's friend, Theodore E. Burton, a member of the House of Representatives, had suggested to him that he send copies of *The Marrow of Tradition* to several members of the House who exerted great influence in certain directions.

* Clarence Winthrop Bowen, publisher and proprietor of the *Independent.*

CLEVELAND, O., March 28, 1902

HON. T. E. BURTON,
WASHINGTON, D. C.
MY DEAR MR. BURTON:

In accordance with the suggestions in your letter of February 10th to me, I have sent copies of my novel, *The Marrow of Tradition* to Messrs. Crumpacker, Littlefield, Olmsted, Moody and Corliss.* Mr. Moody, I believe, is no longer in the House, but in a position of great influence and power which he can often exert in favor of justice and fair play.

As I have quoted you in my letters to these gentlemen, I append an extract from the *Nation* of March 20th, which also appeared in the *Evening Post* of March 22nd, giving some suggestion of the scope and character of the work. This may ease your conscience in case you feel any scruple at having encouraged me to inflict a controversial pamphlet upon any of your colleagues. . . .

Sincerely yours,
CHAS. W. CHESNUTT

The gentlemen in the House of Representatives to whom Chesnutt sent copies of *The Marrow of Tradition* had already been introduced to the Reverend Thomas Dixon's *The Leopard's Spots,* which had just been published. In their answers to Chesnutt they commented upon the fact that the two authors had "entirely different points of view." Mr. Moody, who had become Secretary of the Navy, felt that the determination in some parts of the country "that the colored race should be in a permanently subordinate position" was impracticable, that such a relation could no more permanently endure under our system than slavery, but that he had always recognized the difficulty of the problem for the people of the South.

Mr. Littlefield felt that both books were valuable because they dealt with great questions about which it was very important that the people of the United States should be fully informed. He felt that nothing could be more vital to the welfare of the country than a "full and intelligent understanding by all of the people of the conditions that actually exist in the South where the race problem is acute."

---

* Edgar Dean Crumpacker, Charles Edgar Littlefield, Marlin Edgar Olmsted, William H. Moody, John Blaisdell Corliss.

Mr. Crumpacker thought that the book ought to be read by every man in America. He then proceeded to give Chesnutt a review of *The Leopard's Spots*. Chesnutt answered at once:

May 9, 1902

Hon. F. D. Crumpacker,
House of Representatives,
Washington, D. C.
My dear Mr. Crumpacker:

I have read Mr. Dixon's book. It doubtless represents the views of an extreme and I trust a very small proportion of Southern people. He is a North Carolinian, and for the past two or three years race feeling has been very acute in that State; I was down there about a year ago for several weeks and was surprised at its intensity. Nevertheless I found a number of thoughtful men who regarded that attitude as merely temporary and growing out of certain conditions which would not be permanent. There has always been a great deal of Southern claptrap about the disastrous results that would follow the intermingling of blood. Such intermingling as there has been, and there has been a great deal, has been done with the entire consent and cheerful cooperation of the white race, and I am unable to see any disastrous results that have followed so far.

The race question is doubtless destined to receive a great deal of attention on the part of the public for a long time to come. The Southern people, white and black, are likely to be tangled up in it for several generations, and it is a matter in which the North is under obligation to intervene, in one way or another, and at such times as are propitious, to see that justice is done to all concerned, and that the spirit of our institutions is not sacrificed merely to promote the selfish interests of any one faction of the people—whether the factional line be that of race or anything else. I am sure that your attitude in congress will always be in favor of justice and fair play. There are proper places for matters of race and color to be discussed, and perhaps to very properly regulate social conduct; but I am entirely convinced that under the constitution of the United States, the government should not in any way draw or recognize a color line. If in the matter of suffrage, in the army, and in the navy, and the civil service, and in every other public institution the same rules and restrictions are applied to all citizens, I am unable to see that the white race is in any danger of losing prestige or power, and the colored race will in that event certainly get no more than is coming to it under fair competition with a people who possess tremendously superior advantages.

Sincerely yours,
CHARLES W. CHESNUTT

18

Business and Social Life in Cleveland

THE CHESNUTT FAMILY was very small at this time. Ethel was winning laurels at Tuskegee; Edwin was at Dummer; and Helen, after six unexpectedly happy weeks at Normal School, had gone to Baltimore to teach at the colored high school there on condition that in March she would be free to return to Northampton to complete her work.

Chesnutt again plunged deeply into the business which now became his main interest. The new offices in the Williamson Building were adapted to stenographic work of every description. He was a specialist in taking down depositions of all sorts, as well as many other kinds of reporting. Lawyers from all over the country used his offices as their headquarters while in Cleveland. He reported testimony in court for leading corporation and admiralty lawyers, and no matter how scientific or technical the testimony was, his background in education, law, newspaper reporting, and literature enabled him to understand it and reproduce it with absolute accuracy.

When there was a campaign on, or when conventions met in Cleveland, he was there taking down the speeches and having them reproduced by his office force. The business became a romance in which he was the leading character and to which he devoted not only his days but his nights and often his Sundays. It was enthralling and stimulating, won him many fine friendships, and furnished him with a surprisingly good income.

He became so absorbed in his business that Susan had to assume more responsibilities than she had ever had.

In June Charles was very tired and Susan urged him to take a real vacation. He was already engaged to give a reading at the annual convention of the Western Association of Writers at Winona Lake, Indiana, and from there he went as far west as Colorado.

Edwin came home a very happy lad, for he had passed the Harvard examinations and would enter the sophomore class in September. He started out at once to get a summer job and frightened his mother nearly to death the same evening by coming home with a large fumigating machine, announcing that he was employed as a city fumigator in the district where smallpox was raging. Susan was worried all summer for fear he would take the disease or bring it home to the family, but Charles was pleased with his son's initiative, and Edwin thoroughly enjoyed the experience.

Helen's decision to give up the position in Baltimore and try her luck in Cleveland delighted both her parents. The last drop was added to their cup of happiness when Ethel agreed to give up the Tuskegee position and marry Ed Williams.

That summer was an unusually quiet one. There were no guests, for Susan needed all her time and energy to plan for Ethel's wedding and prepare her outfit. Helen was devoting her time to study in preparation for the teachers' examinations which she would have to take later on, and Charles, thoroughly refreshed by his vacation, was entirely absorbed in his business.

In September Edwin entered Harvard. Ethel's marriage took place in November and Helen began substituting in the public schools. Susan and Charles were content—the plans for their children were working out exactly as they wished.

Once again the Chesnutts went house-hunting. After spending nearly sixteen happy and satisfying years at 64 Brenton Street, they decided that they wanted a larger house in a more pretentious neighborhood. Susan insisted that they buy a house already built, for she did not intend to repeat the experience they had had in the case of the Brenton Street house, when Charles, impelled by a sudden spirit of economy, had had six feet lopped off the side of the house after all the plans had been decided upon. She also wanted the new house to be within walking distance of Emmanuel Church.

The Sunday afternoon walks began again and one day at the

foot of North Logan, they came into a quiet little street called Lamont Street, running between Amesbury Avenue and Republic Street. Here they found a house, on a spacious lot, surrounded by shrubs and trees. There was a ravine at the rear of the lot, through which flowed a little brook between banks covered with wild cucumber vines and spring flowers, where birds and squirrels and little garter snakes abounded.

The house itself was a beautiful place designed by one of Cleveland's leading architects, built of the finest materials, with hardwood floors downstairs and plate-glass windows throughout. It was still occupied by the original owners. The family moved into 1668 Lamont Street in May, 1904, and lived there during the remainder of Charles's life and for several years thereafter.

Charles Orr, librarian of Case Library, and Mrs. Orr came calling almost at once to welcome the Chesnutts to the neighborhood. Within the next few years, Dr. Weston A. Price, Cleveland's widely known dentist, bought the house two doors from the Chesnutts. Dr. John Phillips, co-founder of the Cleveland Clinic, bought the property next door and built a house there. J. Arthur House of the Guardian Trust Bank built a beautiful home next door to Dr. Price.

Other well-known business and civic leaders lived on the street during the following years before moving on to greener pastures and loftier abodes on the Heights.

Susan and Charles invited their daughter Ethel and her husband and baby to move into the new house. Edwin was now a Junior at Harvard, and Dorothy would enter the eighth grade at Hough School the following September. Susan was very happy. Now she had a beautiful home where she could do the entertaining in which her hospitable soul delighted.

The Chesnutts belonged to several interesting clubs. The Dancing Class met regularly now at the Lamont Street house, where the entrance hall furnished an ideal place for dancing. The old Social Circle had developed into the Euchre Club. Others were the Tresart Club, the Chester Cliffs Club, and the Brenton Circle.

Mary Dickerson Donahey * describes the founding of the Tresart Club in her own inimitable way:

"It's not surprising that I am 'the only living person' to whom

---

* Special writer for the Cleveland *Plain Dealer,* 1898-1905, and author of many juveniles.

you can appeal for data of the Tresart Club. I was one of the youngest members. I was also one of the two founders.

"You see, I came to Cleveland from New York, where I belonged to clubs in which I met other folks of my own kind and kindred crafts, and missed such in Cleveland. I came out as a feature writer for the *Cleveland Plain Dealer* but was soon doing all sorts of odd jobs besides features—and of course I interviewed all sorts and conditions of people. During this varied career I discovered how little the people who wrote and sang and painted knew about each other, and I began talking C-L-U-B.

"Charles Grant Miller, then doing editorials on the *Cleveland Press,* was at first the only person to agree with me. As I remember no one else hailed my great idea with any enthusiasm at all! But Patty Stair, composer, organist, piano teacher, was a dear friend of mine, and offered the use of the reception room of the studio she shared with Charles Heydler and Sol Marcosson, in the old Clarence Building on Euclid Avenue at the head of what was then Bond Street.

"We met. We got a club formed. William R. Rose, the columnist on the *Plain Dealer,* provided the name—Tresart from (of course you've guessed it) *tres artes.* A very good name! I think Charles Grant Miller was the first president. Wilson G. Smith was president once, and your father. Edmund Vance Cooke was an enthusiastic member from the first. Of course I already knew all of those eligible, a little if not much; Elroy M. Avery, Mez Brett Smith, Elmie Warner, then society editor of the *Plain Dealer,* who later was Mrs. Herbert Mallory, with the News Enterprise Association for years. Still may be!

"Then there were M. R. Dickey, at that time a musician, though studying law; William Saal, singer and coach; Lucretia Jones, pianist; Mr. and Mrs. Charles MacDonald (she was a singer); J. H. Donahey and Hugh Rankin of the *Plain Dealer* Art Staff; Hugh Huntington Howard and Ora Coltman, artists of renown—the Howards very eager and earnest workers for the success of the venture.

"It was not a newspaper crowd. There were more musicians than anything else. It was a lot of fun while it lasted, but it did not last long. Charles Grant Miller killed it.

"At first as I've said, we met in the Conservatory of Music. Then it was thought we needed a room of our own, and a modest one was rented in the Old Arcade. My memory is that we paid $17.00 a month for it.

"We furnished it adequately and attractively with donated furniture, and most of us were very happy there.

"But Mr. Miller always had delusions of grandeur, and too little respect for a balanced budget. There was an old building on the northeast corner of Erie and Euclid, the Lenox Building, which having been very fashionable as a down town apartment building was on the social downgrade. Mr. Miller insisted that we rent an apartment there at $44.00 a month! We couldn't afford it. The rooms were delightful; we had a kitchen which was nice for our social committee, but we hadn't the furniture—or the rent! I remonstrated, 'Let the club grow slowly. Don't rush anybody into membership. Make it so interesting and important that people will clamor to be admitted. Don't run into debt. Pay as we go.'

"But Mr. Miller's idea was to splurge at once. He won out. We not only took the big rooms but we bought furniture and after several years we busted! It was just too bad! It had had such a healthy start.

"Your father joined the Tresart while we were in the Arcade room. At an early meeting some one—I think it was Hugh Howard—suggested his name. There was a silence. I broke it saying, 'It does seem ridiculous to have a club for writers and leave out the most famous writer in the state!' Of course Edmund Vance Cooke was selling a lot of poetry, but there was no one to come anywhere near Charles W. Chesnutt in prose, anywhere in Ohio. Some one else took up the tale of his success—Wilson G. Smith, I think it was. Novels, short stories in the *Atlantic* etc. Well, the testimony was too much! He was elected to membership at that meeting and as far as I know, only two people left the club. I honestly don't remember who they were, just that two did. I've no desire to cover their shame—I'd proclaim if it I could!

"Every one liked your father, of course, and when your mother came I do think she became more popular than your father. She was a rare woman!"

The Chester Cliffs Club was a country club, an outgrowth of the Tresart Club. At a meeting of the latter during the summer of 1903 a member announced that she had discovered a small country inn at Chesterland Caves which served chicken dinners on Sunday for fifty cents. This evoked great enthusiasm and the club decided on an excursion out there on the following Sunday.

After dinner Charles Grant Miller, Wilson G. Smith, and Elroy M. Avery took a ramble through the woods and came upon a beautiful tract of land which was for sale—eleven acres on a hillside, with big trees and great rocks and a little spring.

In September the Chester Cliffs Club was incorporated with eleven members and their families, shares of stock having been sold to pay for the land. Building sites were assigned by lot, but Chesnutt's site was especially assigned to him because of some cedar trees there, so that he could call his cottage the House Behind the Cedars.

Only three cottages were built, those of Mary Dickerson, Charles Grant Miller, and the Wilson sisters. The rest of the members decided to wait until the roads were improved—they were almost impassable for automobiles at that time and the members had to depend upon interurban cars which had a very poor schedule.

The years went on, some of the members died, others moved away, and no other cottages were built.

The Millers and Mary Dickerson, who later became Mrs. William Donahey, very generously shared their cottages with the other members, and for years many pleasant meetings were held there during the summers and many happy weekends were enjoyed. In 1916 the Wilson cottage was offered for sale, as one of the sisters had died, and the Chesnutts bought it. They spent several delightful summers there, moving out when school closed and returning to the city at the beginning of September.

Here Susan entertained the Women's Guild of Emmanuel Church, or had the inmates of the Home for Crippled Children out for the day, and, year after year, the Garden Club and the Olympian Club of Central High School had their "day in the woods," and produced scenes from *A Midsummer Night's Dream,* or *The Forest Spring,* or other plays requiring a woodland setting. Here these city children became acquainted with Ohio's song-birds and learned to identify many wild-flowers of northern Ohio.

Here Dorothy lay all one summer in a hammock under the trees regaining her health after a serious bout with pleurisy.

Here Chesnutt, in overalls and battered straw hat, spent the days cutting down trees and sawing up wood for the fireplaces at Lamont Avenue; or wandered whistling through the woods, losing his cuff-links or his eye-glasses, but recalling with happy memories the days of his youth down on his father's farm in Fayetteville, North Carolina.

The Brenton Circle was the club Susan liked best. In the late summer of 1904 the women of Brenton Street, which had always had the atmosphere of a delightful little village, decided to form a club to do sewing for charity.

At first only the women who lived on the street were members, but then the happy thought struck them that those who had moved away into other parts of the city would enjoy these meetings; so they also were asked into the club. But the social part of the meetings was so enjoyable that they decided to discontinue the sewing and, instead, to make an annual contribution of money to the Fresh Air Camp.

Every now and then in addition to the bi-weekly afternoon meetings they would have an evening party at the home of a member, or a picnic at Luna Park or Euclid Beach Park, to which the husbands were invited. The following, taken from the secretary's book describes a party at the Chesnutt home:

"On Tuesday evening, January 8, 1907, a goodly number of members of the Brenton Circle and their friends assembled at the home of Mrs. Chesnutt on Lamont Avenue. Everyone felt at home. Conversation was general and when the last guest had arrived, some took partners for the dance, some preferred the card tables, and a few employed themselves looking over postal card albums, the cards of which were collected by the family on their recent trip abroad.

"When refreshment time came we were all accommodated in the commodious dining room where coffee and sandwiches, cake and ice-cream were served.

"The plates were scarcely removed when Mr. Carey rose and said, 'I am delegated to say that Mr. Chesnutt will give us a lecture or a talk or something of that kind, the subject to be left to him to choose. Mr. Chesnutt!'

"But Mr. Chesnutt said, 'I deny the allegation and defy the alligator!' which remark was not the less enjoyed that it was a 'chestnut.' However a compromise was effected and Mr. Chesnutt told a very amusing story—a 'heavenly' anecdote. It was about a man who was admitted to the celestial abode of St. Peter, who noticed shortly that he appeared somewhat dejected. Asking the reason, he was told that none of the man's friends were there. 'Well,' said St. Peter, 'I'll give you a round trip pass to the other place where you'll probably find them.' So the man went to the 'other place' and seeing his friends gathered around a table playing poker said, 'Move up, boys, and make room for me.' 'Have you any money?' they asked. 'No,' 'Then you can't sit in with us.' He left and soon returned. 'I've got money now so move up.' 'Where did you get it?' they asked. 'I sold my pass.'

"After Mr. Chesnutt had been greeted with a round of applause, Mr. Carey gave a well-rendered Irish song. He then kept the ball rolling by calling on one and another until Mr. Clark had given two fine impersonations from poems of James Whitcomb Riley, Miss Grace McConnell two excellent illustrations of elocution, Mrs. Cassler a piece that convulsed the company with laughter, and Mrs. von Ehrenberg *The Baron's Last Banquet*. Mr. Chesnutt varied the entertainment by interludes of anecdotes told in his inimitable manner. When the program was over our host called on all to take partners for the Virginia Reel. This old-fashioned dance was enjoyed by the whole company, and ended the evening. After expressing to their host and hostess the great pleasure they had had, and thanking them heartily for the same, the members of the Brenton Circle betook themselves to their various homes."

19

Chesnutt and Booker T. Washington

IT HAS OFTEN been asked just what relations existed between Booker T. Washington and Chesnutt. They were contemporaries, of practically the same age, each with the purpose in life of working for the advancement of the Negro race. But their philosophies were entirely different. When Washington became recognized as the spokesman of the Negro in the United States, Chesnutt was filled with forebodings. He feared that Washington's policy of conciliation in the South, even though a temporary one as was claimed, was paving the way for complete disfranchisement in the South and a permanent status of inferiority for the Negro.

The work being done at Tuskegee was a great work. Washington's theory of industrial education for the Negro masses was sound; his belittling of the need for higher education, however, was detrimental to their advancement.

The assumption that the ballot was relatively unimportant to the Southern Negro at that stage of his development; that his civil and political rights were secondary to his economic welfare; and that the winning of the friendship of the white South, at whatever cost, was the goal to be desired, did not agree with Chesnutt's doctrine.

When Chesnutt was a guest at Washington's home in February, 1901, he had for the first time realized the greatness of the work that was being done at Tuskegee. At that time he and Washington became warm personal friends, with the highest respect and affection for each other in spite of their diametrically opposed views. Through the years they scrapped and argued and thrashed matters out, but each remained firm in his own belief and could never be converted to the other's way of thinking.

The Boston colored people, who suffered less discrimination than the members of their race in other parts of the country, were bitterly opposed to Washington. The leader of this opposition was William Monroe Trotter, editor of the *Boston Guardian*.

CHESNUTT TO TROTTER

CLEVELAND, December 28, 1901

I enclose you herewith P. O. order for $1.50, annual subscription to the *Guardian*, beginning with the week of January 1st. I have found it interesting, and instructive, and I admire its uncompromising stand on all the questions pertaining to the rights of the Negro. You have the opportunity to conduct a high-class, dignified and helpful newspaper, which can be of much service to the colored race.

I note your various suggestions to myself, mostly with reference to Mr. Washington. I feel quite as deeply interested as any one can in maintaining the rights of the Negro, North, South and everywhere; but I prefer, personally, to do it directly, rather than by attacking some one else. As a public man, Mr. Washington's views are of course a fair subject of criticism, and it is the privilege of a newspaper to express its views on his utterances. I think, however, that you overrate his influence on the course of public affairs; he has merely swum with the current, rather than directed it.

I could not have followed his course; neither do I see my way to adopt the extreme position you have taken. His school has accomplished a great deal of good; I have been there and seen it. I am willing to approve the good, and where I disagree with him, to preach the opposite doctrine strenuously. But I aim to be a literary artist, and acrimonious personalities are the death of art. With best wishes for the *Guardian*, and with the hope that we may all work together, each in his own way, for truth and justice, I remain. . . .

The theme of the discussions between Chesnutt and Washington was always the same, the disfranchisement of the Negro in the Southern states.

CHESNUTT TO WASHINGTON

CLEVELAND, OHIO
June 27, 1903

I have meant for some time to write you again on the subject mentioned in your last letter to me, to-wit, the restricted franchise in the South. . . .

I am squarely opposed to any restriction of the franchise in the South on any basis now proposed. It is wholly and solely an effort in my opinion to deprive the Negro of every vestige of power and every particle of representation. How completely this leaves him in the power of the whites and exposes him to their cruelty and contempt, is indicated by the disclosures of the peonage investigation now in progress in your State. I have no faith in the Southern people's sense of justice so far as the Negro's rights are concerned. Their own public opinion on the subject is hopelessly corrupt, and they have poisoned the North until we scarcely feel that our rights are secure in this part of the country. The time is coming when every man who speaks upon these subjects will have to take sides one way or the other, and if you are going to stand with the Lyman Abbots and men of that stamp, I fear you will be on the side which other colored men who have the interests of the race at heart will feel to be the wrong side. On this proposition I stand squarely with the *New York Evening Post.* I realize some of the difficulty and delicacy of your position, and yet at the same time, I do not see how the recognized leader and spokesman of a people whose rights are in jeopardy can afford to take a stand less high, or demand less for his people than white men do. . . .

I appreciate all you say and have written about education and property; but they are not everything. There is no good reason why we should not acquire them and exercise our constitutional rights at the same time, and acquire them all the more readily because of our equality of rights. I have no confidence in that friendship of the whites which is to take the place of rights, and no expectation of justice at their hands unless it is founded on law.

Pardon my frankness; your letter invited it. I feel deeply on this subject. I want my rights and all of them, and I ask no more for myself than I would demand for every Negro in the South. If the white South will continue to ignore the Constitution and violate the laws, it must be with no consent of mine, and with no word that can be twisted into the approval or condonation of their unjust and unlawful course.

CHESNUTT TO WASHINGTON

CLEVELAND, August 11, 1903

I should have replied sooner to your private and confidential letter of July 7th, but I was very busy and could not find the time to express myself as I should have liked....

I have been reading over some of the pamphlets which you enclosed me in your letter and find them replete with the sane and practical wisdom which has characterized most of your utterances. In this matter of the suffrage, however, I differ from you most decidedly. I see nothing at all to justify what you term "the protection of the ballot in many of the States, for a while at least either by an educational test, property test, or by both combined." It is equivalent to agreeing that the white people in the Southern States may so arrange the election laws as to deprive the Negro of any representation; it means that you are willing in your own county to throw yourself upon the mercy of the whites, rather than to claim your voice and your vote under a free franchise. You may reply that you would have to do it anyway. But you need not approve it....

Nor do I think it the part of policy to be always dwelling upon the weakness of the Negro race. It is altogether contrary to the spirit of our institutions and to the Constitution to pick out any one class of people, differentiated from the rest by color or origin or anything else, make some average deduction concerning their capacity, and then proceed to measure their rights by this standard. Every individual Negro, weak or strong, is entitled to the same rights before the law as every individual white man, whether weak or strong. I think that by dwelling upon and recognizing these distinctions, and suggesting different kinds of education and different degrees of political power and all that sort of thing for the colored people, we are merely intensifying the class spirit which is fast robbing them of every shadow of right. Let the white man dwell upon the weakness of the Negro race; it is a matter which neither you nor I need to emphasize. The question with which, in principle, we have to deal, is not the question of the Negro race; what the black race has or has not been able to do in Africa should no more enter into this discussion of the

Negro's rights as a citizen, than what the Irish have not done in Ireland should be the basis of their citizenship here. We are directly concerned with the interests of some millions of American citizens of more or less mixed descent, whose rights are fixed by the Constitution of the United States, nor am I ready yet to accept the conclusion that those constitutional rights are mere waste paper. The Supreme Court may assent to their nullification, but we should not accept its findings as conclusive. . . . There is still the court of public opinion to which we may appeal. . . .

I have no intention of confounding the good Southerners with the bad. . . . But the white South insists upon judging the Negroes as a class. They themselves must be measured by the same rule and be judged by the laws they make, the customs they follow, and the crimes they commit against the colored people. I think that the Southern white people are, as a class, an ignorant, narrow and childish people—as inferior to the white people of the North as the Southern Negroes are to the whites of that section. . . .

I have taken occasion, in the article which I have written for James Pott and Company, in the volume in which you are also a contributor, to express my disagreement with you upon a matter of the suffrage. I have done so without heat and with what I meant to make ample recognition of your valuable services to the country. But I believe in manhood suffrage, especially now and for the Negro; and I do not believe in a tame or even a patient submission to many other forms of injustice.

I think the feeling with reference to yourself on the part of some colored men, which has resulted in occasional and sometimes very unjust and rancorous criticism, grows out of a realization of this fact: No man who lives and conducts a great institution in the heart of the South, can possibly be in a position to speak always frankly and fearlessly concerning the rights of his people. He is not at liberty to express that manly indignation which is always the natural and often the best and most effective way to meet injustice. I have such a high esteem for your abilities as to believe that no other man in the United States could have said or done as much in that direction as you have; but I still recognize the limitation. You Southern educators are all bound up with some cause or other, devotion to which sometimes unconsciously warps your opinions as to what is best for the general welfare of the race. You are conducting an industrial school, and

naturally you place stress upon that sort of education, with perfect honesty and sincerity, but yet with the zeal of the advocate,
before whose eyes his client's case always looms up so as to dwarf
the other side. Unfortunately, those who would discourage the
higher education of the Negro, use your words for that purpose.
DuBois is in much the same situation. He is connected with
Atlanta [University] and it is hard for him to discuss the abstract
rights of the Negro without ringing in the higher education.
Neither sort of education has anything directly to do with the
civil and political rights of the Negro—these would be just as
vital and fundamental if there were not a single school of any
kind in the Southern States....

Your letter on lynching is fine. As to the "sacred trust," however, acquired by highway robbery of the Negro's rights, the
world is not having much chance to wait or any need to watch to
see how it will be executed. The good Southern whites are still
in the small minority; even Judge Jones announced that by their
verdict in the Turner case, the white people of Alabama had
made known to the world that justice between white and black
could not be expected in the South. Encourage the good ones all
you may; I think the rest of us should score the bad ones; I only
wish we could do it as effectively. Your ability and your influence
are so great that I should like to see them always exerted in favor
of the highest and the best things, which are also, in the long
run, the wisest and the most successful; and on this franchise
proposition, I think you are training in the wrong. I will take
the *Evening Post* and the *Independent* as against the *Outlook*
and *Harpers Weekly* every time.

At the end of August Chesnutt met his family who had spent
the summer with their relatives, the Tysons, on Chesapeake Bay,
and took them to New York for a few days. After their return to
Cleveland Ethel's little son was born.

In September, 1903, a book of essays entitled *The Negro
Problem* was published by James Pott and Company of New
York. Washington, DuBois, Chesnutt, Dunbar, Wilford H. Smith,
H. T. Kealing, and T. Thomas Fortune were the contributors.
It was an absorbing book treating of every phase of Negro life
and informing the public of the Negro's heroic struggle to
advance into American life against the most terrific obstacles.
Chesnutt wrote of the disfranchisement of the Negro; Washing-

ton of industrial education; DuBois of higher education. The remaining contributors discussed other phases of Negro life. The press comments were fine and the book served as a reference book on this perennial problem.

One of the first organizations established by Negroes to influence the American public in their behalf was the Committee of Twelve For the Advancement of the Interests of the Negro Race. This was formed in 1904 in New York City with Booker T. Washington, chairman, Hugh M. Browne, secretary, and Archibald H. Grimké, treasurer.

The aim of the Committee was "to turn the attention of the race to the importance of constructive, progressive effort, and the attention of the country to Negro successes; to correct the errors and misstatements concerning the progress and activities of the race, as well as to make known the truth regarding the acts of the white race affecting us—with a view of perfecting a larger and more systematic effort in the unification of the race."

Twelve of the outstanding colored men of the country joined this committee, among whom were, in addition to the officers, Kelly Miller, T. Thomas Fortune, Charles W. Anderson, J. W. E. Bowen, and other leaders in education, the ministry, politics, the professions, and the arts. When the first vacancy occurred in April, 1905, Chesnutt was unanimously elected to membership and after some correspondence concerning it accepted with the following letter:

Cleveland
June 2, 1905

Prof. Hugh M. Browne
Cheyney, Pa.
My dear Mr. Browne:

I am in receipt of your letter in reply to my letter of inquiry with regard to the Committee of Twelve. Of my interest in the subject and my approval of the objects of the Committee, there is no manner of doubt, and with a personnel including men whose views vary so widely as do the views of some of those on the committee, there is probably room for every phase of thought and opinion in regard to the race question. I think, however, that we are all united, in the wish to overcome, as far as may be, the prejudice against the colored people and to promote good feeling so far as that is possible without the sacrifice of vital principles.

I shall be glad to cooperate with the Committee and to do what I can to further its ends.

Cordially yours,
Charles W. Chesnutt

The work of the Committee was done quietly. It consisted mainly of the distribution of printed matter which tended to create public opinion in favor of the Negro. It was financed by the members themselves with whatever contributions they were able to get from others interested in the cause. Among the pamphlets widely circulated were reprints of articles favorable to the Negro, which appeared in current magazines. Whenever a speech or an address on the race problem was delivered by a man of influence, it was promptly secured, printed, and distributed. The guiding spirit of this Committee was Booker T. Washington. But the methods adopted by these men seemed of little avail in stemming the tide of prejudice and injustice flowing toward the colored people.

During August, 1906, a Negro battalion was established at Fort Brown, Brownsville, Texas. The citizens of the community were very much opposed to this, and engaged in a campaign of insult and persecution of the colored soldiers, who finally showed their resentment. A riot followed, and the blame was put upon the soldiers. They were dismissed from the army without honor and disqualified for further service to the United States.

And then, in September, while the Negroes of the country were filled with deep resentment at this injustice and with forebodings for the future, the Atlanta riot occurred, a race conflict that paralleled in many respects the Wilmington Riot which Chesnutt had described in *The Marrow of Tradition*.

Booker T. Washington at once called a meeting of the Committee of Twelve, and Chesnutt wrote immediately:

Cleveland, Ohio
October 9, 1906

Dr. Booker T. Washington
Manhattan Hotel
New York City
My dear Dr. Washington:

I am in receipt of your letter and telegram from Tuskegee, calling my attention to the meeting of the Committee of Twelve at the Stevens House on October 12. This is one of the meetings at which I should very much like to be present, and I regret exceedingly that I am tangled up here in a lawsuit which absolutely demands my presence during the whole of this week and very probably into the middle of next week; it is of a nature which does not permit of a substitute and I am therefore compelled to forego the privilege of attending the meeting.

I wish also to acknowledge your brief note calling my attention to the issue of the *New York World,* containing a review of the Atlanta horror. I read with great interest Mr. H. G. Wells's article in *Harper's Weekly* on the "Tragedy of Color," and I think you will agree that my views and those of Mr. Wells are very much the same. I do not believe it possible for two races to subsist side by side without intermingling; experience has demonstrated this fact and there will be more experience along that line. Another thing of which I am firmly convinced, in view of recent events, is that no system which excludes the Negro or any other class from the use of the ballot, and leaves this potent instrument in the hands of the people who are alien to him in sympathy and interest, can have any healthy effect in improving his condition. No subterfuge of equal qualifications and just application to black and white alike of disfranchising provisions, can overcome the solemn fact which is brought home every day by reading the newspapers that these State constitutions leave the Negro absolutely at the mercy of the white man.

I have never been able to see how any man with the interest of his people at heart could favor those abominations. I know that your heart is all right, but I think your very wise head is wrong on that proposition, and I should regard it as a much more hopeful day for the Negro in this country when you cease to defend them. There is no hope for the Negro except in equality before the law, and I suspect that hope will be deferred for many a day in the Southern States. At the same time, I think nothing is lost and everything gained by insisting upon the principle. A man weakens his position immensely when he takes any attitude which justifies or excuses his oppressor.

I notice a great deal has been said by colored people about the Atlanta matter. And of course, I have not failed to observe that those best qualified to speak, and whose utterances would carry most weight, have not been in a position to express themselves fully. I appreciate the difficulty of their situation. And so far as the mere matter of speech is concerned, discretion on the part of people who live and work in the South is imperative. I observe that a Georgia editor was expelled from that State for saying a few truthful things about the Jim-Crow law in Savannah. After all, the Northern press, with a surprising unanimity and vigor, has said the things which ought to have been said, much to the chagrin of the South, much to our satisfaction and, I trust, much to the enlightenment of Northern readers.

Negro leaders for some time to come are likely to lead a somewhat strenuous existence. They have my sympathy and will have any small support that I can contribute.

With best wishes for a successful meeting of the Committee and of the council, at which you will doubtless be present to exercise a wise and restraining influence, I remain

Sincerely yours,

CHARLES W. CHESNUTT

Later he wrote to Browne:

CLEVELAND, OHIO
November 3, 1906

PROF. HUGH M. BROWNE
CHEYNEY, PA.
MY DEAR PROF. BROWNE:

I am in receipt of your favor of October 21st, and also of the copy of the address on "Slavery and the Race Problem in the South," by Mr. Fleming. I most heartily approve of its circulation among the leaders of opinion in the South. I should go a good deal further than Mr. Fleming, in some details, but the whole tone of his address is vastly in advance of current thought in the South, and the fundamental propositions of justice to the Negro and respect for the Constitution are so clearly and eloquently insisted upon, that I hope the words of this good man will not be without their weight in the councils of those Southern men who have the immediate fate of the Negro so largely in their hands.

Sincerely yours,

CHARLES W. CHESNUTT

The same day he wrote again to Washington:

CLEVELAND, OHIO
November 3, 1906

DR. BOOKER T. WASHINGTON
TUSKEGEE, ALABAMA
MY DEAR DR. WASHINGTON:

I beg to acknowledge receipt of your letter of recent date. I note what you say about the franchise in Georgia, and while the riot occurred in Georgia, it was not because the Negroes had exercised the franchise or made any less progress or developed any less strength than elsewhere, but because of a wicked and indefensible effort to disfranchise them.

I am quite aware that the Negro will not enjoy any large degree of liberty at the South until there has developed in that section a white party which is favorable to his enjoyment of the rights guaranteed by the Constitution of the United States. The rise of such men as Mr. Fleming indicates that this party, while small, is finding a voice. Surely no colored man can afford to demand less for his race than a white man is willing to concede, and as I read Mr. Fleming's pamphlet cursorily during a busy week, he is willing to give them their rights under the Constitution. The scheme proposed in Georgia for the disfranchisement of the Negro is substantially that enacted in Alabama. This Mr. Fleming condemns. He uses this language: "Let us not in cowardice or want of faith needlessly sacrifice our higher ideals of private and public life." Manhood suffrage is an ideal, already attained in this country except where the reactionary Southern States have qualified it. Surely in a country where everyone else votes and the suffrage is freely conceded to foreigners in a great many states, including I believe Alabama, as soon as they declare their intentions of becoming citizens, it is not only a great lapse from the ideal, but the rankest sort of injustice that any different rule should be applied to so numerous and important a class of the population as the Negro constitutes in the South. I think a little more anti-Negro agitation in the South will very likely result in an effort at the North to see, for the welfare of the whole country, that the Thirteenth, Fourteenth, and Fifteenth Amendments shall become not only the theoretical but the real law of the land. The practical difficulties I admit are enormous, but the value of equal citizenship is so great and so vital that it is worth whatever it may cost. Slavery was as deeply entrenched as race prejudice, yet it fell. And the sound of the trumpets you will remember shook down the walls of Jericho.

If I wanted to answer with the *argumentum ad hominem,* with reference to the Atlanta riot, I could point out the fact that the riot occurred only a few days after your splendid object lesson of the Negro's progress in business and the other arts of peace. The fact of the matter is that this race problem involves all of the issues of life and must be attacked from many sides for a long time before it will approach anything like a peaceful solution. The American people will have to swallow the Negro, in punishment for their sins. Doubtless the dose is a bitter one, but there is no other way out. It only remains for all of us to make the process as little painful as possible to all concerned.

I have read a review somewhere of a book which is described as a very vicious attack on Tuskegee. I trust that this false and reckless publication has not done you any injury.

I also beg to thank you on behalf of myself and Mrs. Chesnutt, for the handsome little volume, *Putting the Most into Life,* which you were good enough to send us. We shall prize it very highly.

Sincerely yours,
CHARLES W. CHESNUTT

In response to a request for funds, Chesnutt wrote to Grimké:

CLEVELAND, OHIO
November 24th, 1906

HON. ARCHIBALD H. GRIMKÉ,
TREASURER COM. OF TWELVE.
MY DEAR MR. GRIMKÉ:

I have today forwarded to Hugh M. Browne, Secretary, N. Y. draft to my order, endorsed to him, as my contribution towards the expenses of printing and circulation of Hon. William H. Fleming's oration, delivered before the Alumni Association of the University of Georgia, on June 19, 1906, at Athens, Ga.

I am no hand at soliciting money for even the best of causes, and this contribution is made from my own pocket. Doubtless, others will be more successful. If there is any deficit, kindly let me know, and I will consider whether I can do anything further.

I read every week, or as often as they appear, your eloquent and forceful letters in the *New York Age.* I am beginning to feel more hopeful concerning the outcome of our problem.

The Atlanta horror was, of course, a dreadful thing, but the unanimous outburst of condemnation at the North, mainly concurred in by the South, is a hopeful sign. The tree of liberty has always been watered with blood; nor does it seem possible to escape the sacrifice. The successful efforts to head off Tillman and Dixon here and there, are also encouraging. The strong protest of the United North and the Army against Mr. Roosevelt's cavalier treatment of the colored troops, and the manner in which it has driven the colored people together, and lent them voice, and made them friends, is a significant sign of the times.

Sincerely yours,
CHARLES W. CHESNUTT

When Andrew Carnegie in 1907 delivered an address entitled "The Negro in America," before the Philosophical Institution of Edinburgh, and the Committee of Twelve decided to circulate it, Chesnutt objected to certain statements made by Carnegie, and this occasioned some correspondence between him and Washington and certain changes in the address:

CLEVELAND, OHIO
November 22, 1907

DR. BOOKER T. WASHINGTON
TUSKEGEE, ALABAMA
MY DEAR DR. WASHINGTON:

Professor Browne sent me the other day a copy of Mr. Carnegie's Edinburgh address requesting my views upon it. It is worthy of all commendation, except that I do not agree with him, or with you, if you are correctly quoted, that it is the "wiser course" to let the ballot for the Negro go, substantially, by default. We may not be able to successfully resist the current of events, but it seems to me that our self-respect demands an attitude of protest against steadily progressing disfranchisement and consequent denial of civil rights, rather than one of acquiescence. Georgia is gone, Oklahoma and Maryland will soon fall into line. I hope at least that Mason and Dixon's line will prove an impassable barrier.

But while I differ from you very earnestly and deeply on this point, I must congratulate you on having won over to such active friendship for the Negro, so able and influential a citizen of the world as Mr. Carnegie.

Sincerely yours,
CHAS. W. CHESNUTT

Washington replied as follows:

PARKER HOUSE
BOSTON, MASSACHUSETTS
December 6, 1907

MR. CHARLES W. CHESNUTT
WILLIAMSON BUILDING
CLEVELAND, OHIO
MY DEAR MR. CHESNUTT:

I have just read your letter to Mr. Browne regarding the interpretation which you put upon Mr. Carnegie's remarks based upon my position bearing upon the franchise, and also what you say regarding my own position. I confess that after reading your letter I have almost reached the conclusion that it is impossible for me to ever get my thoughts regarding the franchise through the brains of any human being; whether the trouble is with my thoughts or with the brains of the other fellow I am not prepared just now to state, but there is trouble in either one or the other direction.

In your letter you say: "On one point, however, I do not at all agree with Mr. Carnegie or with Dr. Washington, whom he quotes, in holding it 'the wiser course' to practically throw up the ballot, or the demand for it."

In the first place, Mr. Carnegie has said no such thing, I have said no such thing. If you can put your finger or eye on a single sentence in all my writing that will bear out this statement I will agree to send you a first class Alabama possum for your Christmas dinner. Suppose you re-read what Mr. Carnegie has said. I feel quite sure that when you wrote Mr. Browne there was something in the lake breeze which was troubling your brain. I have said, and do so now, that to any people living under republican form of government the ballot is a consideration of the very highest importance, and there is no disagreement between you and me as to the importance of the ballot; however, perhaps, we do not agree as to the methods of attaining to the permanent and practical use of the ballot. Some of our people maintain that the ballot is a matter of first consideration in our present condition. This I do not agree with. Practically you do not agree with their contention. Practically, the matter of earning your daily bread and banking your money is a matter of the first consideration. You vote perhaps once in two years. The average brother in the North does not vote even that often, but you earn your daily bread once every day in the year, excepting Sundays. The matter of the next consideration to you is the education of your children, something that you put into practice every week in the year. The next is the matter of attending church, or "should be" with you, something that you practice every week in the year.

If the ballot were a matter of first consideration one would vote every day in the year instead of spending his time in the laying of an economic foundation every day in every year. Take the people of Liberia. They might vote every hour and every day in the year. At the end of the period they would not have improved their economic condition or moral status before the world one iota. There is something deeper in human progress than the mere act of voting; it is the economic foundation which every race has got to have. But I shall not burden you further. We will try to thrash this out when we meet again.

I think after Mr. Browne and Mr. Carnegie have gotten through trying to weave your ideas into the address that you will be satisfied with the changes.

Yours truly,
BOOKER T. WASHINGTON

CLEVELAND, OHIO
Jan. 1, 1908

MY DEAR DR. WASHINGTON:

I received your long and interesting letter. I shall be glad to thrash the ballot proposition over with you sometime. As to the ballot, the importance of a thing is not to be measured by the number of times you do it. Birth. Death. Marriage.

Paramount element of citizenship. Man can earn his daily bread better and bank more money with the ballot than without. You argue the question as though the Negro must choose between voting and eating. He ought to do both, and can do both better together than either alone. It is not the *act* of voting I speak of— it is the right of every citizen to have some part in the choice of those who rule him, and the only way he can do it under our system is through the ballot. It is just as effective if he votes once in five years as though he voted once a day. Would you maintain for a moment that the economic conditions of the South which crush the Negro and drive away immigration could continue to exist if the Negro could vote under wise leadership, such, for instance as your own? I do not, nor do you. It is not all of life to eat or put money in the bank; but, as I say, a free man can do both better than a mere serf yoked to the mule, with no concern in life but his belly and his back.

If the colored people ever expect to cut any figure in this world they must not pitch their ideals too low; though their feet must of course rest on earth, it should not be forbidden to them to lift their eyes to the stars.

I wish you a happy and prosperous New Year.

Cordially yours,
CHARLES W. CHESNUTT

In August two events occurred which shocked the country. Brutal race riots, rivaling in their atrocity similar outbreaks in the South, occurred at Springfield, Illinois. The press of the nation carried many articles on the subject, among which was one entitled "Race War in the North," written by William English Walling, whose article was a ringing challenge to the conscience of America. Chesnutt wrote to Walling:

September 16, 1908

MR. WM. E. WALLING
3 FIFTH AVE.
NEW YORK CITY
DEAR SIR:

I wish to express my appreciation of the very fine article from your pen, in a recent number of the *Independent,* on the Springfield riot. You are in the van of the movement for which you recognize the necessity—a movement to give the Negro equality—not any particular kind of equality, but simply equality, with whatever the word may justly imply. No man is free who is not as free as any other man. By that test the Negro must stand or fall; and the important thing for all of us, is not whether he shall stand or fall, but that he shall have an equal chance.

Cordially yours,
CHARLES W. CHESNUTT

The other event was the decision rendered by the United States Supreme Court in the Berea College case. Berea College had been doing a noble work among the mountaineers of Kentucky and Tennessee. It had received its charter in 1865 and had admitted both white and colored students until 1904, when, by an act of the Kentucky State legislature, education of Negroes and whites at the same institution was prohibited. This act was fought through the courts up to the United States Supreme Court which in 1908 upheld the act.

CHESNUTT TO WASHINGTON, NOVEMBER 25, 1908

I fear that there is not much hope for the Negro's rights in the South, for from recent indications he is going to get very small aid or comfort through the Constitution or the Supreme Court or Congress. I quite agree with the *Evening Post* that the decision in the Berea College case was almost another Dred Scott decision; practically amounts to an absolute abandonment of any Constitutional protection of the Negro's rights anywhere, for what one state may do another state may do. I am delighted to see that Justice Day from Ohio, with whom I am personally acquainted, dissented from the opinion of Justices Brewer, Holmes et al.

I hope that the new President, who is also an Ohio man, will use his influence in favor of the fair and just and Constitutional thing.

20

"The Colonel's Dream"

In 1904 Chesnutt published a story called "Baxter's Procrustes" which dealt entirely with white characters. It was a little satire about a book-collectors' club, "an ingenious and amusing story, extremely well told," as Bliss Perry wrote when accepting it for the *Atlantic Monthly*. It was especially interesting to the members of Cleveland's famous Rowfant Club, who realized with very good grace that Chesnutt was making gentle fun of them.

Although his literary output was small from this time on, Chesnutt was doing valuable work on the lecture platform. He read and spoke before many Cleveland organizations—the Temple Association, numerous church clubs, the College Club, the Cleveland schools, literary clubs, and the like. His message was always the same. The Negro must have all his civil and political rights; he must have equality of opportunity along every line, for only in this way could he advance and be an asset to America's civilization.

This doctrine he carried to other communities also—to New England, the Middle West, Washington, the South. He spoke many times in Washington, D. C., before the Bethel Historical and Literary Association, the foremost institution of its kind, established in 1881, which for many years exerted a potent influence upon the people of Washington and Maryland.

The year 1905 was an eventful one for Chesnutt. In the early part of that year he spent what little leisure time he had in working on a new book, *The Colonel's Dream*.

In June Edwin graduated from Harvard College. His father, mother, and sister Helen went to the Harvard Commencement. On June 25 Chesnutt delivered an address before the Boston Literary and Historical Association on the subject "Race Prejudice: Its Causes and Its Cure." In it he very frankly expressed his convictions on the subject.

He said that originally race antagonism had grown out of the accumulation of differences between the two races, differences that were physical, cultural, and economic. There was "the contempt of the Christian for the heathen; of the instructed for the ignorant; of the fair for those of darker color; of the master for the slave; of the native for the foreigner; of the citizen for the alien; of one who spoke a language fluently for one who spoke it brokenly or not at all."

He said that the remedy for this feeling of antagonism was the "removal of the causes which gave rise to these antagonisms." He showed how many of the differences had been greatly modified before the Civil War. The difference in language had disappeared, the heathen religions had vanished. The institution of slavery and its customs had brought about a constant infusion of white blood into the Negro race, which had greatly though not uniformly modified the original type.

The Civil War removed others of these differences; all men were free, all were voters and all were theoretically equal citizens. But the whites were still relatively rich and instructed, the Negroes poor and ignorant. The control of the social organism, the habit of command, the pride of race and authority still remained with the whites.

He then enumerated the further modification of these differences since the Civil War. Once more the Negro, he said, was practically without the vote in the South. The destruction of slavery, and the marriage laws of the South had checked in some degree the admixture of the races. But the Negroes were better fed and better clothed. They had made a great advance in education and general enlightenment. There were many Negro teachers in the country, several hundred newspapers, several monthly magazines. Thousands of them had been graduated from higher institutions of learning, North and South. They had accumulated property to the amount of several hundred millions of dollars.

But much still remained to be done before these differences

could be adjusted, particularly in the field of education. He advo-
cated both industrial training and higher education as essential
to the growth of the Negro. He stated that the disparity in civil
and political rights must be removed; that wherever men's rights
are fixed by law, those laws should apply equally; that economic
opportunity should depend upon merit and not upon color or
race.

He spoke of the current doctrine of race integrity, which was
then being preached assiduously to the Negro:

"We are told that we must glory in our color and zealously
guard it as a priceless heritage. Frankly I take no stock in this
doctrine. It seems to be a modern invention of the white people
to perpetuate the color line. It is they who preach it, and it is
their racial integrity which they wish to preserve—they have never
been unduly careful of the purity of the black race. Why should
a man be proud any more than he should be ashamed of anything
for which he is not responsible? Manly self-respect based upon
one's humanity, a self-respect which claims nothing for color and
yields nothing to color, every man should cherish.

"Most other people who come to this country seek to lose their
separate identity as soon as possible and to become Americans
with no distinguishing mark. For a generation they have their
ghettoes, their residence districts, their churches, their social clubs.
For another generation they may still retain a sentimental interest
in these things. In the third generation they are all Americans,
seldom speak of the foreign descent, and often modify their
names so they will not suggest it.

"They enter fully and completely, if they are capable and
worthy, into the life of this republic. Are we to help the white
people to build up walls between themselves and us, to fence in a
gloomy back yard for our descendants to play in?

"This nation with the war amendments threw that theory over-
board when it established the equality of all men before the law.
The Northern states have long since repudiated it, when they
abolished discriminating laws, and threw open the public schools
to all alike. . . .

"Race prejudice will not perhaps entirely disappear until the
difference of color shall have disappeared, or at least, until all of
us, white and colored, shall have resolutely shut our eyes to those
differences, and shall have learned to judge men by other standards. I ask you to dismiss from your minds any theory, however

cherished, that there can be built up in a free country, under equal laws, two separate sorts of civilization, two standards of human development . . . events seem to be paving the way to embrace the Negro in the general process by which all the races of mankind are being fused together here into one people. . . .

"And now to close, may I venture a prophecy? . . . Looking down through the vista of time I see an epoch in our nation's history, not in my time nor in yours, but in the not too distant future, when there shall be in the United States but one people, moulded by the same culture, swayed by the same patriotic ideals, holding their citizenship in such high esteem, that for another to share it is of itself to entitle him to fraternal regard; when men will be esteemed and honored for their character and their talents; when hand in hand, and heart with heart, all the people of this nation will join to preserve to all and to each of them for all future time that ideal of human liberty which the fathers of the republic set out in the Declaration of Independence, the ideal for which Lincoln died, the ideal embodied in the words of the Book—the Book that declares that God is no respecter of persons, and that of one blood hath He made all the nations of the earth."

This speech, which was widely discussed, brought much bitter criticism upon Chesnutt. He received abusive letters, many of them from illiterate and anonymous writers, and some unpleasant newspaper notoriety.

The Colonel's Dream, Chesnutt's last book, was published in September, 1905, by Doubleday, Page and Company. It was also issued in England by Archibald Constable and Company. This was an avowed purpose novel written to expose peonage and the convict lease system which were flourishing in certain Southern states and making the lives of the Negro masses more wretched than in the days of slavery. The first copies had the name Chesnutt spelled incorrectly on the cover, but that was quickly remedied with apologies from the publishers.

The Colonel's Dream is the story of Colonel French, the scion of a prominent Southern family which had been impoverished by the Civil War. He leaves the South after the war and makes a fortune in the North. On his retirement from business he returns to the South to visit his old home. He is appalled at the conditions there. Peonage and the convict lease system are flourishing. The baser element of the whites control the town. The Negroes are hopelessly crushed and utterly helpless.

Colonel French tries to rehabilitate the town. He pours out his influence, his energy, and his money in the effort, but to no avail. The whites oppose him so bitterly when they find that the uplift of the Negro is included in the Colonel's plans that he realizes the futility of his dream and withdraws from the scene.

The book, however, ends with a hopeful note: "White men go their way, and black men theirs, and these ways grow wider apart, and no one knows the outcome. But there are those who hope, and those who pray, that this condition will pass, that some day our whole land will be truly free, and the strong will cheerfully help to bear the burdens of the weak, and Justice, the seed, and Peace, the flower, of liberty will prevail throughout all our borders."

This book was not so popular as Chesnutt's other books. Some reviewers considered it his best story but many of them deplored the fact that he was wasting his literary skill in the arts of the pamphleteer. They granted, however, that "the historian of American life who half a century hence gathers together documents for the study of the Negro problem will find abundant material ready to his hand."

One reviewer wrote: "He has a grasp of detail and realistic exposition almost Flaubertian at times, but to clasp that precious quality more closely he must discontinue his preaching or not give it the guise of the novel."

The Southern reviews were characteristic: "The book is a bitter, passionate arraignment of the white people of the South in their treatment of the Negro, and it does not contribute in any way to the solution of 'the problem.'" Another reviewer said, "The story is kindly in its treatment of the better class of Southern whites, but grossly libelous as to Southern conditions in general and tells stories of the practice of peonage and prevalent cruelty and injustice to negroes not only false, but impossible. ... These books do the South incalculable harm. They give an idea to the outside world of malevolent conditions and race rancor here for which there is but little warrant."

The Colonel's Dream was very interesting to the English. They were surprised that the conditions depicted still existed in the South and, having no sense of responsibility for such conditions, gave the book much praise.

21

Mark Twain's Birthday Dinner

IN THE EARLY PART of November, 1905, Chesnutt received an invitation to attend Mark Twain's seventieth birthday party given by Colonel George Harvey, president of Harper and Brothers Publishing Company. The invitations were extended to about one hundred and fifty of America's most distinguished writers of imaginative literature. The party, which took place on December 5 at Delmonico's in New York City, was proclaimed one of the most important events in the history of American literature, and for Chesnutt it marked the highest point in his literary career.

When the daily papers reported the honor that had come to Cleveland through this invitation to one of its citizens, Chesnutt thoroughly enjoyed the little flurry of excitement that it caused, for Cleveland was as usual very appreciative of her native son.

Susan started in immediately on his wardrobe. He must have a new full-dress suit; the other was becoming too small. So he was driven by entreaty and command to go down to Rheinheimer's and order a suit. All the accessories must be perfect, and Susan herself looked after these. Charles's gray eyes did a lot of twinkling during this period of stress, but finally his suitcase was packed and he started off with orders to remain at least a week and take a real vacation.

The dinner was an inspiration. The speeches were brilliant. Autographs were exchanged. Many complimented Chesnutt on *The Colonel's Dream,* which had been published two months previously. Every guest was given a plaster bust of Mark Twain and there was quite a bit of gay rivalry in getting the busts inscribed. Altogether it was a wonderful occasion. The young lad down in Fayetteville, North Carolina, who had filled his journal with his aspirations and hopes, had never dreamed of anything like this. It seemed to Chesnutt his accolade.

While in New York, he went to see his publisher.

> · DOUBLEDAY-PAGE & CO.
> 133-135-137 EAST 16TH STREET, NEW YORK
> December 8, 1905

DEAR MR. CHESNUTT:

I wanted to see you yesterday, and I sent word to you that after Marcosson let you go to come in. I was just at the moment dealing with an insistent poet, and I had to wait a few minutes. When the few minutes expired, and I tried to find you, you were gone. I count this rather a mean trick that you played me.

> Heartily yours,
> W. H. PAGE

> CHAS. W. CHESNUTT
> 1005 WILLIAMSON BUILDING
> CLEVELAND, OHIO
> December 11 1905

MY DEAR MR. PAGE:—

I have your note of December 8th. I should have been glad to see you, but I did not get the word that I was to come in after leaving Marcosson; and I knew you were a busy man, and as I had really nothing of very great importance to say, I did not disturb you. I assure you, however, that the loss was mine.

I enjoyed the Mark Twain dinner very much. It was a great occasion and very inspiring—well worth the trip to New York and something to be long remembered. I spent the week in New York very pleasantly, not the least pleasant feature being the rather long interview which I did have with you.

> Sincerely yours,
> CHARLES W. CHESNUTT

The bust of Mark Twain was put in the library in a place of honor and, as the years went on, it grew somewhat grimy and was no longer ornamental, but no one had the courage to put it away out of sight.

Chesnutt's little grandson was enthralled by the bust and called everyone's attention to it, much to the embarrassment of the family, but finally fate found a way to dispose of it.

Mr. Leslie Pinkney Hill and his wife were dining with the Chesnutts one evening. Little Charles took Mr. Hill by the hand and said he wanted to show him "Mock Twain." The mystified Mr. Hill was led into the library and at once realized what the youngster meant. As he picked up the bust to examine it, it slipped from his hands and broke into fragments. It took much talk and laughter on the part of the family to overcome the dismay of Mr. Hill, who found it hard to believe that he had done the Chesnutts a real service.

22

Chesnutt's Family in Europe

CHESNUTT's main interest for the next few years was his son's future. He said to Susan after Edwin's graduation from Harvard, "Ethel and Nellie are nicely disposed of; now it's Ned's turn." Edwin's health had always been a matter of concern to his parents; he had a chronic catarrhal complaint, and the rugged weather of New England had not improved it.

Chesnutt thought back to his own youth. He remembered Judge Williamson's offer to finance him until he could get a start in England and free his family from the curse of race prejudice. He had sometimes thought that he had been unfair to his children when he had declined that offer. Now Edwin should have the same chance. His son's health, however, was the paramount problem. After talking with Edwin's physician and with several friends who had spent more or less time in Europe, Chesnutt decided to send him abroad for a time. The climate of the Riviera would be good for his health, and later, in England, he could see what openings there were for a young man of his training and education. His mother was reluctant to let him go. Europe was a long way off; Ned was a young, inexperienced lad; and suppose something happened to him! Charles was made of sterner stuff. "He's a grown man, he's been away from home for four years, he has been well brought up and well educated. It's natural for a young man to leave his mother's apron-strings and strike out for himself."

On February 2, 1906, Edwin sailed for Europe. The family

waited anxiously for his letters. Both Susan and Charles began to have qualms about the wisdom of this journey. His first letter, sent by the pilot boat, gave his impressions of the ship and the passengers. Charles and Susan were delighted to learn that among the passengers was Mrs. Azalia Hackley, a friend of theirs who was going to Paris to study singing under de Reszke.

CHARLES TO EDWIN, FEBRUARY 5, 1906

Your mother has written a letter to Mrs. Hackley, which I enclose. Please seal it and send it to her address, which you probably have. We were pleased to know that you had run across her, as she is a cheerful soul, will doubtless prove a congenial spirit, and tide you over any little period of loneliness or depression.

I hope you had a pleasant passage, and that you are enjoying the sights of London. Keep your health always first in mind. It is that for which I sent you abroad. Have as good a time as you like, within the limits of strict economy, remembering that I am not carrying you, but merely boosting you along....

We missed you very much for a day or two, but are getting a little bit adjusted to your absence. The whole family has become wonderfully fond of you since you left; in fact, I can scarcely restrain them from starting off to Europe immediately to look you up. Doubtless they will all swarm over during the summer. Much love and best wishes.

EDWIN TO CHARLES, FEBRUARY 23, 1906

I am now in Paris, having come over from London three days ago. I intended to stay longer at that place, but the climate drove me out. In the matter of weather, I have had the worst kind of luck. I arrived at London on Friday afternoon, and it began to rain shortly after my arrival. It lasted all Saturday, Sunday, and Monday, and spoiled my pleasure entirely. In England there are no furnaces, and for three days and nights I shivered and shook in a temperature of 44 degrees, and a cold drizzle. My feet were never dry, and I was in pretty bad shape. So I grew discouraged and left London on Tuesday morning for Paris via Newhaven and Dieppe. Fortunately, it stopped raining that day, though it was still very chilly. I left London at 10:00 A. M., and arrived at Newhaven at noon.

During the crossing I made friends with a French *cuisinier* who was going to Metz. He could speak practically no English, so we

talked French, at least *he* did. We talked all the way, he telling
me the names of the different objects along the route. I learned
considerable French during the ride. We parted at the Gare St.
Lazarre.

When he left me, for a few minutes I had a feeling of desola-
tion intelligible only to a person, absolutely alone, in a foreign
city, without any great knowledge of the language, and no particular place to go. I had written to Bob Hemmings, and told
him I was coming, but as I walked up and down the platform of
that huge station, I could see nothing of him. At last I started
for the *douane* to see about my trunk and by a stroke of good fortune, ran into him. Then I felt better.

I am fortunate in having Hemmings to depend upon, as I
would be utterly lost without him. He is a typical student of the
quarter and I feel privileged to be with him, as it gives me a very
clear idea of what student life consists of in Paris. Let me say
right here, that Paris in books and Paris in reality are very different. In the first place, even though I can read and write French,
I can no more understand what the Parisians say to me than if
it were Chinese. I catch a phrase here and there, and that is
about all. It is a matter of months, and for some, years.

I am living the same life as the other fellows. Hemmings has
three American friends who are at the Académie Julien and we
eat together, and go around together.

At noon I go to the *atelier,* or the Académie Julien as it's called,
and meet Hemmings, and we all have *déjeuner* together. At 2:30
Hemmings goes back to the studio, and I shift for myself until
5:30, when we all meet again and spend the evening together.
It is not a "fast" life, but rather an indolent one.

There are few who have an entree to the *atelier,* so I am fortunate indeed. The fifteen or twenty minutes a day I spend there
are an education. It is the finest art school in the world as far as
turning out famous painters is concerned, and they are all proud
of it.

There must be thirty or more students there, and they come
from every quarter of the globe. They all speak French, however,
and it is a case of pandemonium all the time. They sing, yell,
fight, "jolly" the models, and paint for dear life at the same time.
The models walk around nude during the rests and everything
is taken as a matter of course. The building itself is an old "barn."

As regards my health, it is about the same—perhaps worse, as

I have a bad cold. It is raining today, and very chilly. The spring won't be here for some time yet, so I am going to Nice.

EDWIN TO THE FAMILY, FEBRUARY 28, 1906

Well here I am at last on the Riviera! It seems an age to me since I left Cleveland, yet it has been less than a month.

This hotel is like all country hotels, plain but good food, and large clean rooms. There are about 40 people here. I made friends right away with a young Pole who speaks good French, and a little English. We eat our meals together, and took a long walk together this morning. We get along very well when it comes to making ourselves understand each other.

As long as I am here, I can't help but improve. The air is fine and bracing, and the sunshine is beautiful today. The rain of yesterday was warm, and harmless. I am going to walk many miles and I shall report faithfully every day.

[And again],

This is the 1st of March, and I am free to say, it has been thus far the best first of March I ever saw, or ever hope to see. The beauty of the Riviera is the sunshine, and it is wonderful what a tonic it is to a weakened system. It is a bright, dazzling sort of sunshine that is never seen in Cleveland, or any other place in which I have been. The sky is a deep blue, the houses are all pink or white, the foliage is dark green, red, or orange, and the Mediterranean is deep blue. When you climb one of the hills in the vicinity, and see the wonderful panorama of mountains, valleys, villages and the sea spread before you, you then begin to appreciate what a privilege it is to be able to come down here.

CHARLES TO EDWIN, MARCH 6, 1906

Am sorry you did not find better weather in northern Europe, but I hardly expected you would find it warm. I don't understand why your feet should have been wet; you surely had money enough to buy rubbers, and you have yourself entirely to thank for not having dry feet, the importance of which it seems to me would have occurred to you with great force. If you had had some flannel underwear, as we have vainly endeavored to induce you to get, you would not have found it so chilly. I very much suspect that, after all, your health is a matter that is in your own hands, and if you want to help yourself off the surface of this earth or under it, you can very much contribute to that result by your own carelessness. . . .

Had I known that you would have such disagreeable weather, I should have had you go from here directly to a Mediterranean port, and you could have worked northward in the summer, thereby saving the double trip. Your mother and Helen speak of coming over in the summer, and in fact are trying to secure passage, in which event you will be expected to meet them in France or England, and act as their guide and attendant. . . .

Edwin's health improved greatly in the sunshine of the Riviera and while there he began to look forward to the future, and to make plans for his own career.

Susan, Helen and Dorothy sailed on the Steamship *Minneapolis* of the Atlantic Transport Line on the twenty-third of June. Mary and David Gibson moved into the Lamont Street house to keep Charles company for the summer.

The trip across was long and restful and altogether uneventful except for the news of the murder of Stanford White by Harry Thaw, for Mrs. William Thaw, the mother of Harry Thaw, was one of the passengers. But she seldom left her stateroom, and the captain had issued orders that no one was to tell her of the tragedy; so she did not learn about it until the steamer reached the other side.

Edwin met the family at St. Pancras Station, and conducted them to a very pleasant boarding house which he had found in Russell Square. Susan and the children had a wonderful summer. They made their headquarters in London, taking various trips from there. Then they went over to Paris and later up to Scotland. Susan could not stand a livelier pace.

In London they were entertained several times by the Coleridge-Taylors and by other friends that Edwin had made while there. They met friends from Cleveland and Washington. They joined some Brenton Street people in a trip to Stratford-on-Avon, and in between times they did the sights of London and vicinity. They rode on the tops of busses and reviewed their English classics. They spent hours in Westminster Abbey and St. Paul's and the Tower, and reviewed their English history. They took boat rides on the Thames to Greenwich and to Hampton Court and Kew. They visited the British Museum, the picture galleries, and the great parks and could not get enough of it all. But Susan began to get tired—it was all too strenuous for her, and she disliked the English food.

CHARLES TO THE FAMILY, JULY 5, 1906

I saw from the paper that the Minneapolis landed on Tuesday. I fear Edwin did not meet you at the dock, but I hope you got safely up to London and that he looked after you properly. The time distance between here and London is about six hours, and when I sit down to my meals I generally calculate what you folks are probably doing at the same moment.

I spent the Fourth in a somewhat humdrum way. It rained copiously the night before, and the grass was green and the trees fresh-looking. I decided to stay at home all day and write on my novel, but after breakfast went down to get my mail, and called at Grant Street on the way back, where I found Ed, Ethel, and Charlie getting ready to go out to one of the parks to picnic. I suggested that they come out to our house, which they did and brought their lunch along; Mrs. Gibson supplied them with coffee. After lunch Ed and I went to the ball game; score 2 to 1 in favor of Cleveland as against Detroit. On the way home we bought some firecrackers for Charlie, who, by the way, cut up all day like the very old Harry. When I went to shoot off the firecrackers he was "fwaid" and didn't want me to shoot off any more; so I gave the whole batch to Ed and told him to take them home and shoot them off where the crowd could enjoy them—there were not so very many.

I suppose you are now in the full enjoyment of your first impressions of the world's metropolis. Have a good time, while you have a chance. Mrs. Gibson is looking after my comfort and I am doing very well. I did a lot of hunting around for the flag yesterday and finally found it and hung it out. . . .

During this summer Chesnutt began to smoke. He and David Gibson would sit on the porch after dinner and discuss current events and philosophy and single tax, and other important matters. He found that he enjoyed an after-dinner cigar and he never dropped this pleasant habit.

SUSAN TO CHARLES, JULY 8, 1906

We are taking this afternoon for rest and letter-writing. We need the rest, for we started out about a half hour after arriving in London and have been going constantly ever since. Though footsore and weary, I have kept up with the children and am now able to climb up the steps of a bus in motion like a real Londoner. We never get inside if there is room on top.

I like the English people. They are polite and quiet. They are way ahead of Americans when it comes to good manners. We all like London, too. There are so many interesting things to see and I think we have put in our time to good advantage. . . .

The English are poor cooks, but we have found one or two French restaurants where we can get something fit to eat. I thought at first we would take our meals in the house, but after two days, I could not stand it.

We take our breakfast here and our other meals out. And such a breakfast! Dot says she lies awake at night thinking of that breakfast. I never tasted such a concoction as they give us for coffee; and the egg shells are so dirty, I have told our landlady that we do not care for boiled eggs in the morning. But we have style! We have a solemn looking butler, and a maid exactly like Eleanor Robeson in *Merely Mary Ann*. We are in the American colony and near the center of things. We can walk to some of the theaters.

Ned is much better in health, but I am afraid he has been too economical in regard to what he eats. I have told him if he cannot get along on his allowance, he had better get back to the States.

[And a week later],

We took tea with Mr. and Mrs. Coleridge-Taylor on Friday, the 13th, where we met Clarence White and Dr. Wilder of Washington, also two ladies from the West Coast of Africa who are living in London. In the evening, Mr. Coleridge-Taylor took the whole party to Croydon—there were twelve of us—to an orchestral concert, given by the students of the Croydon Conservatory, which Mr. Coleridge-Taylor conducted. We had a delightful afternoon and evening.

We have promised to see them again before we leave for Paris. I hear that Portia Washington * is in London and Mr. and Mrs. Washington are coming over in September. Portia doesn't want to go back to America, I hear. Ned feels the same way, but I think he ought to have something to keep him busy. He says he hopes to be able to get a position by November. We shall take him with us to Edinburgh and Paris. . . .

* Daughter of Booker T. Washington.

Susan to Charles, July 17, 1906

We are now located in Paris at 19 Rue Delambre. It is a very nice hotel of six stories. We have two beds in our room, and Edwin's room is quite near us.

We have not been here long enough to know whether we like it or not, as we have been here only one day. One thing we do like is the food. We get good food here which we could not get in England. The stuff I had to eat in London has completely upset my digestion, but I hope to get over that soon.

Edwin gets along nicely with the language and we have no trouble in making our wants known.

Charles to Edwin, July 20, 1906

I had two letters from the folks today, one from Susan and one from Helen. They say you do not eat enough to keep strong. Buck up, and eat your regular meals! I want you to get strong and healthy.

I note what you say about your progress in shorthand, etc. It is very gratifying. Also note what you say about coming home. I shall doubtless hear more from you on the subject—it is up to you. The climate is probably no better here than it was last winter, and the race prejudice is probably the same, though you may be better prepared to stand both.

Try to keep on good terms with the folks, and give them all the aid you can. *Eat plenty of nourishing food;* stay in the open air as much as possible and get strong—it takes a strong man to make a career in this strenuous world.

Dorothy to Charles, July 25, 1906

I have let the others do the writing to you while I rested. We walk so much and the cobblestones hurt my feet so that I almost wish that I didn't have these pretty Sorosis pumps I was so proud of when I left Cleveland. French shoes are terrible. You couldn't give me a pair! They have sharp pointed toes and just to look at peoples' feet when we ride in the trams and busses makes my feet ache in sympathy.

I love the meals at the *Maison Boudet*. We eat outside the restaurant on the pavement where tables are placed under an awning and enclosed by a hedge of bushes in pots to cut off the gaze of the passers-by. The place is frequented by French people

—rarely do we see Americans there. Ned speaks French so well now that we get on fine.

The horses over here work much harder than American horses, and in England they thrive on work, but the French horses look as though they would drop in their tracks. The French beat their horses a great deal.

I hope you are well and do not miss us too much. Much love from your little daughter.

SUSAN TO CHARLES, JULY 27, 1906

We have been seeing the sights of Paris, and drawing in culture with every breath. Dorothy and I have decided that we will have taken in so much culture by the time we reach home, we shall have to offset it by reading all the dime novels we can find.

Personally, I have seen all the cathedrals and castles and tombs of great men, and prisons, and in fact everything except pictures that I ever want to see. I do enjoy the pictures because I can sit down and rest between times. We have seen some fine things and shall put in a few more days at the Louvre and the Luxembourg. We have been leading a too strenuous life, and I intend to go slower as I am about used up. Ned likes to walk and when we start out, he says—"it is only a short distance," and we find when we reach the end that we have walked a mile or two. I can't stand the pace.

Tonight we are invited to tea at Mrs. Hackley's landlady's and Ned has been resting today, as he is to be the interpreter for the party. He says this jargon of French and English uses him up. It would amuse you to be near to hear this English-French conversation. It is very exciting.

We have been riding first-class in the trams here as the cars seem cleaner, and since the first-class fleas nearly eat us up, I don't care to tackle the second-class ones. We eat in the open air nearly all the time. I cannot drink the wine and am continuing the mineral water.

All join me in love to you. I received your letter yesterday, dated July 13. We seem to be cut off entirely from home, when a week passes without a letter.

The stay in Paris was cut short because Susan became ill. So they returned to London where they could get an English doctor.

SUSAN TO CHARLES, AUGUST 3, 1906

We are in London again, after spending two weeks and two days in Paris. The hot wave there drove us out.

We saw Mrs. Hackley several times; she left for the country the morning we left Paris. I like French cooking and the art galleries and the taximetres and the beautiful streets, but I must say the people as a rule are dirty and I do not like the way they live. I was completely exhausted for a couple of days for lack of sleep and the heat, too, perhaps.

You will hardly believe it when I tell you that the street in which we lived was not quiet one hour of the twenty-four. The people sat on the sidewalk and talked and laughed until midnight. When they quieted down, the heavy wagons started in, which annoyed me and prevented me from sleeping after tramping around all day. So I fled. Here, at least, I can sleep.

The children are well and thriving. I have a number of things to say about Edwin, but think I shall wait until I can talk confidentially about him. I am not at all convinced that he is doing as well here as in America, and after all, being able to eat in a restaurant, or having one's hair cut in a barber shop, is not all there is in life.

HELEN TO CHARLES, AUGUST 9, 1906

We have been enjoying London very much this time—it really seems like home. The crowd at our house has changed and is very pleasant—. There are two Americans besides us and the rest are mostly English. Everyone is so nice that I shall hate to leave. An English woman who has just come, thought we were South Americans, and I carefully explained that we were from the States. That mistake has been made several times. In France one of the waitresses thought we were Japanese! Ha! Ha! Everything but the real thing!

The Coleridge-Taylors have been very good to us. Tuesday we were out to dinner and spent the evening with them and became very well acquainted. They are extremely jolly people. Mr. Coleridge-Taylor said that he wanted us all alone so that he could really get to know us. They have given us photos of S. C-T. and the two children, Hiawatha & Gwendolen, so you can know what they look like. The children are beautiful and, as their mother says, a "wonderful contrast." The boy Hiawatha is like an Indian with a great mass of straight black hair, while the little girl Gwendolen is as dainty as a fairy, white and pink, big blue eyes and also a great mass of curly yellow hair. They both wear it long and are remarkable looking children.

Mr. C.-T. read your last book at one sitting and enjoyed it very much. Then I told him how much you enjoyed his Negro Melodies and as a great favor he played us one. We like them and I think the feeling is mutual.

Tomorrow we go to Edinburgh, on a little week-end trip from Friday until Tuesday. By taking this trip we save just half the fare. Mr. Coleridge-Taylor told us about it.

Then we spend three days more in London and then we start on the eighteenth for home. I am sorry we can't stay longer, but that is the best we could do. However, home will look good to us!

When the boat docked at New York Charles's beaming face was the first thing that Susan saw, and they all relaxed—Dad was on the job again!

When Susan had expressed her ideas about Edwin and his opportunities in England, Chesnutt decided that it was best for him to return to Cleveland, after completing his course at the Pitman School. So in November Edwin with few regrets returned home. He had had a wonderful adventure; his health was better; he was an accredited stenographer and typist; and the Atlantic Ocean was awfully wide.

23

The Everlasting Problem

LIFE ON Lamont Avenue had settled into a very pleasant pattern. The Chesnutts were living, for the most part, busy and satisfying lives. Chesnutt, although devoted to his business, found time to spare for many civic duties. He became a consultant on affairs pertaining to the interests of Cleveland's colored population, and was very generous with his time. Publishers sent him books on sociological matters for his opinion. Literary men and women, college professors, philanthropists asked his advice on the problems in which they were concerned. Young men and women sought help and encouragement in their upward struggle. He delivered addresses on the Negro problem in Cleveland and elsewhere. He felt that although he was not at that time accomplishing anything in a literary way, he was certainly helping, as far as he was able, with the world's work. The girls nicknamed him Mahatma.

Susan's happiness consisted mainly in promoting the welfare of her family. She was the mainspring of their existence. The rest of them lived so intensely that her increasing serenity and practical common sense were the salvation of them all. She expended untold efforts in keeping her home inviting and restful. The passion of her younger days for the semiannual housecleaning grew less as she became older. The steady output of electrical appliances made such orgies unnecessary, for which she and the family were grateful. Her sympathetic nature endeared her to all and made it possible to keep really efficient help in the house.

Although the house was much larger than her former home, the problems of keeping house were greatly mitigated. When one of the neighbors said to her one day, "Mrs. Chesnutt, how do you manage to keep your curtains so immaculate? You have the best looking windows in the neighborhood," Susan felt gratified, for the house had forty windows that required curtains, and this was no small compliment.

But her interests were by no means confined to her home and family. She was deeply interested in the work at Emmanuel Church, and arranged her time so that she could spend Wednesdays at the meetings of the Women's Guild, of which she was an active member for many years. Here the women met and sewed to make money for the church; they had luncheon there and exchanged opinions and recipes and gossip and had a thoroughly happy day. When Hedwig Kosbab decided that there ought to be a social settlement house out in the East End, Emmanuel Church helped her start a little club in an empty store out on 89th Street near Quincy Avenue, and Susan sent her daughters, Helen and Dorothy, to help Miss Kosbab.

The children were finding life satisfying and stimulating. Helen had not dreamed that teaching could be such pleasure. Dorothy was absorbed in her lessons and in the pleasant extra-curricular activities at Central High. Edwin was working in his father's office and dreaming of new adventures, for he was not yet ready to settle down.

But the family did not devote all their time to work. They had an active and pleasant social life, and they believed in vacations. They managed to get away, at least once a year, into some other environment where they met interesting people and old friends. They loved the East and their jaunts were generally in that direction. In the summer of 1908 they were widely scattered. Charles had decided on a sight-seeing trip through New England and Canada. Susan and Dorothy preferred Atlantic City, where they would meet their friends. Helen, who had had a serious case of typhoid fever during the previous winter, and Edwin chose Arundel-on-the-Bay, for the boating and bathing and healthy outdoor life appealed strongly to both of them. Charles took his vacation in July and the rest of them in August. Susan still believed in keeping the house open, so that Ethel and her little son came out to keep her father company while the rest were away.

During the fall Chesnutt delivered two addresses—one at the annual meeting of the Niagara Movement in Oberlin, and the other at the opening meeting of the Bethel Literary and Historical Association in Washington. In both speeches he stressed the fact that the Negro had no duties unless he had rights.

CHARLES TO EDWIN, OCTOBER 9, 1908

... I went down to Baltimore last Saturday night, stayed there over Sunday and until Monday noon, met a number of fine people, including Dr. Waring, Mr. Bishop and Mr. Hughes. I stopped at Dr. Hall's and visited the high school Monday morning. I then went on to Washington, was cordially received, and lavishly entertained. Lectured at the Bethel Literary Tuesday night to a very large audience, among whom were all the best people, and strange to say pleased them all with my lecture, which was on "Rights and Duties," referring, of course, to the everlasting problem. I labored like a mountain in bringing forth my arguments, and was greatly relieved that no one seemed to regard them as a mouse. . . .

On his return to Cleveland Chesnutt received a letter from Mrs. Carrie W. Clifford, a leader in the Niagara Movement, and devoted to the interests of the Negro, in which she compared Chesnutt's paper on "Rights and Duties" with Booker T. Washington's utterances as quoted by Ray Stannard Baker in a recent widely read article.

WASHINGTON, D. C.
October 9, 1908

DEAR MR. CHESNUTT:

I did not discuss your paper when presented here the other night, but am availing myself of the privilege of doing so now. The enclosed slip from the *Post* will explain the cause. It is because the white man is forever impressing upon the Negro his *duty,* saying nothing whatever of his rights that the radical Negroes are driven into saying and doing extreme things. *Why,* for instance, do you suppose the reporter saw fit to ignore and overlook all reference in your speech about the *rights* of the Negro, and to emphasize that we should lend all possible aid to the efforts of the Caucasians to better our condition? This makes me furious. What real efforts are the Caucasians putting forth as long as they continue to deprive the Negro of his rights?

The point that pleased me most about your most excellent paper was the clear and explicit manner in which you set forth the declaration that without *rights* there were no *duties.*

The following extract taken from Baker's September article is what set me thinking: "Instead of the foolish agitation for the enforcement of rights which the Negro is not yet ready in most instances to use with wisdom, how wise and humble is the teaching of Booker T. Washington emphasizing *duties* and responsibilities, asking his people to *prepare* themselves for *rights.*"

Now you must admit with me, in the light of your statement that "*duties* are the offspring of *rights*", how very "foolish" any such teaching as the foregoing is, and not in any sense "wise" though I suspect it may be "humble" enough. And in such points as these it is that thinking Negroes must take issue with Dr. Washington. . . .

Yours truly,

CARRIE W. CLIFFORD

CLEVELAND, OHIO Oct. 15, 1908

MRS. CARRIE W. CLIFFORD
1224 YOU ST. N. W.,
WASHINGTON, D. C.
MY DEAR MRS. CLIFFORD:

I am in receipt of your interesting letter of October 9th. Thanks for the newspaper cutting enclosed. What you mention is no new thing. Newspapers are looking for two things—something sensational, no matter how radical it is, or in default of the sensational, something that will fit in with current public opinion and make pleasant reading. It is the fad nowadays to ignore the rights of the Negro and emphasize his duties. The same rule is applied to whatever Mr. Washington says. He does emphasize the duties and says not a great deal about the rights, but what little he does say is practically ignored. That Mr. Washington is not indifferent to his rights may be gathered from the fact that when he makes a pilgrimage through a Southern State, as he is doing in Mississippi at present, he hires a special car for himself and his party.

I note the quotation from Mr. Baker's article. I read it and had it in my manuscript with some comment thereon, but do not remember whether I read it or not, my paper was so long. Agitation for rights is by no means foolish; where rights are denied it is a sacred duty; though of course it can be conducted in a foolish way. And of course you cannot hold Washington responsible for the language of Baker's article. You and I have no quarrel about the principle involved, nor about anything at all. Rights are fundamental; nothing can alter that fact.

I don't blame any one for becoming angry or impatient about the situation in this country. The only way for a colored person to keep calm about it is not to think about it. But there is a certain conservatism in discussion, and a certain philosophical point of view which I think quite as effective as hysterical declamation. But we need both—some to fan the flame and others to furnish the fuel.

With kind regards to Mr. Clifford, believe me,

Sincerely yours,
CHARLES W. CHESNUTT

The Negro's position in the country was actually getting worse. So bad was it that in May, 1909, a group of liberal-minded Americans who believed in democracy, under the leadership of William English Walling, called a great conference at Cooper Union in New York City to discuss the status of the Negro and to formulate a plan of action to improve his position. Chesnutt was urged to attend this conference but pressure of business prevented him from going. It was an epoch-making conference at which was formed the organization called the National Negro Committee, which a year later became The National Association for the Advancement of Colored People.

Among the speakers was the Honorable Wendell P. Stafford, associate justice of the Supreme Court of the District of Columbia. When Chesnutt read Stafford's speech he was encouraged. Here was a man in a high position, who felt exactly as he did and dared to say what he thought. Chesnutt wrote him the following letter:

June 25, 1909

HON. WENDELL P. STAFFORD
SUPREME COURT, DISTRICT OF COLUMBIA
WASHINGTON, D. C.
DEAR SIR:

My friend Mr. James A. Cobb, an attorney of your city, has kindly sent me a copy of your recent address at Cooper Union, New York, upon the subject of Negro rights. I had read it in the newspapers, I believe in the New York *Evening Post,* as an item of news, and have read it again more carefully in the form in which Mr. Cobb sends it.

Permit me to thank you as one equally interested, in a broad and general way, and more directly in a personal way, in the problem which you discuss. You have sounded a very high and noble note, striking at the very root of the matter. The brotherhood of man—the unity of mankind; equal citizenship; justice and equal opportunity for all men; respect for the Constitution and the laws; the danger of class discrimination; a patriotism broad enough to embrace all the people; a humanity wide enough to include the whole world—these are the principles which you advocate, and what better weapons with which to right a civic wrong and to complete the emancipation of both black and white from the lingering effects of the old system?

It has often been said that the future of the Negro in America lies in his own hands. This is only a half truth. A man cannot breathe without air, or eat without food, or develop without opportunity. And the future of the Negro will depend in great part upon the extent to which men like you and the other enlightened spirits who participated in the recent New York convention can influence public opinion to make for every man in this country the conditions under which alone the rapid elimination of the race problem is possible.

Thanking you again, I am

Yours very truly,
CHARLES W. CHESNUTT

In contrast with the noble note sounded in New York by the great liberal leaders of thought was the position taken by the Right Reverend William M. Brown, Bishop of Arkansas. Bishop Brown was born in Ohio and educated in the North but on moving to the South had become more rabidly hostile to the Negro's cause than the Southerners themselves. He and Chesnutt had met in Cleveland and had discussed the Negro problem. At that time Brown promised to send Chesnutt his book entitled *The Crucial Race Question.* One day it arrived with a note from the Bishop saying that he had pleasant remembrances of their meeting at Cleveland and hoped that their paths might cross again sometime. But after reading Chesnutt's letter commenting on the book, he probably modified his hope somewhat. Chesnutt wrote:

CLEVELAND, NOV. 7, 1909

RT. REV. WILLIAM M. BROWN
BISHOP OF ARKANSAS
1222 SCOTT ST.
LITTLE ROCK, ARK.
DEAR SIR:

I beg to acknowledge, somewhat tardily, the receipt of an autographed copy of your book, *The Crucial Race Question,* and to thank you for the courtesy.

For the book itself, I am quite sure that I dissent radically from its views. I could not imagine myself approving a book which condemns to infamy and all kinds of hopeless inferiority so many of my fellow creatures, my fellow citizens, my fellow Christians, and my friends.

The fact that race prejudice is prevalent north, south, and anywhere else, is no argument at all to my mind to establish its justice, its wisdom, or that it has the divine sanction.

I do not know whether it ever occurred to you—it certainly has to me—that if the Creator had intended to prevent the intermixture of races, he might in His infinite wisdom have accomplished this purpose by a very simple method, as he has by the physiological laws which prevent the confusion of genera in the lower animals. I think it very fortunate for humanity that not all the ministers of God agree with you in your views in regard to the Negro. If so, his future fate in the country of his birth and citizenship, would be very sad and very hopeless.

I take pleasure in sending you a copy of a book from my own pen, which treats the same general subject in a very different manner. With hope that you may read it with interest, I remain.

Sincerely yours,
CHARLES W. CHESNUTT

The year 1909 had brought several changes to the Chesnutt family. Edwin had gone down to West Virginia and was now employed at Welch as stenographer in the office of the Hungarian-American Miners and Mine Employees Legal Aid and Protective Society. He was studying law, and also getting some practice in justice court. In September Chesnutt's son-in-law resigned from his position as librarian at Western Reserve University to accept the principalship of the M Street High School in Washington, D. C. Dorothy entered the College for Women of Western

Reserve University in September. The family was small and her mother did not care to send her away.

In February, 1910, Edwin was offered a position as stenographer in the principal's office at Tuskegee. The letter said that they were "in search of a young man who would be willing to affiliate himself with the institution and who would be willing to do a considerable amount of very hard work."

It went on to say that the machinery of the office was rather complicated, and the salaries were not as flattering as they wished, but that they felt that if he could see his way clear to consider the matter favorably he would find there an opportunity which he would in time appreciate. Edwin sent the letter on to his father for counsel.

CHARLES TO EDWIN, MARCH 8, 1910

I have your letter of the 3rd. Pardon my delay in not having answered it sooner. Whether the Washington offer amounts to anything depends somewhat on what you are doing there. Two or three fellows have made good under Mr. Washington's wing, but I imagine he is a very absorbing kind of person and uses his assistants for all they are worth. Of course this is good business on his part. Whether you could get anything out of it or not would depend upon several contingencies. I don't think the salary offer is anything to speak of. I don't know that you are worth any more, but Ethel went down there for a year on the same basis and I had to pay her fare either one way or both—in other words she didn't get enough out of it to keep her and pay her railroad fare both ways.

Of course if you had the literary faculty and could write nice letters and get up nice literature you might be valuable to Mr. Washington. On the other hand, if you go down there you will forego any chances of getting admitted to the bar. I judge from your previous letters that you are aiming at this.

I hesitate to advise you. I don't know what sort of future Tuskegee would hold out for you. You would in any event be only a small satellite of a great man, and I notice that those who are ambitious for themselves sooner or later break away from him. I hesitate to advise you really. I want to see you get nailed down somewhere sometime, if not in some place at least in some pursuit or profession. I have been hoping you might qualify for the bar. If I had thought in the beginning that you were going to adopt shorthand as a profession I should have seen that you were trained in it years ago. Perhaps I made a mistake in that regard. But think it out and do the best you can for yourself.

Early in the spring Chesnutt received a letter from Walling asking him to address the annual meeting of the National Negro Committee which had been organized the year before. He replied:

CLEVELAND, OHIO
April 18, 1910

WILLIAM ENGLISH WALLING, ESQ.
ROOM 422, 500 FIFTH AVE.
NEW YORK
MY DEAR MR. WALLING:

I am in receipt of your letter of April 17th suggesting that I address the National Negro Committee during its approaching meeting in May, on "The Effect of Disfranchisement in the Courts." I see no reason why I should not, in fact many reasons why I should do all that I can to further the work of this organization, and I will very cheerfully undertake to deliver such an address provided you think it worth while. As I have spent very little time in the South for a number of years, I could have little to say about actual experience in southern courts, but I have kept in close touch with the southern situation, and since the argument would in any event be largely upon principle, I have no doubt I can find something to say.

I am reasonably familiar with the proceedings of the conference at the meeting in 1909; at least I followed them closely in the rather full report which was published in the New York *Evening Post,* and I read the address by Judge Stafford, of which Mr. Cobb was good enough to send me a copy, and of course I am familiar with the views and utterances of, I think, every speaker on the last year's program with the exception of two or three. If there was a complete report of the proceedings published I should be much obliged if you would kindly advise me where I can procure a copy of same; and of course I should like a copy of the program for the May meeting as soon as it is completed.

Cordially yours,
CHARLES W. CHESNUTT

Chesnutt returned home in a very enthusiastic mood about this organization, for he felt that at last an organization had been established that could really do some effective work.

Helen had been ill all spring with a serious digestive disorder and had withdrawn from school for the remainder of the year. When Dr. Washington came to Cleveland in April and learned of her illness he promptly invited her down to Tuskegee to visit Mrs. Washington and see his school.

HELEN, AT TUSKEGEE, TO FAMILY, MAY 15, 1910, 6:30 A.M.

This is about the only time I shall have to write today, so I have gotten up early to do it. Have I written anything about social affairs since last Sunday?

There is always a great deal going on here, and one can keep very much occupied, but Mrs. Washington told people when I came that I was down here for my health, and besides the usual affairs which have almost used me up, people haven't given many extra things.

The big annual military hop took place last night in the dining hall. The school is a military school and the student officers are permitted to have this ball once a year. All the teachers attend and it is the greatest social event of the year. The dining hall is huge—large enough to seat 1600 students, so you see that we were not crowded.

Mrs. Lettie Nolan Calloway is also visiting Mrs. Washington and we three went over about half-past eight....

I danced a great deal and enjoyed myself immensely, although at first, I felt terribly stiff. Not being accustomed to much social life, I found it rather hard to be hurled into the midst of a real ball. During a dance one of the men said to me, "Miss Chesnutt, are you having the kind of visit that you enjoy? We understand that you are down here to rest and that you want a very quiet time, so we haven't had as lively a time as we otherwise would have given you."

I responded, "A quiet time! If you call this kind of visit quiet, I should certainly hate to be involved in a lively one. I am nearly dead now."

He thought I was joking, but I told him, though Tuskegee might seem tame to him, it was absolutely hilarious to me.

Even dull as Cleveland is, I have actually been homesick this week. It is quite cold here, and I think that has affected me....

I must tell you about seeing Halley's comet. Thursday night I determined to see it. I shall have to make a little introduction first. The Washington home is guarded every night from five o'clock until five in the morning. They don't bother to lock doors and windows, but have guards who patrol the grounds and thus protect the place. I sleep on the first floor, windows up, and often the guard stalks by my window in the middle of the night.

Well, Thursday night I awoke at 2:30. Dead silence and inky blackness. I got up and put on some clothes and went to the parlor windows to see the comet. No comet visible. Then I opened the front door and tiptoed out, way out to the end of the porch to see what could be seen. I was scared to death all this time. Just as I got to the port-cochère, a great big guard loomed up in front of me. Well, he was scared and so was I. However, he told me that the comet wasn't visible yet, but that when it appeared, he would call me. I walked him around to the other porch and showed him my windows and at 3:30 he appeared with a lantern and called me and we went way down to the end of the grounds where it could be seen beautifully. It certainly was an awe-inspiring experience to see it spreading out all over the sky. . . .

I must stop now and begin to get dressed. We have some distinguished guests for breakfast this morning, and I am going to get ready for church before breakfast. Love to all of you.

In the meantime Edwin was debating with himself whether or not to accept the position at Tuskegee. His mother and Helen urged him to do so. Helen wrote him such glowing letters from Tuskegee that he finally decided to go.

EDWIN TO CHARLES, MAY 29, 1910

I don't think I would ever have reconsidered the matter but for Helen and Ma, but I have a great deal of confidence in Nell's judgment and she is most insistent that I go. I feel that I will get ahead there. I did not ask your advice this time, but that was because I wanted to put all the responsibility on myself. You hesitated to advise me about the same thing three months ago, and I saw no reason why you shouldn't hesitate to advise me again. I think you will agree, however, that it is a step upward.

Ethel writes me she is going to Tuskegee on Tuesday, so I can meet her there and get some pointers. On the whole, while I think that you are not wholly pleased with my decision, the die is cast, and I hope in a very short space of time to convince you that I am doing a wise thing.

24

Honored Citizen of Cleveland

EARLY IN June, 1910, Chesnutt who had never had a serious illness, whose good health and great vitality were the marvel of
everyone that knew him, collapsed in his office one morning and
was hurried to Huron Road Hospital, where he remained unconscious for several days.

After a few weeks he was brought home with a trained nurse
in attendance and by the middle of July had recovered sufficiently to walk around. The doctor informed Susan that he had
had a slight stroke, that he need not necessarily expect another,
but that he could never lead the strenuous life that he had hitherto.

In August Susan, Dorothy, and Helen took Charles to Sea Isle
City in New Jersey.

CHARLES TO ETHEL, SEPTEMBER 1, 1910

Your interesting letter was forwarded to me at Sea Isle City,
New Jersey. At that time I was just beginning a month of recuper-
ation and was not as well as I am now. We spent a delightful
month by the seashore, and I find myself at the end of it rejuvenated and ready for my fall business. The sea breeze was delightful, the surf bathing was bracing, and the town was quiet and
more or less interesting. There was a board walk two or three
miles long; the beach was delightful for walks; there were small
towns in the vicinity, and Atlantic City was not a great distance
away. We managed to put in four weeks very pleasantly, and I
was sorry to feel obliged to come away. Your mother and Helen

and Dorothy profited equally by the vacation and they are all in fine health and spirits and join me in love to you.

At the meeting of the National Negro Committee in May a permanent organization had been formed under the name of the National Association for the Advancement of Colored People, and one important work of the conference was the making of plans for raising funds to carry on the work. It was decided to hold meetings in other cities and to spread the movement in all directions as fast as possible. In September, William English Walling started West to promote the movement.

A letter from Walling in October informed Chesnutt that they had had a very successful meeting in Chicago along the same lines as the New York meetings, with Jane Addams, Rabbi Hirsch, Jenkin Lloyd Jones, and Dr. Davis as speakers. He went on to ask Chesnutt to plan a Cleveland meeting. He would be able to remain in Cleveland only two days, the following Saturday and Sunday, but during that time he wanted to meet some of the leading white Clevelanders who would be interested in such a movement and the leading colored people of the city, with an informal meeting of both on Sunday, to hear important speakers, and thus start a Cleveland movement. Chesnutt replied:

CLEVELAND, OHIO
October 13, 1910

MR. WILLIAM ENGLISH WALLING
4127 DREXEL BOULEVARD
CHICAGO, ILLINOIS
MY DEAR MR. WALLING:

I am in receipt of your letter. I am glad that you had a successful meeting in Chicago. I am sorry Miss Blascoer could not have come on, for I was counting on her cooperation in working up a certain end of this meeting. I am afraid we are going to fall down on the white side. Cleveland is a great and prosperous city, the sixth in the union, but there is a surprising dearth of people like Miss Addams, Dr. Hirsch, and our friends in New York. Racial conditions in Cleveland are peculiar, as I can explain to you when I see you, and I find it difficult to think of half a dozen white people who would take an active, not to say an aggressive part in our movement. However, I think we will have a large meeting for you on Sunday afternoon, and will do what I can toward carrying out your suggestions. If you will call me up by

telephone, Bell Main 2164, when you get to Cleveland on Saturday, I shall see you at the Hollenden and we can talk the matter
over.

Very sincerely yours,
CHARLES W. CHESNUTT

Chesnutt went ahead with his plans; Susan invited Mr. and
Mrs. Walling to dinner on Saturday evening and also invited the
leading colored people of Cleveland to meet them afterwards at
a reception, where plans for starting a Cleveland branch of the
NAACP were discussed. Chesnutt was at the beginning a member
of the General Committee of the National Association for the
Advancement of Colored People, and in January, 1912, he became a Cleveland member of the Advisory Committee, along with
Dr. Charles F. Thwing, president of Western Reserve University,
and the Honorable Harry C. Smith, editor of the Cleveland
Gazette.

Booker T. Washington had been traveling in England and
Europe during the fall of 1910, delivering speeches and optimistic
utterances on the condition of the Negro in the United States.
Several of the leading Negroes in the country were violently
opposed to Washington; his philosophy was so abhorrent to them
that they were unable to see the good in anything with which he
was concerned. An interview published in the *London Morning
Post* stirred up such bitter feeling among them that they wrote a
protest entitled "Race Relations in the United States," in which
they repudiated Washington's utterances. Chesnutt was asked by
W. E. B. DuBois to sign this protest.

His answer to Dr. DuBois is interesting:

CLEVELAND, OHIO
November 21, 1910

DR. W. E. B. DUBOIS
20 VESEY STREET
NEW YORK CITY
MY DEAR DR. DUBOIS:

I have your letter of November 15, enclosing copy of paper
entitled "Race Relations in the United States," and asking
whether I would care to sign it. In view of the very close relations
of members of my family with Tuskegee—my son is in Mr.
Washington's office, one of my daughters has taught there for
several summers, and another was Mrs. Washington's visitor for

a number of weeks this year—and in view further of the fact that I am a nominal member of the Committee of Twelve and signed my name to Mr. Washington's latest appeal for an increase of the Tuskegee endowment, I question whether it would be quite in good taste for me to sign what in effect is in the nature of an impugnment of Mr. Washington's veracity, or at least which it would be only human in him to look upon in the light of a personal attack.

As to the merits of the case—I have read the interview in the *London Morning Post,* which I presume is the expression of Mr. Washington's upon which the protest is based. After all, it is only the ordinary optimistic utterance, to which we are all well accustomed. Mr. Washington is a professional optimist, avowedly so. I imagine the English as well as the Americans understand this fact and take his statements with a grain of salt. The utterances of Mr. Archer, Sir Harry Johnston and Mr. H. G. Wells would indicate that the English understand the situation pretty thoroughly. But after all, it is largely a matter of the point of view. Mr. Washington says in that interview, "The Negro problem in the United States will right itself in time"; this I think we all hope and believe to be the fact. He says further, "I believe, that when America comes to a more accurate understanding of the difficulties which the masses of the working people in other parts of the world have to struggle against, it will have gone far towards solving what is called the race problem." I see nothing wrong about that; it is a philosophic reflection which ought to have a great deal of truth in it.

He says further with regard to the racial problem in America, "I know that some writers draw alarmist pictures, but I look forward to the future with hope, and confidence." Well, I think we all look forward to the future with hope, though the degree of confidence varies so far as the immediate future is concerned. Mr. Washington says further, "any one who lives in the South, where the black men are so numerous, knows that the situation, so far from becoming more difficult or dangerous, becomes more and more reassuring." This is a matter of opinion, and Mr. Washington lives in the South, while not more than one or two of the signers of the protest do, unless Washington be regarded as part of the South. Personally, I have not been any farther South than Washington but once in twenty-seven years.

Mr. Washington says in this interview that "in America as in

Europe and elsewhere the worst happenings are those that get talked about." You have recently published a newspaper letter in which the same statement is made (apropos of the condition of the colored soldiers in the west). Mr. Washington's statement in this interview about the business relations of white and black people is, I think, a little optimistic, but he knows more about them than I do. "Great industrial concerns" is rather a large term to apply to such ventures among colored people; the recent failure of the True Reformers is a case in point. "The racial feeling in America is not nearly so strong as many persons imagine." This may or may not be true; I should like to think that it is. On the whole, if the protest is based solely on this interview, it hardly seems sufficient to bear it out.

If I were inclined to criticize the wording of the protest, I might ask, does it not lean too far the other way; is it not at least equally as pessimistic as Mr. Washington's interview was optimistic? Nowhere does Mr. Washington say that the condition of the Negro in the United States is satisfactory. The protest says among other things that "because of his dependence on the rich charitable people, he has been compelled to tell, not the whole truth but that part of it which certain powerful interests in America wish to appear as the whole truth." Admitting the fact, is the reason clear? If the word "interests" is used in the ordinary sense of political magazine controversy, I am unable to imagine what "powerful interests" could wish to keep the Negro down. The statement is at least a little obscure.

Mr. Washington does not deny in terms that the Negro problem is the greatest of American problems; it is quite consistent with its gravity that conditions should be improved. The statement that "black men of property and university training can be, and usually are, by law denied the ballot" is scarcely correct. They are in many cases denied the ballot, but hardly "by law," as covered by Mr. Ray Stannard Baker's article in the November *Atlantic,* which I read with interest.

There is, it seems to me, a little inconsistency in another respect. In one place the protest states, "No sooner had we rid ourselves of nearly two-thirds of our illiteracy," etc., than the ballot was taken away. Is it true that even in the very narrowest sense of the term illiteracy as used in the census, namely the mere ability to read and write, two-thirds of the Negroes had reached that point fifteen years ago? In a later statement it is stated that "not one black boy in three in the United States has a chance to learn to read and write." This may be true, but if so, it shows in comparison with the former statement a very disastrous falling off. Mr. Washington states in his interview that education is "general"; he does not state that it is universal—as it ought to be. I think the statement about our women in the South is a little broad. Also the statement about the courts. The wording of the protest would seem to imply that universally throughout the South the courts are used "not to prevent crime and to correct the wayward among Negroes, but to wreak public dislike and vengeance, and to raise public funds." I should hate to think that this is true. Negroes, as we all know, do not always, perhaps rarely, get equal justice in the courts, especially where the question of race is involved. But it would be a libel on humanity to charge all the courts of always having such an attitude of mind. The collection of revenue by levying fines is not confined to the South; it is a practice of criminal law everywhere, and our police courts are largely used as a means of revenue North as well as South.

The protest speaks of Mr. Washington suffering daily insult and humiliation. Insult and humiliation are largely subjective, a matter of personal feeling, and I have no idea that Mr. Washington feels himself daily insulted and humiliated. Whether he ought to is a question. As a fact, I imagine he thinks that he is daily honored and uplifted. It is possible that, visiting a foreign country as a distinguished American, he may have thought that the reception accorded to colored Americans visiting Europe would not be improved by making such a statement as that contained in the appeal. We know that our rights in the North are affected by the knowledge of the North of the manner in which we are treated in the South. Possibly Mr. Washington may have been, consciously or unconsciously, influenced by such a point of view. Moreover, the protest is signed by a number of gentlemen, most of whom hold or have held positions of honor and profit, political and otherwise, which they certainly could not have attained without the good will and sense of justice of white people, however imperfect that sense of justice may be in some other respects.

I have always believed that the Negro in the South will never get his rights until there is a party, perhaps a majority, of southern white people friendly to his aspirations. If Mr. Washington can encourage the growth of such a feeling in the South, he will have done a good work even though he should fall short in other respects.

I think the reason first given by me is sufficient for my declining to sign the protest. The other reasons I think will justify me in feeling that I have not failed in my duty in so declining. It would be a lamentable thing to believe that all the money and all the effort on the part of the colored people since the war had not resulted in improving their condition; and if it is improving, it is on the way to favorable solution. There are many things yet to be done; some of them, of which Mr. Washington has fought shy, the NAACP seeks to accomplish. There is plenty of room and plenty of work for both. I make no criticism of any of the gentlemen who have signed the appeal, but personally I should not, as I say, like to "pitch into" Mr. Washington.

With sincere regards and best wishes,

CHARLES W. CHESNUTT

In December, 1910 Chesnutt became a member of the Rowfant Club. This nationally known club was composed of men who loved and collected books. Among them were many of Chesnutt's friends, men who were acknowledged leaders on the Cleveland scene. Some years earlier several of his warm friends and admirers had proposed his name for membership, but one or two members, as he was afterwards told, had thought that "the time hadn't come" for opening the doors to men of Negro descent no matter what their qualifications were. Chesnutt was nothing if not philosophical, and he had said to Susan, who was very indignant indeed, "It would be mighty nice to be a member of the club, but if they don't want me, I can get along without them." But now he had been elected into the club and was one of the chosen. His letter to Mr. Goff in answer to his congratulations explains his attitude:

CLEVELAND, OHIO
December 10, 1910

F. H. GOFF, ESQ.
CLEVELAND TRUST COMPANY
CITY
MY DEAR MR. GOFF:

I have your kind note, and thank you very much.

A month or two ago, Ginn asked me one day if I would care to join the Rowfant Club, observing that he thought there would be no difficulty about it this time. I replied that if they could stand it, I could, but that I would like to have him feel pretty certain about the matter before he put my name up, as I would not care to go twice through the same experience. It went through all right, and I anticipate considerable pleasure from the company of the gentlemen with whom I am "at last found worthy to associate."

Sincerely yours,

CHARLES W. CHESNUTT

Another pleasant event, of 1910 was the publication of "The Wife of His Youth" in the *Journal de Genève*. The story appeared serially in the *feuilleton* of the paper in the issues of November 4, 5, and 6. The translation into French was excellent and the whole family read it with keen pleasure.

The year 1911 was uneventful. Chesnutt had not entirely recovered from the severe illness of the previous year. His sense of humor was dimmed; his exuberance, his delight in singing and piano-playing, his *joie de vivre* were sadly diminished. He wrote a little now and then, played solitaire in the evenings, but lacked the burning enthusiasms of former times. The girls would say to Susan, "Dad never smiles any more—it's like a graveyard around here." But Susan knew that it required time to recover physically and spiritually from such an illness as he had had, and she reassured them.

That fall he was chosen president of the Cleveland Council of Sociology, to which he had been elected in 1905, and of which he had been secretary for some time. The membership of this organization was made up of leading ministers, judges, lawyers, educators, and social workers of Cleveland who studied and discussed the city's civic and social problems and tried earnestly to find solutions for them.

He started off at once with an innovation that won the appreciation of all members. He had someone lead off in the opposition after a paper was read, and the meetings became much more interesting and valuable.

Newton D. Baker was candidate for Mayor for the term 1912-14, and made a very lively and successful campaign, during which Chesnutt accompanied him and reported his speeches. He enjoyed this work very much, for Baker was a brilliant speaker and quoted frequently from the classics, which delighted Chesnutt. He admired Baker for his idealism, his sense of justice, and his scholarship. They became good friends.

Meantime Chesnutt's work in the interests of the Negro continued with unabated zeal:

February 10, 1912

HON. THEODORE E. BURTON
U. S. SENATE
WASHINGTON, D. C.
MY DEAR MR. BURTON:

I presume you have noted the fact that a flood of protest has been pouring into Washington against the appointment of Judge Hook to the Supreme Bench, because of an unfriendly and prejudiced decision of his in a "jim crow" railroad case. I have spoken with you at times about this matter, and you seemed to feel that any agitation in behalf of the rights of colored men was a hopeless cause. I judge from recent newspaper items that this particular protest is likely to prove effective, and I trust that if you have any influence in connection with this appointment, as you certainly will with its confirmation, if made, that you will use it in accordance with the traditions of your party, of your city, and, as I fondly believe, with your own personal convictions.

Yours respectfully,
CHARLES W. CHESNUTT

Senator Burton replied that he had at once spoken with the President about the matter, and that the colored people had a real friend in President Taft. Burton admitted that he himself was keenly disappointed in conditions pertaining to the colored race.

Early in the year some of Chesnutt's business associates, who were members of the Rowfant Club and of the Chamber of Commerce suggested to him that he ought to belong to the Chamber. He was, they said, closely in touch, through his business, with most matters of interest to the Chamber and his active cooperation in its work would be a benefit to the organization.

March 11, 1912

MR. HENRY J. DAVIES
ELECTRIC BUILDING
CITY
MY DEAR HENRY:

I am enclosing herewith my application, duly signed, for membership in the Chamber of Commerce. If I am elected, I shall take pleasure in my membership largely because of the fact that I shall be associated with you.

Sincerely yours,

CHARLES W. CHESNUTT

He was unanimously elected to membership by the board of directors, and served as a member for many years—years pleasant to himself, and profitable to the organization because of his earnestness, disinterestedness, and public spirit.

25

A Summer Abroad

THE FAMILY had been suggesting a real vacation for Charles—a trip to Europe perhaps. Charles refused to go alone. On his first trip abroad he had been terribly homesick and he did not care to repeat the performance. Susan disliked strenuous sight-seeing trips; she found them difficult physically; so Helen was chosen to go with her father and take care of him. Susan and Dorothy decided that they would be pretty lonesome in Cleveland without Charles and Helen, and they made happy plans for an extensive eastern trip with the hope of meeting Edwin during his vacation.

CHARLES TO SUSAN, JULY 3, 1912, ON S. S. MARQUETTE

This is the last evening on the ship. Helen has written you a 12-page letter today, and has doubtless told you all about the trip. We have had a smooth passage, warm weather up to the last three or four days, and an uneventful voyage. There are about 125 passengers, most of them teachers and college students, a great many of them Southerners. Helen was very skittish for awhile, and held me rigidly down; but I had a copy of *The Conjure Woman* with me and lent it to a passenger, and when they were getting up a program for the concert, I was asked and had to read a story, which I did with great success, receiving many compliments, and developing into quite a character.

The trip has been quite long—two weeks less a day or half a day, before we land. We are now in the English Channel having passed the Scilly Isles this morning at breakfast, and the Isle of Wight early this afternoon.

The meals have been fairly good, though we have sighed more than once for home cooking. There is a fairly good library on board of which I have read many books, and with bathing and eating and walking the deck and conversation with the passengers, we have put in the time very pleasantly, though we shall be very glad to land in the morning, as we hope to do. It has really been much less monotonous than I anticipated. There are one or two interesting men on board.

We had a field day—obstacle races, bun-eating contest, broad grin contest, relay races, shoe races, tug of war, needle-threading contest, etc., and a concert with eighteen numbers, of which, as I say, I contributed one. We have had pleasant table-mates, and roommates, and all in all, have enjoyed the first stage of our journey. We reach Antwerp tomorrow, and shall go from there to Bruges; Helen, I imagine, has told you the rest. By the time this reaches you, you will be at the seashore, and I hope enjoying yourselves.

[And a week later],

This is our 5th day in the Netherlands. We have been to Antwerp, Bruges, Brussels, and are now at the Hague, where we arrived yesterday. The clock is striking 10 in the evening, and the air is full of the chimes from a neighboring church. It has been so in every city; the chimes are wonderful. Helen has gone upstairs, and I am writing this in the writing room of the hotel, which is a very clean and pretty one, with an excellent cuisine and good beds, though the bedrooms are rather small here. In Belgium we spoke French and ate coffee and rolls for breakfast. Here, since few speak French and we don't know any Dutch, we speak very little and have Dutch breakfasts—this morning it was veal loaf and sliced dried beef, bread and butter, cheese, stewed strawberries and coffee. Then we went through a couple of museums and saw some very fine pictures of Rembrandt, Rubens, Paul Potter, Van Dyck etc., etc.

Afterwards we took a street car and went out to Scheveningen, the Dutch "Atlantic City," stayed there a couple of hours on the beach and had tea at a restaurant overlooking the sea. We heard part of a concert on a long pier like those at Atlantic City and Cape May; then took the car back to the Zoological Garden, where Helen took snapshots and raved over the flowers. Dutch flower gardens are wonderful; the woods are beautiful. The houses, the streets and public places, the hotel rooms, all are kept spotlessly clean, and the cheeses and sausages, etc., displayed in the windows are simply out of sight and keep us hungry all the time looking at them.

Tomorrow we go in the morning, by electric railway, to Rotterdam, and back in the P.M., stopping at Delft. The following morning we will finish up the Hague and go on to Amsterdam, our last stop in Holland. Belgium and Holland are very interesting countries, and we shall come home loaded with impressions and interesting reminiscences....

CHARLES TO DOROTHY, JULY 18, 1912

I am answering your letter written before you left for the seaside, where I suppose you are now cooling yourself in the same waves that we sailed over for fourteen days; at least I saw a great many of them headed towards America, where I suppose they have arrived ere this.

Helen and I have quite a bit of fun, chasing from city to city. We can't stay long anywhere and cover our itinerary. Day before yesterday we left Cologne at 8 P.M., arrived in Frankfort at 10, to find the city in full possession of a *Schützenfest* or convention of gunnery clubs.

Today we visited Schloss Heidelberg—the castle—and the University, which is coeducational—that is, women attend the lectures and take the academic degrees, and degrees in everything I understand, except law. The students belong to different corps, which are distinguished by different colored caps. For instance, Helen and I dined today at a restaurant frequented, for the midday meal, by students who wear the red caps. Besides the red caps, most of them carried canes, some of them had bull dogs, and most of them had badly scarred heads and faces, the results of the student duels. They are extremely courteous—indeed it is the custom of the country—and take off their caps to one another, all the way down.

At six P.M.—it is now 5:45—we shall take the train for Baden-Baden, after that, tomorrow, to Schaffhausen, arriving at Lucerne for Sunday, where we shall stop for several days, have some laundry done, and rest up for Italy. Helen is "doing noble"— can stand almost as much hard sight-seeing as I can.

Charles to Susan, from Lucerne, July 23, 1912

We are on the eve, or rather the morning of our departure from this beautiful city, set in the bosom of the mighty Alps, by the side of a beautiful lake, flanked by imposing hotels and pretty villas all along its shores from one end to the other. The principal business of the country is hotel-keeping, so far as I can see.

This is our fourth day in Lucerne and we are leaving this morning for Italy. We have steamed from one end of the lake to the other, had some beautiful drives, heard some inspiring music, both sacred and profane, climbed—I should say ridden-up Pilatus, the highest, most rugged and most imposing mountain in these parts, seen the famous Lion of Lucerne, spent four days in a very beautifully situated and well-conducted pension, the first we have tried. It has more of the social atmosphere than a hotel—you get acquainted with people and talk to them and they to you. There are people here of all sorts—Mexicans, Italians, Irish-Americans, Scotch-Americans, plain Yankees, Southerners, and Helen says two new arrivals are colored people from the U. S., tho I don't believe it. . . .

We had a delightful trip here down the Rhine from Cologne, through Frankfort, where we saw Goethe's house and a Zeppelin dirigible airship in flight—we have an aeroplane stabled right across the lake here and have seen it several times in flight, once very near, over a boat on which we were riding. . . .

Susan to Charles, July 28, 1912

This week at Hampton has been a strenuous one but I have enjoyed it. The convention is over and most of the delegates have gone. There are still a few left on the grounds. Mrs. Washington, Mrs. Logan, Mrs. Bruce and Mrs. Napier are still here so we shall not feel lonely for the few days we must remain before going on to Lawrenceville. We are expected there the first of August, and I shall be there just two days and go from there to Atlantic City where we hope to recover from the past few days of strenuous living. The convention was great. There were about three hundred women on the grounds, most of them brainy and doing things for the uplift of humanity. We people who are living in Cleveland can't imagine the great work to be done outside. I have almost decided to go into Club work. . . .

Hampton is a wonderful place. The spirit of helpfulness one sees all around is inspiring. When a young person leaves this place he is able to do things and does not have to waste time in experiments. They have actual experience before they start out. . . .

Helen and her father were certainly enjoying themselves. By the time they reached Italy Charles was as gay as a small boy, and almost as irresponsible. He pretended that they were invisible, that no one could see them or hear them, and said outrageous things about the people around them. Once in a dining car, the young woman opposite him who had been talking volubly in French with her companion, took out a cigarette case and began to smoke. Charles with a twinkle in his eye remarked to Helen "The bold young hussy," and then confidentially, "Isn't it great to be able to talk about people inaudibly, so to speak?"

Helen was somewhat embarrassed for she had caught a glint in the young woman's eye. A minute later Charles was confounded by hearing the conversation slide from French to English so smoothly that for a moment he wasn't conscious of the change. His confusion was so great that the other three began to laugh; the day was saved and the remainder of the time was spent in pleasant conversation.

Another day they had taken a steamer to Sorrento and were put into small boats for the landing. Their boat contained a strange group of people—priests, nuns, market women, a musician with his instrument, a blind man, a cripple. Charles remarked, "This is certainly a weird crew; I never saw such an assortment of characters in my life." Helen replied that they were all pretty queer looking, and then asked her father what he intended to do when they landed. He had no idea at present, he said, but would make inquiries when they reached shore.

At that point one of the weirdest of the group remarked in a pleasant voice that if they needed any assistance he would be very glad to help them.

At railroad stations Charles had a habit of wandering off to buy a cigar or a newspaper without regard to the length of the stop. One day he wandered away and when the conductor was ready to signal the train to proceed Charles was nowhere in sight.

Helen was frantic, but she begged the conductor to wait for him so eloquently that heads began to pop out of the windows;

and then, to the relief of all, he came into view leisurely strolling along with his hands in his pockets, smoking a cigar. Everyone began shouting "Hurry!" in various languages, and when he realized that the train was waiting for him he speeded up and made profuse apologies. Helen never let him out of her sight in a railroad station again.

HELEN TO SUSAN, AUGUST 6, 1912

We are now sailing out of the Bay of Naples up to Genoa, which will take twenty-three hours by this boat. This part of the trip is certainly interesting. The boat we are on is a North-German Lloyd * boat which sailed from China, around India and up through the Suez Canal into the Mediterranean and up to Naples. It is filled with Chinese, Turks, and Orientals; most of the first-class passengers are German. We are the only Americans on board as far as we can judge, although there are several English people. The entire boat speaks German or Chinese. There are some little children who have Chinese and Indian nurses, but although we smile at each other, the children and I can't communicate, because they are German and my German is very rusty.

We have rented two wicker chairs for the trip and they have supplied us with a nice table so that I am sitting out on deck, writing this very comfortably. I am very thankful for this respite, for while in Italy, we were on the go every minute and the heat was fearful, and any spare minute I had I put in resting. Those spare minutes were very few indeed.

Venice was a beautiful place—a dream that lasted too short a time. Florence had wonderful art galleries where we saw the originals of many famous pictures. Rome with its great buildings, its great ruins, its Vatican and Forum was simply overwhelming. Naples is chiefly interesting for its people—the way they live is almost indecent. We spent most of our time outside of Naples—at Capri, Sorrento, Pompeii, etc. I have never really understood about Pompeii and the excavations carried on there, but now it is all quite clear.

As for shopping—we have bought Dorothy's Roman pearls and coral—I have bought some Roman striped scarfs for our Panama hats next summer. We bought your chief gift, a chain with a beautiful lapis lazuli pendant, in Naples, and we have collected

* The Prinz Eitel-Friedrich.

quite a number of pictures. Dad has bought his candlestick for the Rowfant Club, a bronze serpent, which is very interesting. Our money is certainly going, but we want to save enough to spend a couple of days *en famille* in New York. Don't forget to get your permit from the custom-house and meet us on the wharf. The boat is the Anchor Line S. S. California and will reach New York on Sunday, September 1.

I am glad you are having such a fine time. Mother, you won't want to stay buried alive in Cleveland anymore after all your gay summer. Much love.

CHARLES TO SUSAN, AUGUST 13, 1912

This is our fourth day in Paris. Your letter of July 28 met us on our arrival, and was very welcome. Glad you are enjoying yourself; we certainly are having an elegant time. It has rained every day but one. But we have "done" the Louvre and the Luxembourg Museums, the Invalides, Notre Dame and the public squares and places. Helen took me to the *Maison Boudet,* where we had luncheon. We have been to several shows. We called on the Braxtons, and invited them to dine with us last night. To-night we dined with them. They gave us a nice dinner with champagne. They have a beautiful boy baby, just learning to walk. They live in a fine large apartment, beautifully furnished and decorated, have two servants, and seem to be perfectly happy. I wore my evening clothes and Helen her best. On leaving we took a taxi and on the way home had the *cocher* drive out the *Champs-Elysées* and back by the theatres and cafes to our hotel.

On Sunday, Braxton called and took us for a drive in the Bois and we had tea at the Cascade Restaurant.

Paris is a beautiful city and I wish we had more time and more money. This Continental is a fine and expensive hotel, but Helen wanted to stop here and enjoys it very much.

Have met several Cleveland people. One of the Rowfanters is stopping at this hotel, and we have shaken hands several times. Ran across Mr. Emil Joseph at the American Express office Saturday. He is at the Majestic and invited us to call, which we haven't done as yet.

Tomorrow we go to Fontainebleau, with a young woman we met on the boat, a Georgia girl, by the way. We will be here a couple of days yet, during which we shall visit some more public places, call on Mimi Goulesque, leave a card on the American

Ambassador, Mr. Herrick, possibly on Mr. Simmons, the Cleveland artist from whom I hope to learn the address of Mr. Tanner, whose name does not appear in the directory.

We shall leave here for London Thursday or Friday night, and put in the rest of our time there and in getting up to Glasgow, whence we shall sail to meet you September 1, when we will exchange greetings and have a grand lovefeast.

Am addressing this to the place where Helen says you will be when it arrives, or shortly thereafter. Much love to you.

During their short stay in London Charles and Helen spent an afternoon with the Coleridge-Taylors in Croydon. This little visit was one of the most delightful experiences of that happy summer.

Coleridge-Taylor was bubbling over with high spirits—he had just been invited to conduct his *Violin Concerto* in Berlin in the fall. This had been the dream of his life—to conduct an orchestra in Berlin, and now the dream was about to be fulfilled. So the atmosphere was very merry, and Chesnutt and Coleridge-Taylor told jokes and stories, and the room rang with laughter.

Then when it was time for the Chesnutts to go, their host collected some umbrellas—it was raining hard—and took them to the station. They sloshed along through puddles, their gayety not a bit dampened by the rain. The last they saw of Coleridge-Taylor was his brilliant smile and the dashing wave of his umbrella as the train pulled off.

But his dream was not fulfilled; for on their arrival in New York the first thing they saw in the newspaper was the announcement of the death of Coleridge-Taylor.

26

Family and Civic Affairs

In January, 1913, Edwin decided that he had done enough adventuring. He resolved to study dentistry at Northwestern University. And when he started the three-year course in dentistry the family realized that Edwin had finally settled down to his life-work. Now it was Dorothy's turn. She was to be graduated from the College for Women of Western Reserve University in June, and the family were considering her future. She, like the other Chesnutt children, did not want to remain in Cleveland.

CHARLES TO HIS SON-IN-LAW, FEBRUARY 18, 1913

Dorothy will graduate from the College for Women in June. She has prepared herself for teaching, which seems about the only career open to her. There are only three available places for her to teach—at some southern school, here, or in Washington. The conditions of life in the south are not pleasant for a girl brought up as Dorothy has been; the conditions of life in Cleveland are, for other reasons, scarcely more attractive. She would like to teach in Washington, and we should all like to have her do so, if it can be brought about. The place she would naturally think of would be the M Street High School. So I would like to have you write to me as to how best to go about securing this result. You know the ropes.

Since you have not the appointing power, there could be no savor of nepotism in connection with the matter, and her connection with your family certainly ought not to act against her. I know the Washington people think they ought to have all the places, but the Washington schools are supported in part by the

National Government, which interferes with their claim somewhat.

If you think for any reason that the M Street High School is not available, please suggest anything else that may occur to you. She has specialized in English. Help us get the child placed where she can see a little life, and we will appreciate it.

Dorothy went down to Washington in September to see if she would like to teach there but after several weeks she decided that she preferred Cleveland.

When she returned home in January, Judge Addams offered her a position as Probation Officer in the Juvenile Court and she served in that position for two years.

By 1913 the South had come North with a vengeance. In many of the Northern states anti-intermarriage bills were introduced in the state assemblies. When such a bill was recommended for passage by the judiciary committee of the Ohio House of Representatives, the Negroes of the state rose in protest. Delegations were sent to Columbus from all parts of Ohio to acquaint the members of the House and Senate with the Negro point of view on this question. The enactment of such a law, they said, would be equivalent to another Dred Scott decision—"that a black man has no rights that a white man is bound to respect."

Chesnutt went to the Mayor's office to talk with Newton D. Baker and to ask him to use his influence in support of the protest. Baker seemed somewhat indifferent and Chesnutt left him with the feeling that Baker's former idealism was suffering a setback as he went forward into politics. But several days later he received a note from Baker stating that after some independent investigations he had come to the conclusion that Chesnutt was right, that the pending bill in Columbus ought not to be passed under any circumstances, and that he had so advised the members of the delegation from Cleveland.

Chesnutt replied:

April 3, 1913

HONORABLE NEWTON D. BAKER
CITY HALL
CITY
MY DEAR MR. BAKER:

Permit me to express the great pleasure your letter in reference to the anti-intermarriage bill has given me. I fear you thought my silence strange, after our interview. I find it a little difficult myself to account for, except that I am naturally of a somewhat dilatory habit of mind. I did not have the literature just at hand, and more-over I have strained my emotions so much on this Race Problem that I was slightly disappointed and a little discouraged at what seemed to be your attitude at the time. I might have realized from the experience of others that you could not be "rushed," and I am sure that a sober, well considered, balanced opinion on any subject, after personal investigation of the facts, is worth more as a basis of action than a snap judgment, even on the right side.

I assume, of course, that your decision was on the principle involved, rather than on the particular bill, and I shall take care that it is known among those who are more immediately concerned, who, I am sure, will appreciate the wisdom, the liberality, and the real statesmanship of your action.

                              Sincerely yours,
                              CHARLES W. CHESNUTT

Chesnutt was delighted at this time to learn of the honor bestowed upon his friend Page. He wrote at once:

                                        April 3, 1913
HONORABLE WALTER H. PAGE
ENGLEWOOD, NEW JERSEY
MY DEAR MR. PAGE:

I notice from the newspaper that you have been named by President Wilson as Ambassador to Great Britain. It is a signal honor, worthily bestowed. Considering the men who have filled the office, it calls for all there is in a real big man, and I feel that you can meet the requirements. I hope you may have as successful and brilliant a career as diplomat and statesman as you have had as editor and publisher.

I was afraid Mr. Wilson would not find anybody out of the millionaire class who could afford to accept the position. I hope you are in that class, or that you have at least made money enough in the publishing business to uphold the dignity of the office without embarrassment.

                              Cordially yours,
                              CHARLES W. CHESNUTT

DOUBLEDAY, PAGE & COMPANY PUBLISHERS
GARDEN CITY NEW YORK
April 9, 1913

DEAR MR. CHESNUTT:

I wish you to know how heartily I appreciate your kind congratulations and good wishes. The President has great courage to entrust such a mission to a man out of the working ranks of our democratic life; and the confidence of my friends is now very helpful and, I assure you, very pleasant, too.

Gratefully yours,
WALTER H. PAGE

In June Chesnutt delivered an address entitled "Race Ideals and Examples" before the literary societies at Wilberforce University. This was published in the *A. M. E. Church Review* of October, 1913. While he was at Wilberforce, the University conferred upon him the honorary degree of LL. D.

In September Cleveland celebrated the Centennial of Perry's victory over the British in the Battle of Lake Erie. All of Cleveland's civic leaders put their time and energy and enthusiasm into this patriotic undertaking. Chesnutt served as chairman of the Committee on Colored Organizations. He had to spend a great deal of time on this, but he felt that it was well worth while. He had some correspondence at this time with Mr. Charles T. Hallinan, then of the *Chicago Evening Post,* about the segregation pattern that was being imposed upon the colored people in the departments at Washington by the Wilson administration. Mr. Hallinan had written that the situation in Washington needed publicity and that it was hard to get it from the newspapers.

CHESNUTT TO HALLINAN, SEPTEMBER 15, 1913

I have lately had some experience with the "languidness of newspapers in our case." As chairman of one of the committees for the local Perry Centenary Celebration, I prepared and submitted to the publicity department of the Centennial Committee an article setting forth the part played by colored sailors and soldiers in the War of 1812. The article appeared in the *Cleveland Plain Dealer,* but the publicity agent informs me that the *Leader* would not print it. The *Plain Dealer* is much the more

public-spirited of the two papers, in other respects as well as in
this one.

For years Chesnutt and other public-spirited people had felt
the need of a Social Settlement house in the Central Avenue
area. He had, in 1905, at a meeting held under the auspices of
the Negro Board of Trade, delivered a short address entitled
"Does Central Avenue Need a Social Settlement House?"

This address was published in the *Cleveland Journal* and Chesnutt received several offers of help in forming such an organization. William O. Matthews wrote in behalf of the Goodrich
House people, offering any assistance in their power. But the
colored people were poor and unable to finance such a project,
and the wealthy white people were not sufficiently interested;
so nothing was done about it.

Early in 1914 the Men's Club of the Second Presbyterian
Church, located at the corner of Prospect Avenue and East 30th
Street decided to take the matter up. Dr. Dudley Peter Allen
was responsible for that decision. He said to the members of
the club: "The Central Avenue area is practically under the eaves
of this church and it is our responsibility to help those people."

The committee went ahead with their plans. They talked with
several leaders among the colored people, George A. Myers, proprietor of the Hollenden Barber Shop, Thomes W. Fleming,
John P. Green, Chesnutt, and others.

Chesnutt was deeply interested in the plan and spent a great
deal of effort in thinking it through. For several weeks he took
walks along Central Avenue studying the people. He found all
races and many nationalities in the district. There were many
Negroes, but there were also Jews of different nationalities and
Catholics of various origins. This little research delighted him.
He was glad to renew his acquaintance with that part of the city.

One day as he was strolling along he passed a little bookstore.
The window had books and magazines on display. Chesnutt
approached the proprietor who was standing in the doorway. He
would enjoy a chat with this enterprising man. "You have an attractive display here," he said. "Are you interested in books and
writers?" The man replied that he was deeply interested. Chesnutt continued with a smile, "I'm glad to hear that. I'm Charles
W. Chesnutt." The man looked at him blankly for a moment and
then replied, "Of dis city?"

When Charles told the family this story they laughed heartily; whenever any one of them showed signs of becoming the least bit pompous, it was only necessary for someone to say softly, "Of dis city?" and the erring member would realize the mistake amid the peals of laughter that followed.

Having reached some definite conclusions about the proposed social center, Chesnutt wrote the following letter to a member of the committee:

February 18, 1914

A. T. HILLS, ESQ.
AMERICAN TRUST BUILDING
CLEVELAND, OHIO
MY DEAR MR. HILLS:

Replying to the question you asked me the other day, as to how benevolently disposed people could go about social settlement work among the colored people of Cleveland, it has occurred to me, as I said to you in conversation, and also to Mr. Amos B. McNairy, who spoke to me about the matter, that perhaps the most effective instrumentality would be a social settlement up in the colored district, on Central Avenue or some intersecting street between Cedar Avenue on one side and Scovill Avenue on the other. It is a little out of the way of Hiram House or Alta House or Goodrich House, and a similar institution in the neighborhood would find a wide field of usefulness. The settlement houses above mentioned do not deny their privileges to colored young people, but the Y.M.C.A. and Y.W.C.A. do not welcome them with open arms, if at all, and an institution conveniently located, which would combine the facilities of these institutions for young people of all ages, would be, it seems to me, an ideal thing.

As to the lines on which such an institution should be conducted. I would suggest, should it be undertaken, that it not be conducted on race lines. A great many colored people object, and properly so, to the policy of segregation which seems to regard them as unfit to associate with other human beings, and seeks to drive them back upon themselves entirely, and it would be difficult to reach many of them, even with a good thing, coupled with such a suggestion. Of course, they would probably constitute the chief beneficiaries of a settlement house in their district, as do the Orange Street Jews in the case of Hiram House, and the East End Italians in the case of Alta House, and the work could be laid out along lines which might especially apply to their particular needs, so far as these could be distinguished from those of people in general.

Such an institution, if undertaken on the right plan, would probably run into money, not only to build a house but to keep it running. It could only hope for success if promoted by white people, because the colored people are poor, and while they would no doubt contribute according to their means, the bulk of the money would have to come from the same sources which support the other benevolent institutions of the city. There ought to be, to secure the best results, a building somewhat similar to those of the other settlement houses of the city, similarly equipped for the different kinds of work which a social settlement carries on, and it should have at its head an experienced social worker in sympathy with the needs and aspirations of its chief beneficiaries, who would see that it was conducted along right lines. If such a plan should seem too large for the contemplation of your committee, the same work could be conducted on a small scale.

There are also several institutions conducted by colored people themselves, which are worthy of encouragement. One of them is the Colored Old Folks' Home which is doing a good work, and another, The Phillis Wheatley Home for Colored Working Girls, located on 40th Street, which I am informed is well conducted and serving a very useful purpose.

I don't know that what I have said will be of any assistance to you, but if I can make any investigations in order to answer any special inquiries you may wish to propose, or if I can cooperate with you in any way, I shall be glad to do so. I am very much pleased to see an interest in this subject on the part of the better class of our citizens, for the colored element of our population has been more or less neglected, which is not to the credit of so great a city as Cleveland, with its exceedingly generous contributions to philanthropic purposes. I have an idea that a suitable plan for social work among them, properly sponsored and promoted, would receive a very hearty response from the community.

Sincerely yours,

CHARLES W. CHESNUTT

The Men's Club decided to establish a settlement along the lines of Chesnutt's suggestions. They planned to start on a small scale as to buildings and equipment, but they all agreed that the enterprise would need the finest type of social worker procurable. In November Dr. Charles Edwin Briggs went down to Oberlin College to find the right person, and was told about two young people who were both studying in the Graduate School of Social Service at the University of Chicago, to which they had received scholarships at their graduation from Oberlin in June.

Dr. Briggs, having reported to the committee, who were delighted with what they heard, went on to Chicago to talk with these young people and to obtain their services for the settlement.

Property was acquired on East 38th Street between Cedar and Central Avenues and when the Playhouse Settlement was formally opened in June, 1915, Russell and Rowena Jelliffe were put in charge of it.

This little settlement became one of the most important institutions in the cultural life of Cleveland. When the Community Fund was established in 1919, it became one of the Fund agencies; it has now attained national recognition as Karamu House, the name which was adopted some years later.

The month of June was anniversary month in the Chesnutt calendar; June 6, the wedding anniversary; June 10, Susan's birthday; and June 20, Charles's birthday. The June of 1914 was a very happy one. The 6th came on Saturday that year. At breakfast the family were considering how to celebrate the day. "If we owned an automobile, we could have a picnic out at the Chester Cliffs Club," said Susan. The girls agreed that that would be an ideal celebration, but since they did not have one, they might have an early dinner and go to a show. Their father promised to come home in time to carry out their plans.

During the morning Charles telephoned Helen that he wanted her to do something for him. She'd learn more about it in a short time. Some minutes later a shining, new Willys-Overland touring car came rolling up the driveway and stopped at the front door. Everyone rushed out on the porch to see who was in it. The driver said that the car was sent out as an anniversary gift for Mrs. Chesnutt, and that Miss Chesnutt was to take a driving lesson at once. As the young man drove Helen over into Wade Park to carry out her father's instructions, Susan was on the telephone telling Charles how happy she was over such a wonderful gift, and how terribly extravagant he was to spend that much money so rashly.

When Helen had mastered the art of driving she taught Charles and Dorothy. With three chauffeurs in the family Susan thoroughly enjoyed her car, which was a source of very great pleasure to all of them during the remainder of the year. The following year all their joy was turned to bitter sorrow when the car skidded on a wet hillside and caused the death of a young friend whom Susan had invited for a drive. Then, indeed, Susan needed all her Christian fortitude, and Charles all his philosophy, and the girls all their courage, to weather this terrible catastrophe. But at this time they learned what true friendship could be, for the family of the young lady, though heartbroken themselves, showed the greatest compassion for the Chesnutts, and helped them through this bitter period with real nobility.

In July, 1915, Charles decided to go west and visit the expositions in San Francisco and San Diego. Since his sightseeing trips were such strenuous affairs, Susan and the girls chose to remain in Cleveland to entertain Edwin, who was coming home for his vacation. They planned to go East later on. Dorothy, however, became very ill with pneumonia, and when Charles returned he found a trained nurse installed in the house. Late in September Susan took Dorothy to Atlantic City to recuperate before returning to her duties at Juvenile Court.

CHARLES TO SUSAN, OCTOBER 12, 1915

I have your letter of October 10. I cannot say it was unexpected. I quite appreciate that life is expensive, and have no doubt that you have spent your money wisely and I hope you have gotten value for it. I certainly have given value for it, in good work. I am sending you herewith the amount requested by registered letter. It is an awkward way to send money, but is no doubt a little more convenient for you.

I hope you will return by way of New York, so that Dorothy may get a line on it and you both may take in some good shows. I don't know whether the opera is running yet or not, but if so, it might be well to see a good opera at the Metropolitan. I will enjoy it by proxy, through you; you can tell me about it.

I am forwarding to you, by this mail—I see I have opened it and therefore will enclose it with this—an invitation to be present at the consecration of the Rev. Mr. Stearly * as Suffragan Bishop

* A former rector of Emmanuel Church.

of Newark. It takes place at Montclair, N. J., which is very close
to New York. If the date, October 21, should correspond with
your presence in New York, you might find pleasure in being
present; in which event sign and forward the request for admission card as per instructions. I presume this might include
Dorothy as the invitation is for two. Hope you will continue to
enjoy yourselves, and if this is not enough, let me know and I
can probably cough up a little more.

When Charles received Ned's special delivery letter saying that
he had passed the State Board Examination and was licensed to
practice dentistry in Illinois, he was delighted—his son was now
established in a fine profession with every prospect of living a
useful life in his chosen community and contributing his share
to the world's work.

Chesnutt's efforts in race relations never abated. When the
Board of Censors forbade the showing of "The Birth of a Nation"
in Ohio as unfit for exhibition there, he had felt that Ohio was
trying to do justice to the Negro. Later on he wrote the following
letter to the Governor of the state.

CLEVELAND, OHIO
November 23, 1915

HON. FRANK B. WILLIS
GOVERNOR
COLUMBUS, OHIO
DEAR SIR:

It has been called to my attention that Mr. F. P. Riddle, of
Lima, Ohio, who I understand is connected with the State Agricultural Department, and who is promoting what is called the
Buckeye Corn Special Tour, has advertised that as part of the
entertainment of the party en route, it will be shown at Philadelphia the film called "The Birth of a Nation."

Inasmuch as this pernicious picture has been rejected by the
Board of Censors of Ohio, after careful consideration, as unfit
for exhibition in this State, for reasons with which no doubt you
are familiar, and with your entire concurrence, as you have stated
over your own signature, it would seem highly improper that it
should be shown to a thousand or more young people at the most
impressionable age, upon the initiative or with the consent of any
one representing the State in any way, or deriving any office or
authority from the state.

May I and a number of others of the same mind hope that you will exercise your authority, if you have any in the premises, and if not, your influence, to defeat this effort to do by indirection what the state authorities have decided shall not be done.

Yours respectfully,

CHARLES W. CHESNUTT

Governor Willis answered the following day, saying that he had immediately called Mr. Riddle by telephone, stating that he strongly disapproved of his plan to entertain the young people by showing them the film, and that if this feature of the official program was retained, he, the Governor, would at once cancel his promise to be present with the Excursion at Philadelphia to deliver an address to the Corn Boys.

Booker T. Washington's death in November, 1915, caused many white Americans to shake their heads and sigh, "What a pity! Now the Negro has no leadership, no compass, nothing to point the way."

Washington was a great American. He showed the country the value, the necessity, of industrial education. It was through his great work at Tuskegee that America learned the way to technical instruction. He taught the poor untrained Negroes of the South to work efficiently, to save, and to acquire property. A man of the utmost integrity, of indefatigable energy, of dynamic personality, he won for himself a place of distinction and honor and unheard-of power in the council chambers of his country.

But he underestimated one thing—the importance of the ballot. Washington's stand on disfranchisement caused him to be heartily detested by many Negro leaders. The colored people were divided in their estimate of him. There were Bookerites and anti-Bookerites; there were those who considered him the savior of their race, and those who thought that he had sold them out for his own purposes. Well, he was gone, and the other camp, under the leadership of DuBois, now had its chance.

In August, 1916, Joel Spingarn issued invitations to the nation's leading colored men and women to meet in conference at Troutbeck, his beautiful estate at Amenia, Dutchess County, New York. Here, for three days, these distinguished men and women, of every shade of opinion, talked things over quietly and thoughtfully. There were several sessions of the conference, which, though informal throughout, had special topics for discussion, and leaders assigned to preside over them. The topics were comprehensive— Education and Industry, The Negro in Politics, Civil and Legal Discrimination, Social Discrimination, Practical Paths, a Working Programme for the Future. Spingarn had written to Chesnutt asking him to preside over the session devoted to the discussion of Social Discrimination. He had added that personally he hoped that there would be no speeches at the conference (anything over fifteen minutes was a "speech") but there would be no rigid rules about that or anything else.

Chesnutt enjoyed the conference. He lived off the beaten track, and his discussions had generally been by pen rather than word of mouth. To mingle with this group of fine and thoughtful people, to look with them far into the future, to plan with them the best ways of getting at the solution of their terrible and almost insoluble problems was a great inspiration to him.

Another thing that gave him great pleasure that summer was a letter from a member of one of the old families of Fayetteville, who had been reading Chesnutt's books. He wrote a long letter in reply:

CLEVELAND, OHIO, Oct. 16, 1916

MY DEAR MR. LILLY:

Your letter forwarded to me by Doubleday, Page and Company, gave me much pleasure, not only because of what you say about me and my writings, but as a friendly echo from the old town where I was brought up, and the old State where I made my start in life. . . .

I thank you for your kind words about my writings. I wish I could have convinced the whole reading public as well as I did you, of the merits of *The Colonel's Dream,* but it is the least successful of my books. Unfortunately for my writings, they were on the unpopular side of the race question, and any success they may have had must have been due to their merit. Dixon, who took the other side, was not satisfied to present it fairly, but made a fortune by prostituting his talent to ignoble uses. My four books on Houghton, Mifflin and Company's list, sell very well, considering how long they have been out, and my little life of Douglass in the Beacon Biographies is still in active demand. I hope to write more, but a busy life along other lines, in these strenuous times, has given me of late years, little time for literary work.

I do not think I have been in Fayetteville since the occasion on which we met in Colonel Pemberton's office. From my father's letters, however, I have learned of some of the improvements of which you speak, and I imagine the old town is very different from my description of it in *The Colonel's Dream*. My memory of the town as I knew it in my boyhood is vastly more vivid than that dating from my latest visit.

You ask about my family and myself.... I have enjoyed for many years an ample income, from the standpoint of a moderately successful professional man.... Of my four children, all are college graduates, two of my daughters from Smith College, at Northampton, Massachusetts, one from the College for Women of Western Reserve University, and my son from Harvard.... My eldest daughter is happily married and lives in Washington, D. C.... My second daughter has for some years taught Latin and mathematics in Central High School, Cleveland, and is a popular and successful teacher.... My third daughter is a probation officer in the Juvenile Court at Cleveland. My son graduated recently as a dentist from Northwestern University at Chicago, and has opened an office in that city.

Not only have we been well treated in a business and professional way, but in other respects as well. I am a member of the Chamber of Commerce, the Cleveland Bar Association, the City Club, and other Clubs of lesser note, and also of the very exclusive Rowfant Club which belongs among the Clubs, membership in which is noted in Who's Who in America, which includes among its members half a dozen millionaires, a former United States Senator, a former ambassador to France, and three gentlemen who have been decorated by the French Government. It is needless to say that it is not wealth or blood or birth that makes me acceptable in such company. One of my daughters is a member of the College Club, composed of alumnae of the better colleges and universities. Indeed in this liberal and progressive Northern city we get most of the things which make life worth living, and this in spite of the fact that every one knows our origin, and in spite of the fact that this is the United States and that there is plenty of race prejudice right here.... In the North, race prejudice is rather a personal than a community matter, and a man is not regarded as striking at the foundations of society if he sees fit to extend a social courtesy to a person of color.

I have read Mr. McNeill's *Lyrics from Cotton Land,* and like it very much, and before that I had run across occasional poems of his in the magazines. He was a real poet, and the Old North State may well be proud of him. As to entering the Patterson Cup Competition, as you suggest, I see from the Introduction to McNeill's *Lyrics from Cotton Land,* that the competition is limited to natives and residents of North Carolina, so I am barred both coming and going. It is, however, a very pretty conceit, and ought to promote literary effort in the State.

Your letter was a long one, and I fear I have written you almost a book in reply. But it was so friendly and expressed such a genuine interest in me and my doings that I have written at greater length and in greater detail than good taste perhaps would call for, or than your patience will enable you to read, but I shall throw the blame on you for stirring me up; for it has been a long time since I had the pleasure of talking, even at long range, with a gentleman of the old town.

With thanks and best wishes.

Sincerely yours,
CHARLES W. CHESNUTT

Chesnutt's membership in the Rowfant Club brought him invitations to join other clubs of national renown:

CLEVELAND, OHIO, Feb. 3, 1917

MR. H. H. HARPER
TREASURER THE BIBLIOPHILE SOCIETY
308 BOYLSTON ST., BOSTON, MASS.
MY DEAR MR. HARPER:

I received your letter of January 3rd, inviting me to become a member of the Bibliophile Society; also the printed copy of your very interesting talk at the Rowfant Club, which, as I was not at that time a member, I did not have the privilege of hearing when you delivered it. I shall place it among my Rowfant items and treasure it very highly.

I will write you before very long with reference to the membership in the society. In the meantime, I thank you for the invitation and for the pamphlet.

Sincerely yours,
CHARLES W. CHESNUTT

CLEVELAND, OHIO, August 11, 1917

FREDERICK S. LAMB, ESQ.
SECRETARY THE NATIONAL ARTS CLUB
14 & 15 GRAMERCY PARK
NEW YORK CITY
DEAR SIR:

Enclosed herewith please find my check for $10.00, annual dues as associate member of The National Arts Club, together with card containing names and addresses.

If I get a membership card, kindly retain it there until I call for it, as I shall be in New York some time during the coming week, and will call at the club.

Very truly yours,
CHARLES W. CHESNUTT

27

Racial Tension in the First World War

ONCE MORE Chesnutt took up his pen to protest against wrong and injustice at a most critical time in the history of the country.

CLEVELAND, OHIO
April 3, 1917

MR. MUNSON R. HAVENS
SECRETARY, CLEVELAND CHAMBER OF COMMERCE
CLEVELAND, OHIO
DEAR SIR:

The Chamber of Commerce, as the foremost representative body of business and professional men of the community, stands very properly in the forefront of the movement for preparedness, for patriotism, and for the united action of the people in the crisis at present confronting the United States. In view of this position of the Chamber, I think it proper to call your attention, and through you the attention of the Board of Directors or the proper committees of the Chamber to the following facts:

The moving picture film called "The Birth of a Nation," because of its vicious and anti-social character was refused approval by the board of moving picture censors, or whatever its title is, of the State of Ohio, during the last administration, but has been pounding at the gates of Ohio for several years, and finally under this administration has been passed by the present board of censors, and is announced for early exhibition in Cleveland. It seems to me a most unwise and unpatriotic thing to permit its production, at this time especially, without protest, for the following reasons:

The picture was made, of course, to make money, and to make it by stirring up race prejudice and race hatred, which it seems to me is a most unwise and most unpatriotic thing at this juncture in our national affairs. The principal action of the picture is devoted to exploiting the alleged misconduct of colored Union soldiers during the reconstruction period (to say nothing of its glorification of that organization of traitors known as the Ku-Klux-Klan). The principal villain of the story, the would-be rapist, is portrayed as a colored captain in the Union Army. There are already four colored regiments in the regular army with a military history in past wars of which they and the nation may well be proud. There are several complete regiments of colored militia, and battalions in several other states, and similar units proposed in other places. With war declared there will undoubtedly be a large accession to these. The colored people are loyal citizens, without perhaps a great deal of encouragement, in some quarters, to loyalty, indeed in spite of serious discouragement; but it seems to me and those on behalf of whom I speak, that such an insult to the national uniform when worn by men of color, as the public exhibition of such a picture as "The Birth of a Nation," which as a work of pictorial art is a superb and impressive thing, and all the more vicious for that reason, should not be permitted at this time, when all citizens should stand together to support the honor of the nation.

When it is also taken into consideration that there are numbers of colored men in the community who have recently come to the North because of our disorganized labor market, it would seem a matter of doubtful wisdom to do or to permit anything that is likely to breed discontent and ill feeling among these people.

It has seemed to me and to prominent citizens with whom I have talked, some of them members of the Chamber, that it would be a wise and patriotic thing for the Chamber of Commerce to use its influence with the city administration, or the police department, or whatever authority has power in the matter, to discourage this sort of thing at this juncture, and to prevent, if possible, the exhibition of this film.

I am writing as a member of the Chamber, and as a member of the Executive Committee of the Local Branch of the National

Association for the Advancement of Colored People, which, in large part, by its activity, has kept this picture out of Ohio until now, to suggest the hope that the Chamber of Commerce will see this matter in the same light that we do, and will by appropriate action exert its undoubtedly powerful influence to prevent, if possible, the exhibition of this picture in Cleveland.

Sincerely yours,

CHARLES W. CHESNUTT

During this summer the Chesnutts started out on a gay adventure—their first long trip by automobile. Edwin was drafted to help Helen drive the new Hudson touring car to Boston, New York, and other points east. The family invested heavily in linen dusters, automobile veils, driving gloves, touring books and maps, inner tubes, and so on. Mary Gibson, who was going to New York to visit a friend, was invited to join the party. Driving was a slow business in 1917. The journey to Boston took four days.

During the drive across New York State, just as they were passing a little general store high up in the mountains, a tire went flat. There were several men sitting on the edge of the un-railed porch chewing tobacco. At the abrupt stopping of the car they all leaned forward.

"Get out the book, Helen," said Charles. "We'll have to fix the tire."

"Say, Mister, what do you want a book for?" asked one of the men, astounded.

"We need the book to teach us how to fix the tire," was the answer.

"Well, by gosh," exclaimed another, "a book to fix the tire!" "You don't need a book, Mister, we'll fix your tire for you. Come on, boys!" During the time the tire was being repaired, one or another of the men was heard to murmur, "A book to fix the tire, by gosh."

From Boston they went to New York, stopping over at New London for a night. In New York they dropped Mary Gibson and picked up one of the Bishop girls who was going to Pittsburgh to visit her brother. On their way through Pennsylvania they stopped at Gettysburg. The Battlefield was an inspiration. They had hired an excellent guide to drive them over the area and after his talk they could almost visualize the battle of Gettysburg; and as they saw the rows and rows of graves on that field, they thought of Lincoln's immortal speech at its dedication, realized how great America was, that when she really wanted to accomplish a purpose she had the power to do it; and these words came to them: "... that we here highly resolve that these dead shall not have died in vain—that this nation, under God, shall have a new birth of freedom—and that government of the people, by the people, for the people shall not perish from the earth."

During the tour, Charles asked the guide to direct them to a good restaurant. When it was over the car stopped in front of the Gettysburg Inn, and the guide remarked, "Here we are, sir, the best place around for a good meal." With thanks to the man for his very efficient services, the party walked into the dining-room and were ushered at once to a pleasantly located table near the windows.

They had been much moved during the tour of the Battlefield and felt emotionally exhausted. They did not have much to say until Edwin exclaimed suddenly, "Il faut que nous parlions français tout de suite."

"Pourquoi?" exclaimed the girls.

Edwin explained in French that when the hostess had seated them, the manager had appeared on the far side of the room and after some discussion was bearing down on them. They were very much shocked, for they had not had this particular kind of experience before. But they rose to the occasion and were vivaciously conversing in French when the manager and hostess neared the table. That was enough! The relief on the woman's face was comical, as she and the manager passed by the table and out another door.

They had a wonderful meal and soon lapsed into English with now and then a chuckle of pure amusement on Edwin's part, while Charles exclaimed with a grin, "Well, Susan, behold us at last drawing dividends on the fine education we have given our offspring."

As the United States advanced into World War I, the Negro question became very acute. Newton D. Baker had been appointed Secretary of War by President Wilson in March, 1916, and in October, 1917, Emmett J. Scott, Secretary of Tuskegee Institute, was appointed Special Assistant to the Secretary of War to advise in matters affecting the Negro soldiers.

Scott's job was no sinecure. The harsh and unjust treatment of Negro soldiers in southern training camps was deeply resented by the colored people, and protests flooded Scott's office. The question of Negro officers had been bitterly fought out. When Joel Spingarn and James Weldon Johnson, leaders in the National Association for the Advancement of Colored People, went to Washington to see about getting colored men admitted into the regular officers' training camps, they were told by Newton D. Baker that it was absolutely impossible. Spingarn then used his great influence to establish a special training camp for Negro officers at Des Moines, Iowa. From this camp several hundred colored men became commissioned officers in the United States Army. Spingarn was at first widely criticized for sponsoring Jim Crow, but for the training of officers the segregated camp was necessary, and that was that.

Chesnutt received many letters about the situations at the southern camps, and was visited by friends and relatives of the young men, who wanted something done about conditions down there. He did what he could, as the following letter shows:

November 24, 1917

Capt. William R. Green
Company D
Ninth Separate Battalion
Camp Sheridan
Montgomery, Ala.
My dear William,

Mrs. McAdoo was in to see me this morning, greatly exercised over conditions for your battalion at Camp Sheridan. She told me about her son's experience and the incidents connected with it, all of which I had read in the newspapers, and about the order forbidding the colored soldiers to leave the camp; also about their subsequent transfer to the rifle range, which she says is a fever-stricken locality which endangers the lives of the men. She came to consult me about the advisability or propriety of either myself writing or getting some prominent citizen like Mr. Herrick to write Mr. Baker and suggest that he investigate these conditions, and if possible, do something to ameliorate them.

I told her that I had no doubt the War Department, including Mr. Baker, was well aware of all these facts; that they were reported in the newspapers; that I had no doubt the War Department fully appreciated the difficulty of the problem of securing decent treatment of colored troops by the southerners, and that I had no idea that a letter from an obscure civilian, or even from a prominent one, would have any influence upon the general staff or its policies. I told her, however, that I would write you a letter and ask you what you thought about it, and if you could suggest any steps that might be taken by any well disposed person which could possibly have any influence or effect; and that I would be governed by what you might say.

I would like to know, if you can inform me, to what extent the colored soldiers are participating in the benefits of the Red Cross and the Y. M. C. A. and the Knights of Columbus and the other, if there are any other, agencies for the promotion of the comfort and welfare of the soldiers.

If you will write me a letter at your convenience and let me know whether you think of anything that could be done to promote improved conditions among the colored soldiers, I shall be obliged.

Yours very truly,
CHARLES W. CHESNUTT

The welfare of the colored soldier was not the only problem at that time. The great migration of Negroes from the South into the industrial cities of the North had begun. The South tried hard to keep its laborers at home, but hundreds of thousands of them moved to the North during the war years. The problems of housing, of schooling, of race adjustment were very great, but the welfare agencies, especially the Urban League, tried to solve them. White labor was resentful of this importation of Negro labor into its ranks. Racial feeling was very high and race riots occurred in many places.

When the year 1918 arrived, the thoughts of the Chesnutts, like those of other Americans, were centered on the war. In February Dorothy started teaching in the Cleveland public schools as her contribution to the war effort. During the spring and summer the entire family labored faithfully in their war garden, which was extensive. In August they all drove to Chicago to visit Edwin, who was expecting to be drafted at any time. In October he wrote to his father, "Here is the way the matter stands—I am classified as 1-A. If I pass the physical examination I shall be called in short order. There is no chance for a commission. There will be no further commissions given colored men until those already commissioned and walking around have all been called. This is straight from Emmett Scott. I hope you will survive the flu. It is killing more soldiers at the camps than the Germans are in Europe."

And on October 23, "I have passed the physical exam and am awaiting the call to camp. In the meantime I am taking exercises at the Y.M.C.A. so as to harden myself a bit. The flu has killed the dental business, but if it confines itself to the business and lets me alone I shall not howl."

In Cleveland the public schools were closed for several weeks because of the flu epidemic, and Helen spent that period driving members of the Visiting Nurses' Association about the city to their duties in the homes of the afflicted. When the war ended on November 11, the Chesnutts were relieved, for Edwin had not been called to camp, and Helen returned to the schoolroom.

The NAACP was scheduled to meet in Cleveland in June, 1919. The Chesnutts had invited several friends to stay with them during the conference and had planned some entertainment in the way of dinner parties and drives. Susan was in her element, and all the family were looking forward to the event.

One evening in the middle of May, Charles suggested that they go over to the Liberty Theatre to see a movie. It was Friday night and the girls could spare the time, he said. They, however, were both too busy to go. Susan, who never really cared for movies, was not interested. They tried to persuade him to give up the idea and remain at home, but he refused to be henpecked, and went off alone in the car.

The next morning at breakfast he seemed very uneasy. Susan asked him if he felt ill, and the girls began to wonder what could have happened. To set their minds at rest he finally confessed. He had carelessly left the keys in the ignition and found the car gone when he went to get it.

Susan and the girls were filled with consternation—they had to have a car when the NAACP met.

"We'll call up the insurance company right away, and they'll have it back in no time," said Helen briskly.

"Don't feel so badly, Charles," said Susan. "We'll get it back pretty soon. The insurance companies work fast."

Then Charles had to make another confession—he had never

had the car insured. They did belong to the Automobile Club, however, which got in touch with the police and started things moving. Gloom settled down upon 9719 Lamont Avenue.

The fates were kind however, for the week before the NAACP meeting the Cleveland police department telephoned that the Hudson had been found in Detroit and that Chesnutt could claim it by calling at police headquarters there. Charles and Susan decided that Helen should go up on the boat Friday night and drive it back Saturday. But as Charles was getting Helen's reservation, he decided he'd better go along to give her moral support. When he telephoned Susan to that effect, she decided that she would enjoy the ride too, and Dorothy, on learning that the rest were going, joined the party; so the whole family turned the trip into a glorified picnic.

During the week of the conference the Chesnutts and their out-of-town friends found the car very useful, although they were somewhat hampered by the fact that the girls were attending the Foreign Language School at Western Reserve University and their mornings were thus occupied.

ETHEL TO SUSAN, JUNE 25, 1919

Many thanks for asking us up. We are all hard at work and will be all summer. Charlie's school closes today—Ed has some research work which will bring him a salary all summer. I am working for the Red Cross Home Service and have been since last fall. It is very interesting work with the families of soldiers. We help them through all their difficulties; we help them financially, physically, spiritually. We get them homes, work, friends; we send them to hospitals, insane asylums, jail, if necessary, and it is all wonderfully stimulating, not only for our cases but for us, the workers. I enjoy it so much. It takes all one's time and all one's strength and all one's intelligence to do the work, but it is such a worth while expenditure of self. It does not leave me much leisure for anything but I do not regret one thing I have had to give up.

I have bought a home at 912 Westminster St. between 9th and 10th, S and T, a house very much like the one I lived in at 1751 T. St. I saved my money and looked up a house (which was hard work, for Washington is packed full of people and everything desirable is taken overnight). I made my first payment and my terms are good. I can meet my notes unless misfortune overtakes me. Everything is in my name and I am managing. I have proved that I can manage and I am surely delivering the goods—I have had my home papered and put in order from top to bottom. It had to be done because it had been badly treated. I had to watch everything for otherwise things went wrong.

Sorry you lost your car; I hope you have recovered it. You must have enjoyed the NAACP meetings; probably met a lot of people from here.

I am moving into my home tomorrow so my address in the future will be 912 Westminster St. N. W. Best wishes to all.

In July the whole nation was horrified by a race riot that broke out in Washington. Chesnutt was terribly disturbed about Ethel and her family. And then a week later in Chicago a race riot of greater intensity and more savage brutality broke out. Again the Chesnutts were alarmed for Edwin's safety, and filled with anger that such things could happen in a world just made safe for democracy. But these riots kept on occurring, especially in the South, and the future looked very dark for the Negro.

CHARLES TO ETHEL, JULY 30, 1919

We all read with pleasure your account of your activities in the Red Cross, and real estate, and other lines, and I am proud to have fathered so capable a woman. You are displaying excellent judgment in buying yourself a home; I have no doubt Washington property is a good investment, irrespective of the sentimental side of the proposition. With all of the family earning money, you ought to get ahead rapidly and soon assume the rank of substantial citizens; not only intellectually and socially, but materially.

We got our car back and were able to entertain more or less during the NAACP. Emmett Scott was with us a couple of days. Jim and Grace Johnson * were to have been with us, but her mother was taken to a hospital and she was unable to come. Johnson, for business reasons, stopped at the Hollenden, tho he dined with us several times. We entertained at meals a number of the visiting notables, including the Butler Wilsons and your friend Mrs. Gray. On Friday of that week Mr. Villard, Mr. Shillady, Mr. and Miss Grimké, and Miss Ovington dined with us and we took them to the meeting. The following week Helen

* James Weldon Johnson and his wife.

lent Miss Ovington her cottage, which we hadn't been occupying because Helen and Dorothy have been going to the French Summer School—and she spent what she said was a delightful eight days all by herself in the woods. The summer school is over Friday next, and my vacation begins next week, and we are all going out to Chesterland for the month of August. My car was found after 5 weeks, in Detroit, by the police of that city. The whole family went up on the boat to get it.

We have been somewhat concerned about the Washington race riot, and your proximity to it, but it pales into insignificance beside the Chicago riot, the principal center of which has been right in Edwin's block. I was reasonably certain that neither you nor Edwin would be wildly careening through the streets with guns, shooting or being shot. I hope you were able to keep Charlie in the house. Write us the inside history of the riot, and give my love to Ed and Charlie.

EDWIN TO CHARLES, NOVEMBER 11, 1919

I don't remember having written lately, but if I haven't it is because there is nothing interesting going on here in Chicago. This town seems to be dead, and business has been very poor for several weeks.

The streets which used to be filled with people at night, are deserted. Prohibition or the high cost of living, or the recent riot or all combined, have taken the pep out of this breezy town. There is a great deal of agitation and propaganda against Negroes here, fostered by certain property owners who want them segregated. Prejudice is growing and the Negroes are becoming more resentful. Everybody has a job, however, and there is no poverty or hardship apparent, so we all hope that everything will come out all right in the long run.

28

The Chesnutt Home a Mecca

A FRIEND of Helen's once said to her, "How I envy you Chesnutts!"

Helen had replied, "No, you don't! You wouldn't change places with us for anything on earth."

"But I would," the friend insisted. "Your lives are so romantic, so filled with interesting and dramatic situations, while mine is so utterly humdrum."

The lives of the Chesnutts were certainly not humdrum. They lived on a high emotional plane of almost unbearable tension at times, but they thoroughly enjoyed life notwithstanding. Charles was endowed with a philosophy that nothing could undermine and with a gallant sense of humor along with a passion for justice. Susan had a generous spirit, a serenity due to her deep-seated religious faith, and an unwavering belief in the brotherhood of man and the golden rule.

But the children belonged to another generation. To them their parents seemed somewhat naïve. To Susan and Charles who had come from the South to the more liberal North, conditions seemed to be improving. But the observations of the children made it quite clear to them that recognition of the Negro as a human being was rapidly disappearing from American thought. They questioned the philosophy that progress was being made in a country torn by race and class hatred and by greed and self-interest. To them applied Christianity seemed somewhat hollow, and the idea of the brotherhood of man a fantasy.

The years rushed on. Chesnutt was so absorbed in his profession that he had practically given up any idea of further literary effort. His work was very exacting; the personnel of his office was increased from time to time, and the office was literally open days, nights, and Sundays. Yet he was always ready to see people and talk with them and help them if necessary.

The house on Lamont Avenue became a Mecca for all sorts of pilgrims. There was the case of Jason Brown, for instance. One Sunday, several years after the Chesnutts had moved into the house on Lamont Avenue, a tall gaunt old man with deep-set eyes and square-cut whiskers came up the long walk to the porch where the family were sitting waiting for dinner to be served. They watched his approach wondering who on earth he could be. He asked for Mr. Chesnutt and introduced himself as Jason Brown, son of John Brown. He had heard that Mr. Chesnutt lived in Cleveland and he wanted to meet him. The Chesnutts welcomed the old man with unbounded hospitality. To meet a son of John Brown was truly thrilling. They invited him to dinner and in the afternoon settled him in the Gloucester hammock for a nap. When night came he made no move to go; so Susan asked him to spend the night. He accepted the invitation gladly, but insisted that he did not want to put her to any trouble; he would simply sleep on the porch in the hammock if he could have a rug to cover him. Susan and Charles both assured him that it would be an honor, and no trouble at all, to give him a bed—the son of John Brown could have anything they possessed—but the old man was firm and with utmost serenity camped out on the porch in the hammock, coming in the next morning to wash up and eat breakfast.

Jason Brown lived in a small town near Cleveland, and now and then the urge would come upon him to go somewhere. Several times during the summer he came to the Chesnutts, spent the day with them, and slept on the porch in the hammock, his very presence being an inspiration to the whole family.

People came from every walk of life seeking advice and help. One woman asked for a loan of three hundred dollars to help buy a fur coat. In her business, she said, one needed to dress well, and a fur coat was a necessity to a well-dressed woman. Chesnutt told her that many well-dressed women did not own fur coats. His wife and three daughters had never owned such luxuries and they were well-dressed, he thought. He told her that buying clothing on time was very poor business; as a business woman she ought to know that. He gave her some good advice and sent her away more satisfied with her economic status.

There was a little meek-looking woman who came one evening to talk with Chesnutt about a fine altruistic plan she had in mind. She owned an eight-suite apartment house in an exclusive neighborhood and had decided to rent the suites to colored people if she could find eight really first-class families who wanted them. She wished to know what Mr. Chesnutt thought of the idea.

Chesnutt replied that that depended upon several things. First he'd like to know how she proposed to get rid of her present tenants. That would be easy—put in one colored family and all the other tenants would move out immediately. What about rents? Well, the rents would be reasonable; they might be a little higher than she was charging her present tenants, but that was a matter of business, after all. How long might they expect to occupy the apartment? She would give every tenant a contract for a year's lease, of course. But, replied Chesnutt, the kind of people she wanted in her apartment house were not in the habit of moving annually. They owned their homes for the most part and were a pretty stable segment of the city's population. He said he had heard some of his friends say that they were tired of the responsibilities of home-owning and wished there were some decent apartment houses into which they could move. The only ones available for colored people were worn-out, rat-ridden buildings in the slums. Well, said the woman, she couldn't possibly guarantee more than a year's occupancy, but that would all be ironed out as time went on.

Chesnutt studied her for a moment and then asked, "Would you object to telling me your real motive for wanting colored tenants?"

She blushed brightly and replied:

"Well, Mr. Chesnutt, mine is one of a row of several apartment houses, and the owners of those on either side of mine have been very nasty to me, and so I want to pay them back. I can think of nothing that would hurt them more than to fill mine with colored people."

"I had reached some such conclusion," replied Chesnutt thoughtfully.

The woman was embarrassed, and after talking with Chesnutt for a while longer, left with profuse words of thanks for his advice and kindness, and then and there abandoned that particular scheme for revenge on her neighbors.

An incident which filled the women folk with deep indignation, merely amused Charles, "The poor souls are ignorant and narrow; they deserve pity, not indignation," he would say.

One evening Dorothy answered the telephone. She remained at the phone for several minutes.

"Well, this is the limit!" she exclaimed as she hurried into the library, followed by Susan and Helen.

"Calm yourself, Dottie," said her father," and tell us what it's all about." Dorothy repeated the conversation:

"This is Miss Blank speaking for Mrs. A——. We understand you have a very nice home out there on Lamont Avenue."

"I beg your pardon?"

"I said that I have learned that you have a very nice home and keep a well-trained maid."

"Really, just —"

"Mrs. A—— has had in her household for many years a very fine colored woman. She has served them as nurse and companion for a generation, and is really almost a member of the family and very superior, I assure you. Now she is too old to work and we want to arrange things for her so that her remaining years will be happy and free from anxiety."

"That is very fine, but what —"

"I am coming to that. We have done a little investigating among colored people and find that you are splendid people with a very pleasant home, and that you always keep a maid. I have been asked to talk with you and tell you that we think that your home would be just the place for this woman to live. My friends will pay you generously and will pay your maid also for special services to her. You see we want her comfortably placed among her own people where she will have the advantage of a pleasant social life of which she has been deprived owing to her employment, and where she will be well cared for and well waited upon."

"Are you suggesting that we take this person into our home as a member of our family?"

"That's it exactly, Miss Chesnutt. We want her to be among her own people."

"But we are not 'her own people.' We've never heard of her before. The people to whom she has given so many years of service would seem to me to be 'her own people.' Besides, this is a family that values its privacy and we shouldn't dream of taking a boarder and spoiling our family life."

"But we understand that Mr. Chesnutt is very much interested in the welfare of the colored people of Cleveland, and this surely seems a worthy occasion for him to show that interest."

"Let me speak plainly," replied Dorothy, who by this time was burning up at the effrontery of this seemingly cultivated woman. "You are suggesting that we have our home invaded by an utter stranger, that we adopt into our family a person about whom we know nothing at all, because your friends want to cast out from their home a woman who has served them faithfully for more than thirty years."

"But—"

"Let me finish please. Our home is a private home. We do not take boarders. We should not be willing to board our best friends, much less a woman of whom we've never heard. Please give your friends that message. Goodnight."

But they called up again several times, unwilling to accept the fact that money could not buy what they wanted. Finally they were convinced and placed their protégée in another home.

One evening the Chesnutts were serenely engaged in their usual occupations. Charles was sitting at his desk in the library playing solitaire; Susan was in the parlor absorbed in the evening paper; while the girls were preparing for the next day's work at school.

When the doorbell rang. Helen answered it. A well-dressed man with a harassed expression and a diffident manner asked if he might speak with Mr. Chesnutt. He was shown into the library and introduced himself as Mr. Blank, of one of Cleveland's suburbs.

"What can I do for you, Mr. Blank?" said Chesnutt.

Mr. Blank after several false starts burst out with, "I'm in a terrible mess, Mr. Chesnutt, and I thought that you might be willing to help me."

"Why do you think I shall be able to help you?" inquired Chesnutt.

"I have heard that you have a deep interest in what concerns the colored people of Cleveland."

"But," said Chesnutt, "you are not a colored man, are you?"

"No, but at the present moment, I am inclined to wish that I were, for then there would be no problem."

"Well," replied Chesnutt pushing aside his cards, "this is really interesting. Tell me what is on your mind."

Mr. Blank began: "My wife and I had been married for a long time, but we had no children and we both wanted a child. We decided finally to adopt an infant soon after its birth so that it would be wholly ours. We arranged with a hospital to keep us informed about any possible adoptions and received word one day that there was a fine child, a few weeks old that we might have. The records of the hospital indicated that he was white, of American parentage, with practically perfect health.

"In a fever of anticipation we went to the hospial and found a charming brown-eyed baby with pretty, curly hair and most enchanting little ways."

Mr. Blank paused for a moment and cleared his throat.

"Finally after a great deal of red tape had been unwound he became our legally adopted son. The child really resembles Mrs. Blank and we decided that we did not want people to know that he was adopted. Moving later to Cleveland we found that there was no trouble about this deception. He has grown to be a beautiful child and is now about two years old. We are both utterly devoted to him and he loves us dearly."

"But, where do I come in, Mr. Blank?" inquired Chesnutt.

"I cannot bear to continue with the story," replied Mr. Blank in a breaking voice, "but he begins to show signs of Negro blood, and the neighbors are whispering. We are very unhappy, for they are beginning to suggest that we are Negroes too."

"I'd like to see the baby," said Chesnutt thoughtfully.

"I'll get him, he's out in the car with his mother." Mr. Blank, a moment later, ushered in Mrs. Blank and the baby.

Mrs. Chesnutt and the girls promptly joined the party, and admired the pretty baby, who flirted with them and played peek-a-boo from his mother's arms.

He obviously had some dark blood. It might have been Italian or Syrian or Negro, but the chances were that it was a strain of Negro blood. It was also quite apparent that the parents worshipped the child and that he loved them.

Chesnutt studied them a moment. "Just what do you intend to do?" he finally asked.

Mrs. Blank wound her arms more closely about the child as Mr. Blank replied, "We'll have to get rid of him."

"Just how do you intend to get rid of your little son, who is your son by law?"

"That is why we have come to you. You surely must know some fine colored family to whom we can hand over our little boy. We will support him and pay them for their trouble and keep in touch with him, for we really love him dearly, but if we keep him the price will be too high for us to pay. We are not heroes or martyrs, but plain ordinary people who must live in a world that is intolerant and inhuman."

All the women were sobbing by now, and Mr. Blank's eyes were filled with tears.

"I'll do what I can for the child's sake. I suppose it is too much to expect any white American to assume voluntarily the burdens he will have to carry if he becomes involved in the race problem. I hope to God that the time will come when it won't be considered a disgrace to have a strain of Negro blood."

When the Blanks had departed, the house settled down again. Charles started a new game of solitaire. Susan remarked, "He really is a beautiful baby," and became absorbed once more in the evening paper. Dorothy went upstairs, and Helen put her Latin papers into her briefcase and announced "I'm going to bed. This has been too much for me."

The baby's story did not end unhappily, however. He was soon adopted by a well-to-do couple known for their good works, who reared him carefully and sent him to college.

29

The Passing Years

THE PROCEEDINGS of Saturday night became almost ritualistic in the Chesnutt household. The ceremony would start at dinner.

"Are you going to the Rowfant Club, tonight?" Susan would ask.

"I really don't know," Charles would reply, "I haven't decided yet."

After dinner Charles would walk into the library and begin to read. Susan would go upstairs and lay out Charles's clothes. Helen would go out to the garage and bring the car up the driveway to the door. Then peace and quiet would prevail for a while.

Suddenly Charles would dash toward the stairs, and begin, "Susan, where are my dress clothes?" "On your bed," Susan would reply, as she turned the page of the evening paper. At this point Dorothy would go quietly upstairs to be on hand in case of emergency. The emergency always arose—a collar button would fall to the floor; the studs had a habit of disappearing; the tie was usually the wrong one. But finally, with the combined efforts of Dorothy and Susan, who by this time was helping too, Charles was ready for the Rowfant Club. Then Helen would put on her wraps and say, "I'll take you down, Dad." Susan would add, "I'll go, too, for I don't want you to drive back alone." Then Dorothy would remark that she'd go along for the ride; and in the end the whole family would take him down.

On their return they'd all become absorbed in their own affairs. Then about 10:30 or 11:00 o'clock the telephone would ring and

Charles would tell them that he was ready to come home. Again they'd all climb into the car and drive down to get him. Saturday night was dedicated to Dad, and neither Susan nor the girls would have dreamed of making an engagement for themselves.

Chesnutt enjoyed these Saturday nights at the Rowfant Club. There he met, in delightful fellowship, some of the finest and most scholarly men of Cleveland. In that atmosphere he was able to expand mentally and spiritually; and there he basked in the warm rays of friendship for which his lonely heart had yearned in the days of his youth in North Carolina.

When his turn came to contribute to the Saturday night programs he was delighted, and spent a great deal of time in research and in writing. His first paper entitled "Who and Why was Samuel Johnson" was read in November, 1911. Then followed in April, 1914, "The Life and Works of Alexander Dumas," and in March, 1915, "François Villon, Man and Poet." Chesnutt had for several years been devoting his spare time to the study of French poetry and had been collecting editions of François Villon's works, both in the original French and in translation. "George Meredith," "The Diary of Philip Hone," "The Autobiography of Edward, Baron Herbert of Cherbury" were titles of other papers that he presented as the years went on.

In 1920 Chesnutt had another serious illness, appendicitis followed by peritonitis. This experience left him with his health impaired, and from that time on his activities were greatly curtailed. He played solitaire in the evenings, and worked out crossword puzzles, spending hours at these pastimes.

A new interest came into the lives of the Chesnutts a little later. They discovered Idlewild, a beautiful little resort in Lake County, Michigan, about four hundred miles from Cleveland and somewhat nearer to Chicago.

In the summer of 1921, the family separated. Dorothy spent the entire summer doing graduate work in Education at the University of Chicago. Helen taught Latin at the Foreign Language School at Western Reserve University. In August Susan went to Idlewild, where Edwin joined her, while Charles and Helen went west to the Pacific coast.

The western trip was a mad dash from beginning to end. There were so many places that Charles wanted to see that they stayed nowhere very long. They spent several days in Yellowstone Park, went as far as Victoria, British Columbia, and returned through the Canadian Rockies, stopping off at Lake Louise and Banff; then on through Winnipeg and home.

Susan's discovery of Idlewild had far-reaching results, for from that time on the summer vacations were westward—the East had lost its charm.

Chesnutt never forgot his friends and nothing pleased him more than to hear about them. The following letter from Martha M. Smith, a former teacher at Central High School, to his daughter gave him a delightful picture of an old friend and made him homesick for the past!

WARWICK, BERMUDA
January 23, 1922

DEAR HELEN,

As you know, my chief diversion here is walking. Usually I have no special aim other than to enjoy the charm that exists wherever one turns. Yesterday, though, I did have a definite objective in mind. I wanted to find Southcote because my Boston friends had told me to be sure to look up the cottage. They said they would try to rent it for the season if they ever came to Bermuda again, that it was charming and I'd love it, etc.

I thought I knew just where to strike off to reach it quite directly. Anyway the "tribe roads" as they are called are tempting by-paths. Well, somehow I didn't come upon anything like Southcote as I had pictured it, and I kept walking about until my two feet were more than tired. Finally, I saw a woman sitting on the porch of a cottage, and while I was sure it wasn't Southcote, I thought I'd make inquiries. If the lady was kind, she might invite me to rest a bit. She did just that and somehow conveyed a welcome, though she was shaking-shaking with palsy, I suppose. Anyway, we began to chatter quite briskly about Bermuda and Bermudians, their ideas in the matter of vegetables compared with our own, other resorts—Pass Christian was mentioned—people who flitted across our paths, here and there. She had met Michael Strange in a shop a day or so before.

From this, you may well conclude that nothing was said worth repeating and yet I felt the woman with whom I was talking was a very interesting person. She quite absorbed all my attention until very suddenly a little man appeared. I think he darted, rather then walked onto the porch. One eye looked as if it were glass. He wore a gray smoking jacket or house coat, bound with black, shabby, decidedly worn braid.

Southcote? Certainly he knew Southcote. If I must be on my way, he would go with me, at least far enough to set me right, so that I couldn't stray again. All at once in the midst of conversation, he began to demonstrate the German goose-step, insisting that I try it, too. So we went goose-stepping along until he could point out Southcote.

By this time, my guide knew my name, and so it seemed fitting as I turned to thank him that I should indicate I still did not know his. "Cable," he said, and darted off, vanishing in just no time. Wasn't I a stupid fool not to realize at the moment that the man is George W. Cable! Miss Leon has confirmed absolutely my after-thought. I might have called back, "Then you know Charles W. Chesnutt!" No doubt, Mr. Cable would have darted my way again and we should have walked on and on forgetting Southcote altogether. Anyway, I think the incident may interest your father.

Love to you and the family,

As ever,

MARTHA

The home on Lamont Avenue had always given the Chesnutts great pleasure, it was so spacious and comfortable and beautiful. Susan, who was constantly planning some improvements, never failed to receive the happy cooperation of the others. "Home" was a magic word to them.

CHARLES TO ETHEL, DECEMBER 20, 1922

Enclosed find a small check, of which please give Charlie what you like and keep the rest for yourself as an earnest of my love and good wishes for my eldest daughter and my only grandson.

We have done the old house pretty well over during the year. In the late spring and summer we had the old soapstone sink taken out of the kitchen and replaced with a modern sanitary white sink of the approved level for dishwashing; a new toilet and washstand installed in the bathroom and new linoleum to replace the old.

Recently we have had the hall, parlor, library and vestibule refinished in the new sand color, the dining-room ceiling repainted, kitchen repainted and back halls and sewing room repainted or kalsomined. There are new pongee curtains in hall.

parlor and library. In the way of furniture we have bought a
brown mahogany five-drawer table-desk for the library, Sheraton
model inlaid, a dream of graceful beauty, 60 x 30 inches; a large
overstuffed chair upholstered in taupe mohair, with a brown
mahogany end-table on which to put your book or whatever you
like. And the final extravagance, we have just bought an electric
victrola, and have been dancing ever since. Up at Idlewild, where
your mother and Dorothy and I spent August, I danced every
night until the home waltz.

I also spent a lot of time fishing and rowing; caught so many
black bass and blue-gills that your mother got tired of cooking
them. . . .

Edwin came home for Thanksgiving, his first visit since my
operation a couple of years ago. He got in at 11 o'clock in the
morning and left by the night train. He is very good looking and
seems to be doing very well.

We wonder why he does not get married, but he seems to have
no inclination that way. Unless you should get busy, or Dorothy
should marry, Charles seems likely to be my only descendant in
the second generation. Helen is a hopeless case.

The family all join me in love and the season's greetings.

CHARLES TO ETHEL, JANUARY 23, 1923

I don't believe I ever acknowleged receipt of the handsome
necktie you sent me at Christmas. I have been wearing it, to the
great improvement of my personal appearance.

We have been having quite a lively season since we had the
house fixed over. First Dorothy gave a large party, over fifty
guests, during the Christmas week. She had a tall Christmas tree
in the stair-well in the hall, two pieces of music, dancing, and
nice refreshments. Everybody enjoyed it immensely. Then Susan
had the new rector and his wife to dinner. Last Saturday night
Helen gave a party to all the Central Senior High School women
teachers. As soon as it was mentioned her friend Miss Mallory
asked permission to join as hostess, which Helen granted. Immediately another friend, Miss Sowers, demanded the same privilege,
so the three of them shared the labor and the expense. There
were thirty-two guests. The party began at 4 P.M. with music by
an orchestra of five of the high school students conducted by
Mrs. Parr the musical director. When the music was dismissed
supper was served. After this delectable meal the ladies played

cards—bridge and five hundred; and after that I gave a victrola concert; and about 11 o'clock the party broke up. Everybody commented on the beauty of the house, the perfect harmony of the lamps and the flowers, and certainly, with the ladies all togged out in their best clothes it was a beautiful sight. The thing this house is best adapted to is social entertainment and I fear now that it has been put in apple-pie order we shall be bankrupted by hospitality. Dorothy's club, The Young Matrons, meets here next Friday afternoon to round out the circle.

I have been reading with interest the newspaper articles concerning Roscoe Bruce and Harvard University. I am glad he raised the question. I don't know that he or anyone else can change President Lowell's decision, but it is a dirty shame to spoil a fine old tradition by a petty surrender to a low and unfair prejudice. All send love and best wishes.

Chesnutt's interest in Harvard University's attempt at this time to exclude colored men from its dormitories was very deep. When he opened *Cleveland Topics* one day and saw some flippant remarks about the outcome of the controversy, his indignation was extreme.

April 20, 1923

Mr. Charles T. Henderson
Editor Cleveland Topics
319 Caxton Building
City

Dear Sir:

I have been a subscriber to *Cleveland Topics* for several years. I began to take it at my wife's suggestion that you had been a classmate of my son at Central High School, and that she had known your mother. It is one weekly paper that all the family have been reading from beginning to end, and I have for some time been saying to my friends and acquaintances at the Chamber of Commerce, the City Club and elsewhere, that it was the best edited paper in Cleveland, because of its sane and sensible views on public questions, and its outspoken courage in expressing them.

Imagine my feelings therefore, when I opened my paper last week and ran upon the following gem of liberality, broad-mindedness, fair play, and good taste:

"So it has been decided that negroes shall not be excluded from

Harvard dormitories. We should like to say what we think of this but there is a constitutional amendment against such language.

"Anyway, we are interested to learn that the all wise Harvard overseers voted that 'men of the white and colored races shall not be *compelled* to live and eat together.' That must be a great relief to certain gentlemen of color who otherwise might find themselves 'compelled to live and eat' with white folks."

If this utterance had emanated from a Florida "cracker" or a Georgia "red neck," or even an Alabama senator, I should not have been surprised; but from a man brought up in Cleveland, educated in the public schools where he went to school with colored children, and with a mother such as yours, who was widely known as a generous and broad-minded woman, who to my personal knowledge has eaten in public with colored people, it came as a surprise, to say the least.

I really cannot understand the basis of your emotional turmoil, which is apparently so great that you cannot find decent language to express it. I suspected that you did not know what you were writing about, which I have verified by ascertaining that you are not a Harvard man. Colored students have always lived in the dormitories and eaten in the dining halls at Harvard; I have paid the bills of one of them and ought to know. The "living together" and "eating with white folks" involves no more intimacy than life in a hotel, and you know or ought to know that colored men are received as guests at some of the best hotels in Cleveland, that eight or ten of them are members of the City Club and eat in its dining room, and I have seen brown men eating in the sacred precincts of the Union Club, and at the University Club.

I am quite sure that had you had any such feeling against Jews, you would not have expressed it publicly in any such manner, nor, had you had a hundred subscribers whom you knew to be colored, would you have gone out of your way to insult them, if only as a matter of policy, to say nothing of good taste.

I shall not indulge in the childish gesture of saying "Stop my paper," since I have paid for it in advance, but I shall hereafter take it up with suspicion and qualify my admiration with reflection.

Yours truly,
CHARLES W. CHESNUTT

Chesnutt was unjust to Henderson, for he had had nothing whatever to do with the offensive article, explained the managing editor of *Topics*. The criticism, however, was absolutely just, and he asked Chesnutt to accept his personal apology, and his thanks for calling their attention to the "unpardonable stupidity of the 'smart' item," and promised that that particular columnist would be supervised thereafter.

Dorothy, who had been teaching French and English at Willson Junior High School since 1920, was married in March, 1924, to John G. Slade, a young man who was studying for his Master's degree at Ohio State University, and who afterwards entered the Medical School at Howard University. Dorothy remained at home and continued with her teaching. When her son was born in June, 1925, Susan, with the help of a nurse-maid, undertook the care of the baby.

In 1925 the Chesnutts, who had tried out Idlewild in a rented cottage for several seasons, decided to build a summer home of their own there. Charles bought a plot of land bordering the lake and planned with a contractor to have the cottage built and completed by June of the following year. They spent the winter planning the furniture for the cottage. The house on Lamont Street had an enormous attic, and whenever Susan had bought new furniture she had stored the old furniture in the attic, so that now it was a gold mine for them.

They gradually got the things together and in June hired a mover to take them to Idlewild. There was Charles's cherry rocker with leather seat, from which Susan had with difficulty divorced him several years previously, and the oak library table at which he had written his books so long ago. The girls selected several old walnut chairs that would give an air to the living room, the oak desk which had seen all four children through Central High School, and some oak bookshelves.

Susan was very practical. She selected the bedroom set which had been her pride and joy when she had first moved into the Brenton Street house; the Jenny Lind bed which Charles had bought to help furnish the first little home on Willcut Street, and a huge brass bedstead which had been the acme of luxury during their early years on Lamont Street. Dorothy added an antique oak chest which she had inherited from an old friend of the family, and Helen contributed one of her choice possessions—a fire-place set, including andirons, shovel, tongs, and poker.

And then they started to Idlewild to spend one of their happiest summers in organizing—Helen's favorite word—the cottage where they spent the remaining summers of Charles's life.

Idlewild was situated in the western part of Michigan, between Reed City and Ludington, about five miles from Baldwin, the county-seat of Lake County. The Chesnutts either drove all the way, a distance of about four hundred miles, or they halved the distance by taking the boat from Cleveland to Detroit and driving only two hundred miles from there. The trips, up and down, contributed greatly to the family's enjoyment of the vacation.

At Idlewild Chesnutt relaxed in the clear, pine-scented, health-giving air. He spent his days fishing, sitting in an old willow chair at the end of his little pier, absorbing the golden sunshine and catching a blue gill now and then with bamboo fishing-pole. Or, feeling more energetic, he would row out into the lake in his flat-bottomed boat (Susan had insisted on this type of boat) to cast for bass with rod and reel. He was not always successful, but he had a great deal of fun with his fishing. The girls and Edwin, who spent his short vacations there, drove him for miles around the countryside in search of bait, and whenever they heard of a well-stocked lake anywhere in the vicinity there they would drive him to try out his luck.

If the weather was rainy or too cold for fishing, he would sit before the log fire in the living-room and read, or play solitaire, or do cross-word puzzles, which he enjoyed immensely, calling in all the members of the family for assistance which he never needed at all. Susan was equally happy there, for her love of social life was always strong.

Many of the cottagers were elderly. They came from Detroit and Grand Rapids, Chicago, Cleveland, Columbus, and other cities of the Middle West as well as from Canada. Some of the cottages were beautiful places. Across the lake from the Chesnutt's was the summer home of the eminent Chicago surgeon, Dr. Daniel H. Williams, affectionately called "Dr. Dan" by his friends. Dr. Dan's house was immaculate; perfect order and system pre-vailed even in the garage and tool-house. Whenever Susan and the girls went to call at Dr. Dan's house they developed such an inferiority complex while there, that on their return home they began picking up the books, magazines, and newspapers which littered the living-room; or they tried desperately to tidy up the front porch, which faced the lake, by removing the oars and the boat cushions and the fishing-tackle and the sun-hats and bathing shoes to the back porch. But the attempt was abortive; for no sooner was anything put tidily away than Charles demanded it, and within an hour or two things were exactly where they had been in the beginning.

Nature was lavish at Idlewild. Brilliant blue skies reflected in the lake; the most gorgeous sunsets imaginable, fading away gradually to let the night come on, its sky studded thickly with brilliant stars and constellations that a city-dweller could never dream of. The sunrise was equally beautiful if one rose early enough. Nothing could surpass the thrill of seeing at that hour a crane stepping daintily along the shore of the lake, stopping now and then to dip its bill into the water in search of breakfast. No place could have been more enchanting to Susan and Charles, in their advancing years, than Idlewild.

But sickness dogged Chesnutt's steps and caught up with him again in the spring of 1927. The unsparing expenditure of energy in his younger days was taking its toll.

Fred Charles, of the *Plain Dealer,* learning of his illness, went out to Lamont Street to interview him, and found him in his library working on a new novel. During his illness his mind had been busy with the incident of the Blank baby told in a preceding chapter, and he had begun the novel on which Fred Charles found him engaged. The next day's *Plain Dealer* had a headline on the front page—"Muse Lures Pencil of Chesnutt Anew," and a flattering article about him and his literary fame. Among other things it said, "Chesnutt's office in the Union Trust Building is one of the few in Cleveland where tea is served each afternoon punctually at four." Chesnutt received quite a little flurry of attention when this article appeared.

March 23, 1927

MR. FRED CHARLES
C/O CLEVELAND PLAIN DEALER
CLEVELAND, OHIO
DEAR MR. CHARLES:

I read with interest and pleasure your very flattering "Write-up" in the *Plain Dealer.* Several gentlemen have called me up, commenting on the fact that a newspaper gave me so much space while I was still alive, and many others of my friends have made favorable comment. My family was very much pleased with it.

Our four o'clock tea business has picked up since your article appeared. In fact, we have had quite a rush. Miss Moore and I suggest that you come around to the office some afternoon about that time and have a dish of tea.

Cordially yours,
CHARLES W. CHESNUTT

That year the family went to Idlewild as soon as school closed, for they wanted Charles to have as long a vacation as possible. But early in August he learned that some of his business affairs needed his personal attention and returned to Cleveland accompanied by Dorothy, with her baby and Sadie the nursemaid, to keep house for him. Susan and Helen remained at Idlewild, for they had invited guests to visit them in August.

CHARLES TO SUSAN, AUGUST 9, 1927

We all arrived home safely this morning, reaching Cleveland at 6:00 o'clock. The baby stood the journey very nicely indeed. We took a taxi up to the house, I skimmed up to the neighborhood grocery and the A&P and bought some emergency rations and we had a nice breakfast; peaches, oatmeal, boiled eggs, toast, and coffee. Then I skimmed out to my property on Superior Street and found that I had to pay a bill of $125.00 for repairing pipes in the stores, collected some rent, and during the day have arranged for the collection of more tomorrow. Going out tonight to see about still more. One of my tenants is moving out Saturday and I shall put a sign on the house. Found everything in good shape at the office.

Don't worry about us. Dorothy is taking excellent care of me and we will take good care of the baby. Love to you and Helen and regards to Jessie.

CHARLES TO EDWIN, AUGUST 23, 1927

The baby announced last evening at the dinner table that he was "gonna wite a long letta to Unka Ned." Although his intentions were praiseworthy, I knew he had bitten off more than he could chew, so I am writing a letter in his place.

I received your letter at Idlewild inclosing the cutting from the Chicago paper, telling of Mr. Mencken's views on the future

of the colored race. I put away the cutting in order to talk it
over with you. It is probably in a drawer or pigeon hole of the
desk in the living room.

I am sorry I could not wait to see you, as I like to see my only
son at least once a year. Perhaps you will find it convenient to
come and see us in Cleveland.

I left some bass in the lake for you with the necessary equipment to take them out. However, fishing for bass is a business in
itself. I had better luck than last year, but not anything to boast
of as it was.

I hope you will enjoy yourself in Idlewild, and will drop me
a line from time to time when the spirit moves you.

Again misfortune entered the Chesnutt household. Early in
November Helen was rushed to the Cleveland Clinic Hospital
with a ruptured appendix. Peritonitis set in and for several weeks
her parents were in a state of great anxiety. The strain on Susan,
who was not well, was so great that the family feared she would
collapse. When early in January her brother-in-law, Dr. Ben
Henderson, died at Fayetteville, she was persuaded to go to North
Carolina, which she had not visited since her mother's death
nineteen years before.

SUSAN TO FAMILY, JANUARY 7, 1928

I arrived safely last evening at seven-thirty. I was the only passenger for Fayetteville. The train was filled with New Englanders
and rich Germans bound for Jacksonville.

Charlie bought me a seat in the Pullman and I had no trouble
whatever. Both the conductor and porter were very courteous
and looked after me all the way down. From the time I arrived
there were callers up till one o'clock this morning. The old custom of sitting up with the dead is still in vogue. I have been up
just long enough to have breakfast, and knowing how anxious
you must be to hear from me after that terrible rush to the train,
I am writing a line or two before callers begin to arrive. Dot, I
hope you did not strain yourself taking the hat-box up those
steps. It was a hectic get-a-way, but I am here among relatives and
friends, and for the first time in months I have really relaxed.
Everybody is glad to see me but can not understand why my hair
in not white and why I am not *old* and wrinkled.

I reached Washington at 7:55 and found no one waiting as
Dad's telegram read 8:55. I telephoned Ethel who said that Ed

and Charlie had just left for the station. When I saw those two swagger young men coming toward me I was proud of the way they looked. Both are handsome; Charles has grown taller and is certainly handsome. I was treated royally by all of them. Was taken out to the house for breakfast, and came back to the station and left at 10:55 for Fayetteville. Jane came down to the station and we had a little visit. Lots of love to all of you.

CHARLES TO SUSAN, JANUARY 9, 1928

We got through Sunday very nicely. Had codfish for breakfast out of my box, roast lamb for dinner, all very nice.

When I left this morning, Nick was working at the house. He cleaned out the furnace, and found some more boxes and baskets in the cellar and was shifting the ashes from a big box in the back yard to some smaller containers which the ashman could handle without tearing up the lawn.

Hope you are having a good time and that the funeral went off satisfactorily. Stay and get your rest and see your old friends and have as good a time as you can. We will worry along without you until you come back.

I don't know any more news, and I suppose the girls are writing you right along. Love and best wishes.

[And a week later],

. . . Have got in three tons more of coal. The baby is in fine fettle. His literary taste is much in evidence. He has four or five *Mother Goose* books and several others, and can repeat most of the rhymes. He got out a volume of the *Encyclopaedia Britannica* the other day and in his thirst for information tore out one of the pages. His mother is going to paste it in. . . .

Stay as long as you like, but we shall all be glad to have you back. With the best intentions in the world nobody and no bunch of people can quite fill your place.

We called you Long Distance last night but you were out.

My love to the Williams family. Ethel knows how to entertain people and loves to do it. Tell Charlie if he can pick up a *House Behind the Cedars* to do so by all means. I would pay up to three or four dollars for a good copy, not more than two dollars for a *Conjure Woman*.

We all send love and are looking forward eagerly to your return.

Susan read between the lines of these letters and realized that she was needed at home. She was met with open arms.

30

The Spingarn Medal

CHESNUTT had been writing pretty steadily for some time. When Carl Van Vechten's *Nigger Heaven* was published in 1926 containing some flattering comments on his books, he had felt the urge to write again, and the incident of the adopted baby had so stirred his imagination that he started a new novel based on this. It was this novel that Fred Charles had found him writing. His friends had seemed so delighted at the prospect of another book from him that he had put aside his cards and his cross-word puzzles, and was devoting his waning energies to this work.

In March Chesnutt once more took up the cudgels for the Negro by appearing, on behalf of colored labor, before a Senate Committee at Washington, against the Shipstead Anti-Injunction Bill. This bill was proposed and promoted by the labor unions. Its object was to limit the power of injunction vested in Federal Courts with the view of strengthening the hands of the labor unions in labor disputes. Chesnutt was opposed to strengthening the power of the labor unions, because of their unjust and inhuman stand toward Negro labor. Armed with affidavits telling of the brutal treatment of Negro workers by many unions, he, accompanied by Harry Davis, under the auspices of the Cleveland Chamber of Commerce, made a plea for Negro labor.

CHARLES TO EDWIN, MARCH 20, 1928

Just returned this morning from a trip to Washington and New York. I went to Washington to appear before a Senate Committee in opposition to a certain bill. Stopped over night with Ethel and found them all well. . . .

In New York I met James Weldon Johnson, who introduced me to some publishers relative to certain designs I have upon the reading world. I also called on Carl Van Vechten at his apartment. I had had some very interesting correspondence with him about the time of the appearance of his *Nigger Heaven,* and found him a very amiable and affable gentleman. He remembered in the course of the conversation that he had met you in Chicago at the home of a Dr. Glenn, if I recall the name correctly.

The family are all well. Helen has recovered superficially from her distressing experience and is back at work, although I am not sure that she is yet entirely out of the woods. They all join me in love to you.

The month of June was eagerly anticipated by all the Chesnutts. There were now four anniversaries to be celebrated, for the baby's birthday also came in June. But the great day, the day par excellence was the golden wedding day of Susan and Charles. The children planned a family reunion, and later in the day a reception, so that their parents' many friends could congratulate them and wish them happiness. But in May Helen had to return to the hospital, and all plans for the celebration were stopped.

On June 8 the whole family drove over to the hospital after dinner with some interesting news. Charles had just received a telegram from James Weldon Johnson announcing that at the meeting of the Spingarn Medal Award Committee that day, the medal had been awarded to him for his pioneer services as a literary artist and his distinguished career as a public-spirited citizen. The telegram went on to say that the medal would be awarded at the annual conference of the NAACP at Los Angeles by the Lieutenant Governor of California, on July 3, if Chesnutt could be present. If not it could be presented by proxy, and then presented personally in a special ceremony in Cleveland in the fall.

The award of this medal was a great surprise to all of them. There had already been thirteen annual awards since its founding by Major Joel Spingarn in 1914, and there was no more reason for Chesnutt's receiving it at that time than there had been for the last thirteen years. So the girls suggested that he decline the award, especially since to receive it necessitated that long trip across the continent.

Susan wanted to go. A trip in a special car filled with friends would be an enjoyable way of seeing the West, and would not be as taxing as a regular sight-seeing trip. The girls, knowing how difficult long trips were for their mother, begged them not to go. But Charles wrote to Johnson:

June 11, 1928

MR. JAMES WELDON JOHNSON
SECRETARY, NAACP
69 FIFTH AVENUE
NEW YORK CITY
MY DEAR MR. JOHNSON:

I received your telegram on Friday and answered it on Saturday, expressing my appreciation of the honor and stating that I hoped to be at Los Angeles in person.

I assure you and wish you to assure the committee that I appreciate very highly the honor conferred upon me. I was under the impression that the medal was awarded for current achievement, and am all the more pleased because the committee seems to have made it retro-active in my case. However, I shall try to finish my novel and bring my work a little more down to date.

Mrs. Chesnutt, who has never been to the Pacific Coast, has decided that it has been the dream of her life to visit California and that this is her opportunity. As a married man, you know what this means, and she will accompany me.

A personal question: On these occasions, what kind of clothes are usually worn by the candidate? Is a dinner jacket permissible, or is one supposed to wear a long cut-away or a dress suit? I don't do this every year and I want to do it right.

Is it necessary to make arrangements in advance with regard to entertainment, or will some committee take charge of that, or just what is the situation in that regard?

Please advise me as promptly as possible so that I may know what to do.

Yours cordially,
CHARLES W. CHESNUTT

Chesnutt enjoyed very much the congratulations by telephone, telegram, and letter that began to come in. Many of his friends congratulated him on the "belated honor" and said that it should have been awarded to him long ago. Such statements as "the medal gains lagging prestige in this year's award"; "the honor if belated, is surely deserved"; "the Spingarn Medal Committee has covered itself with glory"; "to have one's achievements recognized by one's own people is so rare an occurrence in the case of our people that it is wonderful and most encouraging indeed"; these were very interesting to all the family. *The Cleveland Plain Dealer* expressed the sentiments of the community in the following fine editorial:

FITTINGLY BESTOWED

Cleveland is honored by the honor to be conferred on Charles W. Chesnutt, novelist and lawyer. To him is awarded the medal which goes each year to the one of African descent and American citizenship who achieves the most distinguished service in some field of honorable endeavor. The medal goes to Mr. Chesnutt for his "pioneer work as a literary artist depicting the life and struggles of Americans of Negro descent, and for his long and useful career as scholar, worker, and freeman of one of America's greatest cities."

It is a bestowal fittingly made. Mr. Chesnutt has been an untiring worker for good causes, a writer of strength and grace and sound purpose. Some of his earlier books have been all but forgotten by a generation always eager for the new, but they will long remain as an expression of a brave soul pouring itself out in effective protest against racial prejudice. Charming tales they are too; readable romances created by a word artist.

This service medal could not be more appropriately awarded. Cleveland congratulates Charles W. Chesnutt.

SUSAN TO ETHEL, OCT. 16, 1928

... I was hardly in condition to take the trip to California but when the news came that your father had received the Spingarn Medal, and it was to be awarded at Los Angeles, it seemed such an opportune time to go to California that I decided very hastily to go.

I enjoyed the journey going very much—then we planned to return by the northern route—through the Canadian Rockies—which was gorgeous and wonderful. The return trip was a little too long for me. We were ten days, after leaving San Francisco, before we reached Chicago. We spent one night with Mr. and Mrs. Jesse Binga and met Clarence Darrow at dinner there, then went on to Idlewild where I collapsed from fatigue. From then until now I have not been quite myself. However, I would not have missed it for anything.

I intended to write you of my trip as I went along, but did not figure on your father. He gets fussier every day, and he nearly drove me wild while traveling, trying to do all the things that he wanted to do. But on the whole, it was a great trip. The meetings were well attended—six or seven thousand people every evening. The people of Los Angeles are very hospitable when it comes to entertaining.

31

End of a Rich, Full Life

THE LAST YEARS of Chesnutt's life were happy years. Each season found him physically a little frailer. His hearing became impaired, which brought his pre-eminence as a court reporter to an end. He no longer ran his office. His associate, Helen C. Moore, was now in charge, but he still enjoyed meeting the world which came to its doors, and nothing could induce him to retire. When "my office" became "the office" Susan realized that Charles was beginning to accept old age with its infirmities. He began to spend more time at home. Some days he did not go to the office at all, but more often, after he had yielded to Susan's entreaties to remain at home, the office would telephone and ask him to come down to attend to something that no one else seemed capable of doing. So she would call a taxicab and start him off, little realizing that Charles submitted to this indignity merely for her peace of mind. At the corner of Euclid Avenue and 93rd Street he invariably dismissed the cab and took the Euclid car down to the Union Trust Building where the office was located.

But his business inactivity had its compensations, for he gradually began to write again. The publicity gained by the Spingarn Medal award in 1928 had caused a demand for his books, but as they were out of print the demand could not be filled. So Chesnutt, who had been writing in a desultory way for some time, decided that he had better settle down and finish his novel about the adopted baby. In between times he amused himself by writing for his little grandson a series of short stories about wonderful animals who could talk like human beings, with which both of them had a great deal of fun.

When he finished the novel, he sent it on to Harry Bloch of Alfred A. Knopf, who had suggested that he write something new for publication, and thus take advantage of the special publicity being given to his work.

But Chesnutt was old now, and frail, and tired, and his last novel, *The Quarry,* lacked the magic touch which had won him fame a generation before. Harry Bloch returned the manuscript with a note to which Chesnutt replied: "I am sorry, of course, that you had to decide against my book, but thank you very much for reading it. I note what you say about the central idea in the story, and my failure to carry it out successfully, and the lifelessness of the characters and the 'priggishness' of the hero. I suspect you are right about all of this, and in the light of your criticism I shall, before I submit the book elsewhere, see if I can put some flesh on and some red blood in the characters. . . .

"Houghton, Mifflin and Company has published a new edition of *The Conjure Woman,* in a very beautiful format, with a foreword by Major J. E. Spingarn. I hope its sale will justify Mr. Greenslet's enterprise. Perhaps I am too old to write another live book, but if some of my first ones could be revived, that would be something."

This new edition of *The Conjure Woman,* issued in February, 1929, just thirty years after its publication, delighted Chesnutt. Elrick Davis, the literary editor of the *Cleveland Press,* wrote such a glowing tribute to him that the whole family felt rejuvenated and begged Charles to keep right on working at *The Quarry.* But he did not have the vitality to rewrite the book, and put it aside until later.

Again he became ill and was confined to his home for several weeks, and later on started a series of treatments at the Cleveland Clinic.

CHARLES TO ETHEL, MAY 13, 1929

We should like very much to have you with us this summer. The NAACP will meet here June 25 to July 2, I think the dates are, and as soon as it is over we shall trek northward. If you could come to the convention you could drive up with us after it and save R.R. fare.

Your mother and I are getting older every day and you and we live so far apart that we seldom meet, and we should like to enjoy a little of your society while we are still alive—really alive and not just hanging on to save funeral expenses.

Your mother will write, and would have written sooner, but she has been in indifferent health and working too hard because of the rottenly incompetent and unreliable help that she has to put up with. All join me in love and the hope that you can be with us. Please let us know soon.

EDWIN TO CHARLES, MAY 15, 1929

Your letter received. Hope that you can have a good long stay at Idlewild this summer and regain your health.

Right now, I am looking at a big headline in the evening paper stating that 90 people were killed in an explosion and fire at the Cleveland Clinic. Isn't that Dr. Phillips' hospital? And was he killed? That's really a big tragedy, and it certainly shows the uncertainty of life and the illusory nature of happiness. There must be a lot of grief in Cleveland tonight.

I expect to catch quite a few bass with you this year if we can get good weather. Also we might make a trip to Woodland where the fishing is very good. They tell me that with better roads and electric current coming from Ludington, Idlewild will be much improved. It also has street lights along all the main streets. . . .

CHARLES TO EDWIN, MAY 17, 1929

The Clinic catastrophe was a dreadful thing. I have been going to the Clinic this winter for treatment, and was due for a treatment on last Wednesday morning, the day of the explosion, but fortunately had not gone, by which I probably escaped death.

The newspapers have been full of the affair ever since, and I am sending you some papers today.

Dr. Phillips was in the Clinic at the time of the explosion, but he got out. A friend of his, standing nearby with his automobile, saw him sitting on the steps and went over and offered his automobile to take him home. He had just got in the car when Dr. Crile came out of the Clinic and wanted to look after him. Dr. Phillips said no, there were a hundred people in the Clinic who needed attention more than he did. He went home, was taken ill from the gas, and died that night about 8:00 o'clock.

They had moved up to Wade Park Manor a few months ago leaving their house next to ours vacant.

You will see from the list of names that seven or eight of the doctors connected with the Clinic lost their lives. It is all commented on at length in the newspapers, both as news and editorially, and will undoubtedly occupy the public mind to the exclusion of almost everything else for some time.

We all join in hoping that you are well and doing well, and look forward to seeing you at Idlewild this summer.

CHARLES TO ETHEL, JULY 15, 1929

We are nicely located for the summer and are looking forward to your visit. Helen is in Europe, landed in London yesterday if her boat arrived on schedule. Her friend Alta Bien is with her.

Your mother hasn't got rested yet but is taking it easy. Dorothy and I do the work, with the assistance (the other way) of the baby. Hope the fish will bite when you come, they have been rather shy so far.

Hope your husband and son are well. Now that you are alone perhaps you can give your old dad a little of your society.

All join me in love and the hope of seeing you.

Ethel spent the month of August at Idlewild to the great delight of her parents. It had been nearly twenty years since she left Cleveland for Washington, and they had seen very little of her since that time. They enjoyed talking of the past, and living over again with her their early life.

In December Ethel's husband became seriously ill and the family were very much concerned about him.

CHARLES TO ETHEL, DECEMBER 18, 1929

No news being good news, and not having heard from you for several days, we are assuming that Ed is improving.

Our family is staggering along as usual. Your mother and I are just able to get around; the baby has a bad cold; and the girls are pretty well tuckered out with their term examinations, and grades, and school parties and plays, and other professional activities. Love to Ed and Charlie.

But Ed did not improve, and for the first time death entered the family circle of the Chesnutts.

In 1930, Chesnutt, who now had some leisure time to dispose of, made an extensive survey of the economic, civil, and social status of Cleveland's 75,000 colored people. This article appeared in *The Clevelander,* the monthly journal published by the Chamber of Commerce, in November, 1930, under the title "The Negro in Cleveland."

In this he brought out clearly all the injustices suffered by Cleveland's Negro population. He touched upon the restrictive covenants by which people of Negro descent were barred from the great suburban developments; and told of the ill-kept neighborhoods where the laboring class lived in "dilapidated, rack-rented shacks, sometimes a whole family in one or two rooms, as a rule paying higher rents than white tenants for the same space." He referred to the labor situation, telling how many of the unions barred the Negro from membership and thus deprived him of a chance to earn a decent living. He wrote of the difficulty that the colored boy had in learning a trade, and told how the tax-supported trade schools run by the Board of Education were so dominated by rules and regulations dictated by the unions that the attendance of colored students was discouraged by the officials. He told how the Cleveland Street Railway Company did not employ Negro motormen or conductors; how the great public utilities employed Negroes only in the humblest positions; and how the huge department stores and commercial concerns employed no Negro clerks or salesmen, with few exceptions.

But there was a brighter side to the picture. In public service the Negro had a better chance owing to his voting power, which was well organized under very efficient leaders. In the learned professions also the Negro was well represented.

He spoke of the widely varying attitude toward the Negro of the social service agencies supported in whole or in part by the Community Fund. The Y.M.C.A. and the Y.W.C.A. did not admit colored members except at the Cedar Branch of the Y.M.C.A.; but the Phillis Wheatley Association under the guidance of Jane Hunter was doing noble work with Negro girls; and the Playhouse Settlement under the direction of Russell and Rowena Jelliffe had long been doing a great cultural service for the Negro.

In summing up he said: "There is a race problem in Cleveland, but it is not acute. From the Negro's side it is mainly concerned with a fair living, a decent place to live, making his way in the world on equal terms with others, and living at peace with his neighbors. With fair play the Negro makes a very good citizen. Abuse him and he becomes in his own eyes a martyr, and the martyr complex is not conducive to good citizenship. . . .

"The better class of white people in Cleveland are in some ways very generous toward the Negro, and can generally be relied upon to respond liberally to any call on their part for money for any worthy purpose. But they could render the Negroes a better service by cultivating fraternal or, if that be too much, at least friendly relations with them, not so much by way of condescension, as from man to man, thereby making their advancement easier along all lines. For they still have a long and hard road to travel to reach that democratic equality upon the theory of which our government and our social system are founded, not to desire and seek which would make them unworthy of contempt."

Chesnutt's last literary production was an essay entitled "Post-Bellum—Pre-Harlem," which appeared in Part Five of *The Colophon* issued in February, 1931. It was one of twenty essays by writers of international reputation telling how their first books were published, which *The Colophon, a Book Collectors' Quarterly*, published during the years 1930 to 1937. Chesnutt enjoyed writing this essay. He exhumed his scrap books, reread old letters, and had such a happy time with his memories that he nearly forgot to finish the essay.

These twenty essays were later collected by Elmer Adler, one of the editors of *The Colophon,* and published by Simon and Schuster in 1937 under the title *Breaking into Print*.

Chesnutt's love of life was so great, his interest in the world and its problems so vital that he seemed to those who loved him perennially young. His gallant humor, his love for people, his keen enjoyment of all the little things in life never grew less. A passion for human justice possessed him; for justice he worked throughout his life.

His conception of human rights was simple. Rights are fundamental. Man does not have to earn them; does not have to struggle to be worthy of gaining them at some far-off future time. Rights are given by God and are inalienable, and any human being that does not demand his rights, all of them, is lacking in integrity and is something less than a man.

His philosophy for himself and his family was characteristic:

"We are normal human beings with all the natural desires of normal individuals. We acknowledge no inherent inferiority and resent any denial of rights and opportunities based on racial discrimination. We believe in equality and all that it implies. We shall live our lives as Americans pure and simple, and whatever experiences we encounter shall be borne with forbearance, and fortitude, and amusement if possible."

His children were nurtured on this philosophy which became a part of their mental and spiritual inheritance.

Chesnutt enjoyed a rich, full life. Starting out at the age of fourteen to earn his living, he had been able by his own efforts, with the assistance of what tutors he could find, to acquire a fine liberal education. He was an ardent reader and loved all kinds of books. In his later years the books on his bedside table showed his wide range of interest. *The Odes of Horace,* the latest French book, a mystery story, a current best-seller; the *Story of Philosophy,* the *Atlantic,* the *Crisis, Opportunity,* the *Nation,* the *New Republic*—all gave him interest and pleasure. He loved music and the theatre and, until his health became too poor, attended with his wife and daughters the many concerts and plays that have enriched the lives of Clevelanders. He loved beauty and was able to store his mind with the beauties of nature by extensive travel in America and in parts of Europe.

But he was human and had his weaknesses. He was not a good business man. His real-estate ventures were always a hazard because of his forbearance—some of his tenants exploited him outrageously. He, like many others, suffered serious financial losses in the crash of the stock market in 1929. But he never grew cynical. Life to him was a beautiful thing.

He experienced in abundance the things that make life beautiful—aspiration, high endeavor, noted achievement, and widespread recognition; then disillusion, readjustment, service to mankind, the respect and affection of all who knew him, abiding love and devotion from every member of his family.

In November, 1932, he came home from the office one day and told Susan that he was a bit tired and would go to bed. He was not at all anxious to get up, a very unusual state of mind; so Susan called the doctor, who told her to let him rest. Several days later the doctor suggested a nurse—even then his wife and daughters had no idea that Charles was mortally ill, for to them he was the essence of immortality. On November 15 at 5:30 in the afternoon, the nurse summoned Susan and the girls. As they entered the room Charles smiled at them, held out his hand to Susan, and with a little sigh breathed his last. That tender little smile was on his face when they buried him.

The simple Episcopal service was held at the home in which he had spent so many happy years. He rested in his library surrounded by his beloved books. The room was filled with flowers sent from all over the country. There was even a beautiful wreath from the State Normal School at Fayetteville, North Carolina, where he had been principal fifty years before.

The friends who attended his funeral brought into focus and made quite clear the pattern of his life, the threads of which had spread into so many directions, and touched so many levels of society. The people who had served him—those who had been at one time or other employed in the house or yard; the plumber, the painter, the carpenter—those who had kept his property in repair. His business associates—the stenographers, lawyers, judges with whom he had worked for so many years. Cleveland's educators—the president of Western Reserve University, a member of the school board, school administrators, and teachers. A former Secretary of War; his friends of the Rowfant Club, the Cleveland Chamber of Commerce, the National Association for the Advancement of Colored People, the City Club, the Cleveland Bar Association; remnants of the Social Circle, the Brenton Circle, the Tresart Club, all of which had long since died out.

Jew and Christian, Protestant and Catholic, black and white, rich and poor, underprivileged and highly cultured, old and young were all there showing their love and respect for the gentle, unassuming man lying so peacefully before them.

There for an infinitesimal period of time Chesnutt's dream seemed to have come true, the vision which had guided him throughout his life:

"Some time, we are told, when the cycle of years has rolled around, there is to be another golden age, when all men will dwell together in love and harmony, and when peace and righteousness shall prevail for a thousand years. God speed the day, and let not the shining thread of hope become so enmeshed in the web of circumstance that we lose sight of it; but give us here and there, and now and then, some little foretaste of this golden age, that we may the more patiently and hopefully await its coming."

Index

Académie Julien, 218

Addams, Jane, 239

Adler, Elmer, 311

Afro-American journals, as reviewing media, 119, 120, 127, 129, 130

Alden, Henry Mills, 103

Aldrich, Thomas Bailey, accepted "The Goophered Grapevine" for the *Atlantic*, 43

Allen, Dr. Dudley Peter, 260

Allen, James Lane, 96-97, 100, 149, 172

A.M.E. Church Review, 259

Amenia Conference, 266

American Negro, The, by W. H. Thomas, Chesnutt's criticism of, 160-63

Anderson, Charles W., 197

Archer, William, 241

Archibald Constable and Co., English publishers of *The Colonel's Dream*, 211

Atlanta riot, 198, 202, 203

Atlanta University, 159, 196

Atlantic Monthly, The, Chesnutt's stories published in: "The Goo-phered Grapevine," 41, 43, 68; "Dave's Neckliss," 49, 68; "Po' Sandy," 43, 68; "The Wife of His Youth," 95-96, 97; "Hot-Foot Hannibal," 106; "Baxter's Procrustes," 208; Howells's article on Chesnutt in, 147-48; mentioned, 114, 170, 242

"Aunt Mimy's Son," by C.W.C. in *Youth's Companion*, 84, 143

Avery, Elroy M., 186, 188

"Bad Night, A," by C.W.C. for McClure Syndicate, 40

Baker, Newton D., as mayor of Cleveland, 245-46, 257-58; as Secretary of War, 274-75

Baker, Ray Stannard, 229-31, 242

Battle of Lake Erie, Centennial of in Cleveland, 259

"Baxter's Procrustes," by C.W.C. in *Atlantic*, 208

Beacon Biographies of Eminent Americans, 112, 116, 267

Berea College, 206

Bethel Literary and Historical Association, 124, 208, 229

315

Dummer Academy, South Byfield, Mass., 174, 183
Dunbar, Paul Laurence, 88, 110

Edwards, Harry Stillwell, 54-56, 109
Emmanuel Episcopal Church, Cleveland, 49, 118, 184, 188, 225
Erie Street Cemetery, Cleveland, 4
Euclid School, Cleveland, 48
Eustis, Senator James, 43-44

"Fabric of a Vision, The," story by C.W.C. submitted to *Atlantic*, 84, 85
"Fall of Adam, The," story by C.W.C. in *Family Fiction*, 40, 84
Family Fiction, publishes stories by C.W.C., 40, 54-56
Fayetteville (N. C.) *Examiner*, 22, 29
Fayetteville (N. C.) *Observer*, 33
Field, Cyrus W., 34
Fleming, Thomas W., 260
Fool's Errand, A, by Albion W. Tourgée, 19
"Fool's Paradise, A," by C.W.C. in *Family Fiction*, 40
Fortune, T. Thomas, 133, 140, 197
Forum, the, 43, 77
"Free Colored People of North Carolina, The," article by C.W.C. in *Southern Workman*, 170
Freedmen's Bureau, 4, 5
Fugitive Slave Law, 3
"Future American, The," article by C.W.C. in *Boston Transcript*, 149
Future of the American Negro, The, by Booker T. Washington, 119, 124, 129

G.A.R. National Encampment, 173, 174
Garrison, Francis J., 146
Gettysburg Battlefield, Chesnutts visit, 273
Gibson, David, 220, 221
Gibson, Mary R., 220, 273
Gilder, Richard Watson, and Chesnutt's stories, 56-59, 102-3
Ginn, Frank H., 244
Goff, Frederick H., 244
"Goophered Grapevine, The," story by C.W.C. in *Atlantic*, 41, 68; in *The Conjure Woman*, 84, 92, 101
Gould, Jay, 34
"Grass Widow, A," story by C.W.C. in *Family Fiction*, 40
"Gray Wolf's Ha'nt, The," story by C.W.C. in *The Conjure Woman*, 94
Greeley, Horace, 28
Green, John P., 260
Green, William R., 275
Greenacre, summer school in Maine, C.W.C. lectures at, 113-15
Grimké, Archibald H., 197, 202, 279

Hackley, E. Azalia, 217, 224, 225
Haigh, George, 6
Haigh, T. D., 17, 25
Halley's Comet, 236, 237
Hallinan, Charles T., 259
Hampton Institute, 251, 252
Harper and Brothers, and Mark Twain dinner, 213
Harper's Magazine, 103
Harper's Weekly, 196, 199
Harris, Cicero, 5, 9, 10, 15
Harris, Edward L., 164, 165
Harris, Moses, 6
Harris, Robert, 5, 6, 9, 15, 19, 25
Hart, Albert Bushnell, 144, 145